West Kent Within Living Memory

West Kent Within Living Memory

Compiled by the West Kent Federation
of Women's Institutes from notes sent by
Institutes in the County

Published jointly by
Countryside Books, Newbury
and the WKFWI, Maidstone

COUNTRYSIDE BOOKS
3 Catherine Road
Newbury, Berkshire

ISBN 1 85306 349 5

The cover photograph shows the Chelsfield
Sunday school outing, 1938.

Designed by Mon Mohan
Produced through MRM Associates Ltd., Reading
Typeset by Paragon Typesetters, Queensferry, Clwyd
Printed by Woolnough Bookbinding Ltd., Irthlingborough

Contents

Foreword

Traditionally, Kent has been divided into West Kent and East Kent, the dividing line being the river Medway with Kentish men and women living to the west and men and women of Kent living to the east.

Over the years large areas of West Kent have become part of Greater London. West Kent Federation includes all the land of Kentish men and women plus that part of east Kent lying to the west of a line drawn through Rainham, Lenham and Tenterden.

West Kent is a county of tremendous contrasts; it has a long history of hop and fruit growing, horticulture and agriculture, with a more industrialised region to the north. We have the smaller village institutes to the south and east of the county and the very large town institutes to the north and west. In fact, many of our larger institutes are situated in the London boroughs. It therefore follows that our 'remembrances' are all very different, providing a colourful picture of our half of the 'Garden of England'. Concrete motorways now bisect the county, soon to be joined by the Channel rail link from London to Folkestone.

As County Chairman, I have many opportunities to meet members in their institutes, all so very different and yet working for the same aims and objectives. Our members' living memories, in some cases, go back to early in the 20th century. Memories of two world wars, when Kent was in the front line, of quiet village life, of hop pickers travelling down from London for their annual holidays, of fishing, sailing barges and Chatham Dockyard.

This book has given the members of West Kent Federation the opportunity to record some of their stories for future generations to enjoy and to gain an insight into life in the county during the first half of the century.

We are grateful to all those members who provided the collection of memories and to Davina Digby and Margaret Adams who co-ordinated the project.

Jean Garrett
County Chairman

Acknowledgments

West Kent Federation of Women's Institutes would like to thank all WI members, their families and friends who sent contributions for this book through their institutes and independently. We appreciate the tremendous interest shown in the project. Unfortunately we were not able to include extracts from every submission; this would have meant some duplication of content and, of course, we had to take into account the total amount of space available in the eventual publication.

All the contributions, without exception, were of value in deciding the shape and content of this book. We are grateful for them all.

Special thanks are due to Irene Brierley for the delightful line drawings and to Vivienne Staniforth for the map of West Kent.

Davina Digby and Margaret Adams
Co-ordinators

TOWN & COUNTRY LIFE

SOME TOWNS AND VILLAGES REMEMBERED

It is not so long since the lamplighter toured the streets of Gravesend at dusk, or every high tide on the river Thames saw a mass of shipping moving to and from London's docks, or Biggin Hill was just a few farmworkers' cottages. Children played in roads disturbed only by the odd horse and cart, and fire fighting depended on horse power, a bucket and a pump. It is all within living memory, as these recollections of just a few towns and villages show.

SIDCUP SHOPS AND CHARACTERS

'Along Sidcup's High Street, in the 1920s, all one's requirements could be satisfied so that no one needed to shop in the larger nearby towns. There were butchers, bakers, grocers, fishmongers (also selling game), greengrocers, drapers, shoe shops, ironmongers, jewellers, photographers, stationers, art shops and restaurants. One could "shop around", there was such a good variety of goods and prices. Saturday evening was the time for bargains at the butcher's. Polish eggs were on sale, very cheap, at some of the cheaper grocer's shops, but buying them was false economy as almost half of them were bad when opened. Customers could be seen smelling each egg to try and avoid the bad ones. A rotten egg has a disgusting smell.

Some of the baker's shops would sell their left-over cakes and bread the next day and children could be seen queuing outside the shop before they went to school, with a clean pillowcase to buy bread and cakes for the family for a few coppers. Each child was eager to compare their contents with the others and there was great rivalry, especially if someone had cream cakes in their pillowcase.

Deliveries of bread and meat were made daily and orders were taken for groceries, fish and greengrocery. Every "Boots Cash Chemist's" made deliveries of their goods by the messenger boy on a bike. There was always a group of telegraph boys, with their bicycles, outside the main post office, waiting to deliver an incoming telegram.

Morris's had two shops, a gentlemen's outfitters on one side of the High Street and a ladies' on the other side. Mr Morris was in charge of the gentlemen's shop. He was a tall, upright and slender man,

10

with grey hair and a moustache. He always wore a black jacket and pin-striped trousers, a black bow tie and winged collar. Miss Morris, also tall, grey haired and dignified, ran the ladies' shop. As the customer entered the shop, she would enquire the nature of their requirement and conduct them to the appropriate counter, where a chair would be placed for them to sit on. Upstairs were the millinery and glove departments. A cloth would be placed on the glass-topped counter and gloves were brought and displayed on the cloth. If the gloves were a little tight in places, they would be eased by stretching with glove tongs. Farthings were never given as change, but instead a strip of coloured paper with a row of dress pins stuck into the paper.

Dawson's was a draper's shop selling ladies' clothes, materials and all the requisites for embroidery and knitting. This was one of the shops which had overhead rails for conveying cash. Money paid was placed in a wooden type of cup, with a screw top, which was then screwed into a holder on the overhead rail. Immediately behind this holder was a strong spring which was activated by pulling down and releasing a wooden handle which sent the money speeding towards the waiting cashier. Sometimes there were junctions in the rails and the holders would come to a halt and change their direction. All this was repeated in reverse to give the waiting customer her change and receipted bill.

Stanger's sold household linens and materials only and both Stanger's and Dawson's had live-in accommodation for some of their young assistants.

Popplewell's sold mostly underwear, male, female and children's. It was a fascinating shop run by the two Miss Popplewells and a friend. All were rather slight, grey haired smiling ladies, who seemed to have always looked the same, never ageing. They seemed always to be able to meet one's requirements. The walls of the shop were lined with shelves full of brown paper parcels and many more parcels were stacked on the floor. They had a single wooden ladder, which they would place against the wall and climb up to bring down the parcel containing the required garment. The parcel would be placed on the counter, the string unravelled and the brown paper opened to reveal its contents. Once the customer had left satisfied, the parcel would be repacked, and placed back on its shelf. They had the uncanny knack of being able to memorise where everything was kept.

The streets were always fascinating to us as children, as we never knew what we might see. Once a rather swarthy man with a large brown bear on a heavy chain came into our district. As he played his mouth organ, the bear moved his feet and swayed in time to the music. "Whistling Rufus" would walk through the streets playing on a tin whistle. He was a tall man who always wore a belted tweed jacket over which he wore a long loose-fitting coat, and knee breeches, long socks and boots. On his head he wore a Tyrolean-type felt hat. The children thought him very clever and followed him around.

"Hot Dinner" was a rather large policeman. He could often be seen popping a steaming hot potato chip into his mouth from the paper he was holding. In very hot weather he always carried his helmet and was continuously mopping his brow. He was a good policeman though. Occasionally a drunken person would cause a disturbance in the street and the police would be called. When this happened the offender would be strapped on to a trolley similar to a costermonger's barrow and wheeled off to the cells in the police station.

Children and their parents would go into the fields once the harvesting was over and pick up any crops the harvesters had left behind. Potatoes were one of the crops which were most worthwhile. Successful gleaning would provide enough for a family for many weeks.

On Sunday evenings in the summer and on Bank Holidays, it was a favourite pastime, for families and courting couples, to sit on the banks of the Sidcup bypass and watch the cars and charabancs returning from a day at the coast and heading back towards London. On Derby Day, children would wait for charabanc parties to return from the races and standing at the side of the road, would call out to the passengers: "Throw out your mouldy coppers." There would then be a mad rush into the road to retrieve any money the fortunate winners would throw.

Smokey Joe was a tramp who frequented the locality. He always pushed or propelled an old bicycle or engine-less motorbike, very often without tyres. There was always an old pail on the handlebars containing hot coals from which smoke poured out. He played the mouth organ and some people would encourage him to play a tune and dance. Some gave him money, but somehow it seemed demeaning to make him do this. It was said that the police would take him in from time to time to give him a good scrub down. Sometimes he was so black from his fire that only his eyes looked white. There were various stories told of his origin, one that he was shell-shocked from the First World War, another that he came from a wealthy family living not many miles away. On one occasion he was reported dead and a large article appeared in the local newspaper, only for him to be seen again later in the streets with his "bike". A few years later he passed away. The last of Sidcup's characters.'

BRASTED

'On the road from Westerham, over 70 years ago, lying well back down a narrow lane but visible from the road, was Park Farm, in a beautiful rural setting at the foot of the North Downs in the Darenth Valley. The cowman's cottage was just at the top of the lane, fronting the main road, and the garden was of great interest to the inquisitive eyes of childhood, with its pieces of intimate washing spread over the bushes in full view of passers-by.

Next came the allotments, very neat and beautifully kept, many with an attendant scarecrow, source of much admiration from the youngsters and of competitiveness and ingenuity amongst the allotment holders.

The fresh spring bathing pool which was situated at the bottom of the recreation ground was a wonderful amenity to the village, and how terribly disappointing it was when the Union Jack was not flying, which meant that the pool was closed for the day, and old Mr Thomas who looked after it was busying himself with more important matters. No amount of tugging at the bell would avail, and the would-be bathers went sadly away.

Further along the street, opposite the Baptist chapel, was the first pub, the Bull Inn, sitting comfortably on the corner of the High Street and Church Road, which led past Mill Farm, more familiarly known as "Spinkses". From here fresh milk was supplied to the villagers, served from a milk cart fitted with a brass-tapped urn from which the metal cans complete with hinged lids were filled, pints and quarts and even half-pints.

And so to the Stanhope Arms, snuggling close to the lychgate into the churchyard. St Martin's church, somewhat squat and solid, appeared to be overlooking the village with a benevolent but sternly watchful eye. On Ascension Day the children from the elementary school, dressed in their Sunday best, would march two by two to the church for a special service, after which the rest of the day was a holiday.

Church Road led on to the railway station, complete with the stationmaster's cottage and the name "BRASTED" in white-washed stones alongside the railway lines. On the platform was one of those exciting machines which dispensed thin little bars of chocolate for one penny. A short distance from the station was the bridge over the road across which the train of two carriages and a steam engine puffed to and fro between Westerham and Dunton Green, stopping at Brasted and Chevening Halt on the way.

To return to the High Street: the next buildings of importance were the village school on one side and the village hall on the other. The children were called to school, morning and afternoon, by the ringing of a bell, which could be heard all over the village. This was a much coveted chore by the bigger boys. "Fuggles" bakery and cakeshop were almost opposite the school, and children were given permission to run across in playtime to buy two delicious ha'penny buns, or even more luscious, a pastry confection containing home-made mincemeat and covered with pale mauve icing.

After that the busy little shops came thick and fast. Hann's Stores, Woodham's and Markwicks Stores were grocery shops, and Markwicks also had a drapery counter. There were two more bakers' shops, West's and Cowlard's.

A rousing sight was the butcher's pony and trap, clip-clopping along in fine style, with Mr Shorey's eldest daughter driving on the rounds delivering the meat. There were also a second butcher's, a chemist and two or three sweetshops, a newsagent and the post office.

One of the sweetshops was known amongst the children as "Rosie Rice's" because she always served in her father's shop, which stood at the corner of "Lucy's Lane", Lucy being Rosie's sister! There one could buy 40 aniseed balls for one penny, enormous gobstoppers for four a penny, and a liquorice ribbon for a farthing.

It was an enthralling sight in Mr Broad's cobbler's shop watching him produce a seemingly unending supply of nails from his mouth and tapping them into the leather soles and heels. Other intriguing places were the saddler's tiny establishment and Swann's the draper's and haberdasher's, where you could also take clothes to be sent away to Perth to be cleaned and dyed. So on to the village green, in two sections, surrounded by white wooden posts and iron railings, with a quaint water pump between, which was the main source of water for the cottagers living by the green. Here also was the blacksmith's, where one could watch the horses being reshod, and a complex of other workshops run by Mr Kember – including a paintshop and a carpenter's shop. One of the most entrancing sights to children's eyes was the fitting of iron rims to the wooden wheels of the farm waggons. A big bonfire was built in which the rims were brought to white heat. They were taken from the fire with long tongs by leather-aproned men and dropped onto the cartwheels, which had been made in the carpenter's shed, whilst one or two apprentices would pour water onto the flames licking at the wood, producing a gorgeous hissing, steaming noise. Riveting too was the production of horseshoes in the forge. The hand-operated bellows hoarsely squeaking, keeping the fire glowing, the hammering and shaping of the red-hot metal on the anvils, the plunging of the horseshoes into the water.

On the other side of our house came the motor repair works, opened in 1911 by my father, Mr F.A. Smith, where repairs were

The forge at West Malling, which closed in 1927. Mr T. Longhurst is holding the horse's head, his son beside him. Blacksmiths were to be found in every town and village in West Kent.

carried out to the new-fangled machines, an exciting and very progressive venture. There was a local coal merchant, who delivered the coal by horse-drawn coal waggon, a small hand laundry and, of course, Durtnell's, the famous builders from generation to generation.

The White Hart Hotel and the King's Arms were also to be found in the High Street, and two doctors had their homes and surgeries in the village, with their own dispensaries for making up medicines, pills and potions. Every possible need was catered for in this one small community.'

GRAVESEND

'I was born in Gravesend in 1919 just after the end of the Great War, in a three-storey house at the end of a terrace of six, with gas lighting on the two lower floors but oil lamps or candles for the bedrooms. A gas street lamp was positioned outside our house and, like R.L. Stevenson, I used to watch each evening for the lamplighter to arrive complete with a short ladder.

Life was very different from today, the majority of leisure pursuits being linked to one's church (in our case Methodist). Apart from the regular Sunday services with Sunday school morning and evening there was the PSA (Pleasant Sunday Afternoon) at which talented instrumentalists and singers entertained with light classical works or excerpts from oratorios. Then during the week there were class meetings and various social groups, Brownies, Guides, Cubs and Scouts for the younger members and Wesley Guild with lectures, as well as a dramatic group producing annually a well known play for three nights and a matinee, badminton and tennis clubs, sewing meetings and various sales, tea and dinners.

Travel abroad was very rare. The most that could be expected was one or maybe two weeks at a convenient seaside resort staying in a boarding house where, if food wasn't provided the landlady would shop and allow her kitchen to be used for one's own preparation of a meal. Travel to one's destination was usually by train – a snorting steam-driven monster which puffed along at a sedate rate stopping at many stations en route. At the end of the journey boys would be waiting to carry luggage for sixpence.

There were no supermarkets – the nearest to these were branches of chain stores (Home and Colonial, World Stores, Liptons, David Greig and the Maypole) all of which had small stores in the main shopping streets. There one could purchase certain packeted items and butter which was in a huge slab, the amount required being broken off by wooden paddles which were then used to pat it into shape. Some stores finished it with a pattern of a swan or cow stamped on the top with a wooden mould.

The more usual way of grocery shopping was for the grocer's representative to call at the beginning of the week to take one's order which was delivered later. Butchers called with meat and took orders for next day. Milkmen made an early morning delivery for which a can was left out overnight, and a mid-morning delivery when one took out a jug and the required amount of milk was ladled into it from a brightly polished brass-topped churn in the back of the cart. The baker came round at 7 am with hot rolls in a wooden tray balanced on his head and later with bread. In my home cakes were never purchased from the baker – all were home-made as was jam, marmalade and pickle, but buns and cakes were available at the baker's with prices at around a penny each and always seven or 13 for threepence or sixpence. Things delivered to one's door were usually placed in large flat open baskets carried on bicycles by young boys of approximately 14 to 16 years who cheered the streets by their whistling of popular songs of the day.

As now, the library was at the lower end of Windmill Street. There was no children's department, one had to be eleven to be issued with a ticket and two rate-paying adults had to back up the application. Books were bound in dark bindings and apart from the classics there was very little fiction.

There were two small cinemas, the Gem in New Road and the Plaza in Windmill Street, and a theatre, the Grand, at the bottom of Harmer Street. During the summer there was an open air theatre on the Promenade where a company of actors put on a variety performance. Next door to the theatre was the open air swimming bath surrounded by trees from which leaves dropped into the water – in large numbers in the autumn. The entrance charge on Sunday morning when the water was clean was sixpence and this was gradually reduced as the week progressed until Saturday afternoon when it was twopence. The Promenade was a notable feature and resembled a miniature seaside resort with swimming in the river and play on the shingles lining the river bank. There was a bandstand with Sunday afternoon concerts by local brass bands (Fort Gardens was not opened until the 1930s).

There were frequent passenger ferries from the Town Pier at the bottom of High Street to the landing stage at Tilbury (one shilling and sixpence) and from there trains to Southend and to London Fenchurch Street. Also car ferries from West Street Pier. The river Thames provided the main influence on the town and the bulk of the town's employment – river pilots, lightermen etc, plus dock workers and staff at all levels for the P & O cruise liners which started and completed journeys at Tilbury, where regular passenger and cargo liners also embarked and disembarked.

Looking back it seems incredible that things should have changed so very much in 60 years or so.'

'I was born in Gravesend and the river Thames governed life in my youth. To see the empty river today it is hard to believe that, in the 1940s and 1950s, every high tide saw a mass of shipping carrying every kind of cargo to and from London's docks. Maritime noises were taken for granted, like bird song, as ships' sirens signalled "port", "starboard", "astern" etc all on a different note.

Gravesend was the official boundary between sea and river and Trinity House ran its Thames and Channel pilotage from the Royal Terrace Pier. My grandfather and uncle were pilots. The latter once took me with him on a Dutch cargo boat from a wharf in the Pool of London – through Tower Bridge's raised arms, round the bends and turns of the many Thames reaches until, at Gravesend, he handed over to the sea pilot and we clambered into the bobbing pilot cutter to be taken ashore.

High tide, no matter what day of the week also meant that the shellfish shops would be open as soon as the catch was cooked. I liked the brown shrimps best and was an expert at shelling them –

unless they were very small and then I would pinch the head and tail together, biting off the body, shell and all.

Inevitably, the Thames was a wartime target and Gravesend got its share of bombing. During the doodlebug phase we had an "umbrella" of barrage balloons – the moving ones were attached to the stern of ships, still going up and down the river despite raids.

After the war I crossed the river regularly in the chuddering old ferry boats (*Edith, Catherine, Rose* and *Gertrude*) on my way to boarding school in Essex. I loved seeing the liners at the Tilbury landing stage and the busy tugs, but best of all were the brown-sailed Thames barges which, because of fuel shortages, were used well into the 1950s to transport goods to the estuary and round the East Coast. The big white ships of P & O and Orient Lines were frequent visitors to Tilbury and, sea-struck as I was, it was not really surprising that in 1959 I went to sea myself.

I think the thing I miss most now is the cacophany of ships' sirens heralding the midnight arrival of a New Year. These days there are not enough ships left on the Thames to perform the ceremonial "cockadoodle-doo".'

FARNBOROUGH

'Farnborough village lies on the London to Hastings main road, dating from the Middle Ages, and was an important stopping place during coaching days. On the outskirts of Farnborough, at the turn of this century, was a police station, one of the oldest in the country. Next door was the White Lion, an old coaching house. As the road rose to Union Hill, there was a large, pleasant house and garden, with forge and workshop, where lived the artistic March family of sculptors. Here was created Bromley war memorial and the world famous memorial of the First World War in Montreal. After 1950 the house was pulled down.

At the top of the hill was the workhouse, built by the Board of Guardians in 1845, with room for 250 inmates. The children were marched to the local school for education till the 1940s. In 1910 two wards were built for the infirm, manned by untrained nurses, 1913 saw the first telephone installation and 1915 the first ambulance. A training school for nurses was set up (sister's pay £25 per annum). Buildings were heated by gas and portable paraffin lamps; there was no heat during operations. In 1936 part of the workhouse was demolished and new wards and a nurses' home erected, so that by 1940 870 beds were available. Many hutted wards were built in 1940 so that there were 1,200 beds. Guy's medical and training staff came from London and Dunkirk army casualties were housed in the hospital. In 1953 an outpatients department opened and in 1956 an

Locksbottom police station at Farnborough in 1908. The right hand side was home to the station sergeant.

operating theatre. It is a large hospital now with plans for building a new one on the site.

Along the road to the village were a few groups of cottages, some behind larger houses at intervals leading to the Common and Farnborough Green, with the school on one side, two buildings and a school house. The lower building was for boys, who played on the village green. An infants' school was built in 1910.

In the late 1920s a bypass was built, through the green (leaving a small patch on either side), through an orchard and strawberry fields, taking many cars away from the village.

Past the green, veering to the right, was the High Street with a few shops and cottages (with a communal washhouse), and two alehouses where ale was brewed and sold; a small front room was the bar! The alemaking finished early this century and in 1910 two shops were erected on the site, a butcher's and a greengrocer's. A large laundry flourished too, with washing drying on a green near an old, large house. On the opposite side of the High Street was a farm, where the cows could be seen coming in to be milked, with the bull peering over the half-door of his stall.

Corn and soft fruit were grown in the fields till the late 1950s, when the farm closed, except for fruit growing on a Pick Your Own basis. A cluster of houses in Pleasant View overlooked the farm and still look out over the fields. An open field faced allotments by the village pond and Cosy Nook Tea Garden.

Many people came to the village in horse-drawn vehicles at

19

weekends (and later by No 47 bus, started in 1914 from Shoreditch), to stroll in the fields and have tea in one of the tea gardens in the village. In the 1940s and 1950s there were many visitors at weekends as buses ran every ten minutes.

From the Square by the George the old coaching road veered to the right with cottages and a few shops to the church facing the fields. The post office was in a room of a house opposite, though in the 1950s it was transferred to premises newly erected as shops in the main road, so that Farnborough people's needs were well catered for – three grocers, three greengrocers, two butchers, a draper's, three bakers, two shoe repairers (one selling new shoes as well and still doing so today), a chemist, hardware, hairdresser and barber, a dairy, two newsagents and confectioners.

In 1900 at the end of the village, a narrow winding lane with a few houses at intervals led to Orpington. Some larger houses in large gardens, including Farnborough Hall, the home of the Stowe family, were on one side of the hill leading out of the village. These were demolished 1950 onwards, and a large estate of smaller houses and bungalows was erected.

Near the church was a mansion on a large estate, the home of Lord and Lady Avebury (the August Bank Holiday originator), called High Elms. The house was used by Guy's Hospital staff during the 1940s, but was gutted by fire. At the back of the hospital are three plots of land which until the 1940s were occupied by gypsies in small cottages. Urania Boswell, Gypsy Lee, queen of the Kent Romanies, and head of the Lee-Boswell clans, lived there, her caravan too. She died in 1933, when 200 family mourners followed her funeral to the churchyard, while it is said thousands of people lined the route as well. Each year till well before the war, a Gypsy Horse Fair was held in the village, the horses being trotted along the High Street for prospective buyers to see.'

ALLINGTON

'In January 1939, my family moved to a lovely rural setting at Allington, two miles west of Maidstone. It was a quiet area with just the occasional trains to be heard. Even the quarry was quieter. There were no houses along the northern London Road beyond Grace Avenue. Allington Way, Conway Road, Ash Grove and Poplar Grove were all cul-de-sacs. The most memorable noise was one which always caused a thrill and a romantic sense of adventure. It was the roaring of the lions at Maidstone Zoo. Other animal cries were sometimes heard, like the cackling laugh of the spotted hyena. This was usually between 4 and 4.15 pm. The private zoo was owned by Sir Garrard Tyrwhitt Drake, a fine figure of a man who, as mayor

20

of Maidstone many times, led Civic parades riding his magnificent white horse, later to be replaced by an equally eye catching black and yellow Rolls-Royce.

The zoo was a great attraction. There was a miniature railway which conveyed one a half mile or so to the main entrance. As it went it passed through fields in which grazed a unique herd of white miniature ponies which on occasions pulled a Cinderella coach. There was also a rare collection of smelly wolves which lurked in a wooded area. Gert and Daisy were two lovable elephants on whose howdah we enjoyed many a ride. There was a camel, monkeys and much more, a very impressive collection and as far as I can remember, they all looked well.

Having waited six months for our house to dry out before moving in, my parents set about creating a garden from the field in which we found ourselves. Much grassland surrounded us and in the field behind the scenes changed rapidly, with corn, beet, swedes, cabbages, cauliflowers, sheep, cows, black, red and white currants and gooseberries. An apple orchard too and wild horseradish. Rats lurked in the farm buildings in the valley below and in one severe winter came right up to the house, as did the field mice when we first moved in. We used to watch them pop up through a hole by the fireplace then chase them around the room.

By the time war broke out, in 1939, number 18 Allington Way was built and remained the end of the road until building resumed in 1947. Stacks of breeze blocks and bricks were left and later became a haven for us children, building our own camps and houses. Trestles too and huge planks which made see-saws of gigantic height. These were hidden conveniently between rows of beech hedges. Beyond these hedges was a five-bar gate leading to a farm track which wound its way through corn fields for a quarter of a mile to a picturesque colonial style wooden bungalow complete with verandah. It belonged to Mr George Bunyard, a much travelled botanist and market gardener. The garden with its bamboo canes, large magnolia tree and other exotic plants was testimony to his achievements.

A great many of Cox Brothers' (builders) houses were built on Bunyard's land which stretched down to the railway line in places north of the London Road. The cherry, apple and plum orchards north of the London Road were farmed by William Talbot Edmunds, who lived in the large Allington House which stood in a big garden. This is now the site of Palace Wood infants' school. During the war years, the local schoolboys used to help the Land Army girls with fruit picking and some of the root crops. At the top of Castle Road, on the left hand corner, stood a couple of farm cottages and alongside these were the farm buildings, where the machinery was kept and apples were loaded on to lorries bound for Covent Garden market. Castle Road was quiet during the war years. Potatoes were always grown on a wide strip of land on the left hand side between the road and orchard.

We often walked our rabbits on lead and collar down to the footpath on the far side of the first railway bridge and followed it west to meet up by the next bridge which crossed the narrow lane running down from opposite the Sir Thomas Wyatt Inn. Sometimes, after rain, it was too flooded for us to negotiate. The working ragstone quarries, which stretched from Castle Road west to the present 20/20 industrial estate, belonged to D. Bensted and his house, together with a cottage, was set in the midst covered in dust. We would skirt round the quarries and along to the hop farm of Mr Kennard, which stretched from the railway line almost to Preston Hall. The smell of hops was delicious, especially when they were being dried in the kilns. For years the church had its own bin, enthusiastically manned by the rector and some stalwart followers, who were there by 8 am armed with lunchtime sandwiches and flasks of hot tea and coffee. Obtaining money for church funds in those days was a slow and painful business but great fun and so healthy. Many children joined their parents for the annual event.

As well as the working quarries there were the "burnt out" ones which lay between the present Mid Kent Shopping Centre and extended down to the Castle gatehouse. They were surrounded by spindly fences with staves that could be easily dislodged for us to wriggle through. Home to disused iron trucks and rail trucks, spooky corridors of creepers and trees; paths which led up, down and round, we had a marvellous time. With five or six of the neighbours' dogs, a regular motley band of at least seven of us would spend hours happily running, tracking and bird nesting. We never took all the eggs, just a sample to blow and catalogue. In springtime catkins and pussy willow were out in profusion and the ground was carpeted with primroses and violets, bunches of which would be carefully picked and taken home. In summer there were the wild strawberries. Very little traffic used Castle Road, except to service the quarry or visit St Laurence's church, the Castle or Locks. St Laurence's was a lovely church with a beautifully painted frieze. The churchyard had many graves and a memory which sticks is of how many children had died by drowning when only four or five years old. The river at Allington used to flood quite considerably before the locks were enlarged.

The woods down there were "Private", out of bounds, but one winter, when the snow was thick, we made our way there to play "Tarzan" on the extremely tempting hanging vines. Unfortunately the snow was never as deep again and the experience wasn't repeated but it was wonderfully memorable. On the southern side of the London road, Ted's Snack Bar was a popular landmark for all lorry drivers. Situated in a rough stony lay-by close to Allington House and east of Tudor Garage, it was a mere hut with wooden shutters and a wide shelf on which to serve the dishes. He was helped by his cheroot-smoking wife and they provided hot meals. The smell of bacon cooking was tantalising to say the least. Alongside was the newsagent's hut, more like a garden shed, and here in the early hours the local schoolboys would gather on their bicycles ready for the early morning deliveries. At the top of Grace Avenue, Mr Davis had the general stores and post office and next door was Lindridges the greengrocer. Later Mr Davis owned both and made them into one shop.

Tudor Garage has altered considerably. It previously had been known as Trinion's Garage but Mr Buck senior took over after the First World War and had a Tudor-style house built alongside. During this time there were certainly fewer petrol pumps and the workshop behind was an invaluable addition to the community. As was the large clock on the front by which we children regulated our lives. Strangely, in spite of never possessing watches, we always arrived home on time for meals, albeit running like mad after the first glimpse of that clock. Mr Buck loved animals and his son, Billy, was very fortunate. He had a beautiful St Bernard dog and a monkey kept in a large cage in a big fenced off yard. In other outbuildings there were a piebald and a skewbald pony. They were often seen trotting around drawing a little pony trap or being ridden by Billy and his friends.

Milk was delivered, by horse and cart, twice a day with a milk churn and aluminium half pint and one pint measures. We would run out with our jugs to collect it and be very careful not to spill any on the way back. Bread was also delivered in the same way, as was coal, but much larger shire horses were used to pull the carts. Nearly every day when we were around, we would vie with our friends to see who, armed with bucket and spade, could reach the precious droppings first. I don't think we bought any fertilisers in those days, I can only remember the welcome smell of hot horse droppings!'

OLD BEXLEY

'To most people the traffic hold-ups on the Heath are chaotic but much the same sort of things have been going on for years. Before the motor car became so popular it was not unusual for the traveller, whether by cycle or pony and trap, suddenly to find himself surrounded by a herd of cows. In those days the hospital authorities and local residents exercised their common rights and turned their stock out for grazing, so cattle from the hospital and donkeys belonging to one of the local residents were always being met.

One of the events of importance to us youngsters occurred every Tuesday. This was cattle market day in Dartford and sheep and cattle were driven along the road to Bexley. These usually arrived just as we were coming out of school so we assumed the roles of assistant drovers running ahead to prevent the animals taking the wrong road.

These were the days of steam trains and a long goods train could take a long time to pull up the incline towards Sidcup. This was very annoying to the cricket club as the batsman at the bottom end became distracted and play was held up.

Nearly all of the shops had their errand boys complete with carrier bicycles and there was much rivalry on the "delivery stakes". Probably the plum job was at the chemist as he had only bottles of medicine and boxes of pills which were carried in a black metal box slung over the shoulder. Chuter's the bakers also ran a tea room. One of the features of this was the invasion on Saturday afternoons by the students of the Osterberg College in Oakfield Lane. In the absence of buses they arrived on bicycles and one side of the High Street was packed with them. The girls used to look very smart as they were all in uniform complete with straw hats, far different from present day students! The post office was originally on the site later occupied by the National Westminster Bank; the postmaster, a Mr Gammon, was quite a character and was always seen wearing a skull cap and smoking jacket when serving behind the counter.

The Freemantle Hall was the centre of entertainment. On Saturday nights it was used as a cinema; these were the days of the "good old silents" when Pearl White, Charlie Chaplin and Buster Keaton shared stardom with the "Keystone Cops". Admission was threepence, sixpence or ninepence and there were two separate performances. The orchestra consisted of a piano with the same tunes played to suit the various films and anyone caught whistling the tunes was promptly removed, as were the schoolboys who persisted in throwing nutshells on the floor much to the discomfiture of patrons who wished to leave their seats discreetly, as all that could be heard was the sound of crunching underfoot!

This was also the scene of many private parties and one could stand outside and watch the "elite" arrive in their own carriages as there were very few motor cars at that time. Inside the Master of Ceremonies, a Mr Lincoln who was also the cinema's "bouncer", could be heard calling out such things as "side lines", "top and bottom couples" and various other terms which meant nothing to us outside. Many years later, however, when Old Time Dancing became more popular these terms associated themselves with the

Lancers and Quadrilles. On other occasions one could listen to pianoforte recitals given by Sir Granville Rubeck who lived in Park Hill just beyond St John's church.

Nearly all commodities were delivered by horse and cart; milk, bread, fish, groceries and coal too. There were three coal merchants in the village, one operated from the station siding, another at the top of the High Street and the third in Bourne Road and they would deliver as little as a half-hundredweight which was about a shilling! Milk was brought round by three different people; the main one operated from the dairy farm opposite St John's church. Sterilised bottles were unheard of and the milk was ladled into customers' own jugs or into small pewter pots and it was a recognised joke that when it rained the milkman would take the lids off the churns in order to add to his supply! Chuter's did most of the bread with Groom's in opposition coming from Erith. The fish suppliers were Razzles. Ale was also delivered; Reffells brewery had several horses in use and bottles from the off licence and goods from the railway were also delivered by horse and van. The railway owned two pairs of horses and these were stabled under the arches by the railway bridge – as you may gather manure was plentiful and free for the taking.

The taxi services were horses and cabs and in addition to their normal work these horses were used to draw the fire engine! Although they had no need to hurry when pulling a cab, as trains were very few and far between, they looked altogether different when going to a fire complete with trappings and brass bells. The fire alarm was given by firing a rocket and the sound of this seemed to inspire the nags to ferocity. Ironically these poor creatures met their death when their stable caught fire.

On the corner opposite the Millers Arms stood the old forge where it was an everyday occurrence to see a line of horses awaiting their turn to be shod (incidentally this was also where the local children took their hoops to be repaired). At the back of the forge was a high wall up which hops were trained to grow and the blacksmith's wife, for the sake of her health, would lean out of an upstairs window and inhale their powerful aroma.

The old mill, since destroyed, was a flour store, the flour being brought from Erith daily from Cannon and Gaze's who were the mill's owners. The horses, when unharnessed used to refresh themselves in the stream which came well up to their bellies being as deep as four or five feet in places. The stream at the back of the mill was the recognised "swimming pool" for the local children and it was not unusual to see trout there too.

Towards St Mary's church, just inside the gate, is a small brick building which at one time was used as a mortuary where suicides were taken before burial. At the far side was a window and when

25

news got around that there was a corpse inside there was a general scramble of morbid minded schoolboys eager to have a look.'

BEARSTED

'My family moved to Bearsted in March 1919 – I was then 22 months old. Our first home was The Lodge, Milgate Park, on the estate of Sir Walter Fremlin, owner of Fremlins Brewery, Maidstone. Milgate estate was very large, taking in most of Bearsted and Thurnham. He was a great benefactor to the village, building the Men's Institute, providing the pump at Roundwell and giving the ground for the WI hall to be built. A large part of the estate was covered by his hop gardens, situated at Sutton Street, Yeoman Lane, Barty Farm, Spot Lane and Caring Lane. The families living at Milgate were expected by Mr Walter to go hop picking, and had their bins next to the Londoners who came down every year to pick hops. They started at 6 am and I had to walk at the age of five and six considerable distances to the hop gardens on my own, and had to pick an umbrella full of hops before I was allowed to play with the other children. The rate paid was threepence a bushel and at the end of about six weeks everyone went to Tollgate House to be paid their monies due.

The village in the early 1920s consisted of The Street, Sutton Street, Roundwell, Church Lane, The Green, a few cottages in Yeoman Lane and Plantation Lane and Ware Street and Thurnham Lane, which came in Thurnham parish.

There were two bakers, Mr Datson and Mr Rowland, who baked on the premises, two butchers, Mr Moss and Mr Raggett, two village stores, Mr Corps and Mr Bates, a drapers owned by Mr Perrin and a post office. Milk was supplied by Mr Foster who owned a farm in Ware Street and Mr Hodges in Thurnham. Bread was delivered daily, being carried to the door in large baskets. Milk was brought in large cans and measured with a dipper straight into a jug.

The village was surrounded by orchards, fields and hop gardens. Transport was by horse and cart or pony and trap. There was one bus a week (quite small, rather like a mini-bus), which came from Leeds Village, waited in Maidstone while people shopped and returned in the afternoon; it held about 15 to 20 people and was never over full. Later on a few delivery vans and cars appeared on the roads, but were very scarce. People walked mostly, unless lucky enough to get a lift on a cart. I remember bowling my hoop from Milgate to Bearsted school, without meeting any traffic. If someone was very ill in the village, The Street was strewn with straw to keep down the noise of carts passing.

On the day I was five years old I walked with my mother to

Bearsted school. The school consisted of three classrooms. There were about 80 to 100 pupils with one teacher having to teach two or three different levels in the same room.

When Sir Walter Fremlin died, the new owner of Milgate Park, a Captain Bence, required our lodge for one of his servants, so we were moved to Byfrance just behind Thurnham Mill on the river Len. In 1922 my father together with Mr Filmer had rebuilt the water wheel, nine feet in diameter and weighing five tons. The river ran through our garden and the water wheel was driven by this. My father also generated electricity for Milgate House and he had a power house further up river. I loved to be allowed into the mill by Mr Wratten and to climb to the top floor with him. It was extremely noisy when working. At the side of the mill was a well, from which we drew all our water. There was no water at Byfrance and my father made daily journeys to the well using a yoke to carry the buckets. There was no lighting, so it was oil lamps and candles at bedtime.

One doctor and one district nurse served the community, which although mainly centred on the village covered considerable distances to outlying farms and cottages. The surgery was then at Dr Wittome's house in Yeoman Lane and later moved to The Limes, The Green. It was nothing to sit there for up to three hours waiting to see the doctor, as he was sometimes called out for an emergency. Treatment and medicines were of course paid for, as were visits to a patient.

Weddings and funerals were always well attended by villagers as being a small community everyone was known to each other. When anyone died the death bell tolled the age of the person. Weddings always drew a crowd and were talked about for days, particularly what everyone wore.

A Dramatic Society was formed in the 1930s which was the highlight of the village entertainment. There were weekly play readings and the productions filled the WI hall for a whole week.'

OTFORD

'When I was a child in the 1920s, Otford village relied almost entirely on agriculture for its living. We were surrounded by farms, apple orchards and hop gardens which kept working no fewer than seven oast houses. Twice a day the dairy farmers' cows wandered across the green from their grazing fields on the Sevenoaks Road to their milking parlour at Hilldrop Farm. Horses were also often about the village street waiting their turn to be shod at the forge. The clang of the blacksmith's hammer rang out and the singeing smell of red-hot shoe on horse's hoof scented the High Street.

27

Another familiar sound was the baying of the West Kent foxhounds whose kennels were at the top of the hill on the way to Shoreham. The hounds were let out and fed at six o'clock every morning and their excited clamour roused us all. We often met the hounds out on the road, the whole pack in the charge of a couple of mounted huntsmen. Although I was quite small they never frightened me or knocked me over as they swept past us like a silent white, tan and black flood, the only sound the clicking of their nails on the road.

There was very little traffic, of course, only the hourly Sevenoaks bus, red, noisy and open-topped, the occasional delivery van, the milkman's horse-drawn float delivering our milk in gleaming silver milk cans and, most excitingly, magnificent traction engines and steam rollers, chuffing and snorting with brasswork gleaming and names such as Bertha and Edith.

I only remember three private cars in Otford and one of those was driven, most unusually and daringly, by a young woman, but then she was an Australian! On Mondays, we had to remember to keep our garden gate securely closed to prevent invasions of livestock being driven in to Sevenoaks market. This lack of traffic is evidenced by one of my earliest and most vivid memories of a village funeral. I watched this short procession come slowly up the High Street, across the green and into the church. First came the coffin carried by six men, then the mourners two by two, the black clothes showing up the brightness of the flowers carried by the women. I must have been too young to understand what I was seeing but the silence and stillness of all the bystanders impressed me greatly and I still think it was the most dignified and moving funeral I have ever seen.

Although the village was small, so that everyone knew who everyone else was, it was also very divided. There was a distinct division between the village and the gentry. The village largely consisted of several large families very much inter-related and most of the men worked on the local farms or in farming related trades. Many of the women worked in the fields seasonally – hop picking, apple picking and so on – but more of them were in domestic service. The gentry lived in the large houses about the village and employed the village women to do their housework.

Without electricity and with oil lamps for lighting, coppers and flat irons to cope with the laundry and open fires for heating, everyone who could afford it had either daily help or a resident maid, often both. At a time when everyone grew their own fruit and vegetables and probably kept chickens too, there was at least a part-time gardener too.

Another deep split that divided the village was that between Church and Chapel (the Methodist church). It was in 1921 that the

WI President wanted to hold a whist drive in the church hall during Holy Week. This the vicar would not allow and the subsequent furious remarks recorded in the WI minutes declared that the vicar had been "most arbitrary".

Earlier there had been a much greater controversy concerning the village war memorial. One party – mainly Church – thought that a suitably inscribed ornamental lychgate between the church and the green would be just the thing. Everyone else, headed by the same WI President, wanted a new village meeting hall, thus providing an alternative to the church hall. After much argument, the hall party won and an ex-army hut was purchased and erected in a corner of the recreation ground, under the grand title Otford War Memorial Hall and Working Men's Club, although it was known to everyone as "The 'Ut".'

BITS OF BECKENHAM

'All along Beckenham Road there were very large houses, right up to Queens Road. From Queens Road a parade of shops led to Clockhouse station. These shops included a sweet shop that opened on a Sunday afternoon, very unusual in those days. There was also a cycle shop, chemist, butcher, hairdresser, newsagent, greengrocer, ironmonger and a tailor's where, at the appropriate time of year, the inter-school sports trophies were on display. Clockhouse station was at the top of the hill. There was an exit from the station in Clockhouse Road where the horse cabs awaited passengers alighting from the trains.

During heavy rain, Clockhouse railway track used to become flooded and the water, on occasions, reached the level of the platform. This problem was overcome, much later, by culverting the river Chaffinch. At the bottom of Clockhouse approach, in Beckenham Road, on the corner of Sidney Road, there was a very large house surrounded by trees and a high fence. The original West Beckenham Conservative Club was built in part of the garden at the back of the house.

Opposite the club, in Sidney Road, was Ouseley's yard and byres where they kept their cows. The dairy was on the corner of Blandford Road. The cows were driven from the yard, down Clockhouse Road and beyond the river to pasture. In Beckenham Road, on the other corner of Sidney Road, there was a large grocer's, Sherlocks, and every morning Mr Sherlock could be seen standing in the shop doorway, dressed in brown boots, long tweedy socks, plus-four trousers and a dark smock topped with a white apron. His two daughters worked in the shop with him.

There was another parade of shops to the corner of Churchfields

Road where there was the public house, the Prince Arthur. Sadly, this parade of shops plus the houses on the opposite side of the road were demolished, with loss of life, by a doodlebug during the Second World War.

There used to be a tram service that ran from Penge to Croydon. At the terminus the driver changed the overhead arm to change the direction of the tram. They were open-topped and the seat backs were reversible to face the direction of travel. On each seat there was a heavy mackintosh apron provided to cover your legs when it rained.

A Saturday evening shopping trip was made to Penge market. My special memory is of the man with the boiled sweet stall and the overhead pressure lamps. Also, Penge Empire, where some of the great music hall stars like Nellie Wallace, Marie Lloyd, Billy Bennett, Max Miller and many others appeared. Whilst waiting to go in there were the buskers to entertain the queue and the peanut and roasted chestnut vendors. When the doors finally opened there was a stampede up the stone stairs to get a good seat in "the gods", an evening's entertainment for sixpence.'

BIGGIN HILL

'As a village at the turn of the century, Biggin Hill was practically non-existent and never appeared as such on any map. It was part of the parish of Cudham and consisted mainly of the manors of Aperfield and Cudham. Isolated farms and farm workers' cottages were almost the only habitations.

On the main Westerham Road, adjoining Jail Lane, stood Biggin Hill farm, probably the origin of the name of the village. In front of the farm building a piece of green land became the centre of various rural activities. Alongside the green stands the Black Horse Inn, at that time a coaching stage on the road to Westerham, whilst further along on the opposite side of the road stood the smithy under the proverbial "spreading chestnut tree". This closed down in 1944. There never was a jail in Jail Lane, but it is probable that convicted prisoners would be accommodated overnight in what is now the Old Jail Inn on their way to prisons within the county. In 1923 a cattle trough and drinking fountain, now filled with flowers, were installed on the green and a memorial was erected to the fallen of the First World War.

As the name implies, the region is extremely hilly, climbing up from a deep valley on the Surrey border to around 800 feet above sea level. From the top of the valley, breathtaking views of woods and open spaces extend as far as the eye can see, although increasingly the open spaces have tended to become residential areas. In 1900 the population was around 500. Much wildlife roamed the woods – foxes, squirrels, badgers and many varieties of birds.

There was no school in Biggin Hill until 1913, before which time local children had to walk along Jail Lane to Cudham Voluntary School, paying three halfpence per day to attend. Considering that the first bus service through Biggin Hill did not commence until 1913, it says much for the stamina of our grandparents, many of whom, particularly those living in the valley, must have walked at least two miles each way every day to school. The headmaster and headmistress were each paid £70 per annum, plus a house and fuel. One of the founders of the school was Charles Darwin. Much later, his name was given to the secondary school, which was the first comprehensive school to be built in the Borough of Bromley.

Aperfield Estate was sold to a London businessman, and in 1902 he offered for sale plots of land surrounding the manor house at £10 a time. Payment was £1 down with the remainder in 18 instalments spread over nine years, but even on those terms they were not easy to sell, probably because of the difficulty of transporting building materials to the area.

Nevertheless, weekend bungalows began to spring up in the valley, once called the most beautiful valley in Kent. Some of these were little more than shacks, built of wood, breeze block or asbestos with corrugated iron roofs and used by townspeople as weekend holiday accommodation. Most had a frontage of from 40 to 60 feet and with a fair sized surrounding area. A few of the bungalows were of much better presentation and, although mainly wooden, had slate roofs and a verandah. One or two of the latter remain, giving a touch of Edwardian charm to the village. Legend has it that one well presented bungalow in Oaklands Lane, once an old Roman road, was the weekend retreat of a very prominent member of the Royal Family. Foxhunting occasionally was one of his pursuits, but if local folklore is to be believed, there was a more personal attraction. It is fortunate that newspaper reporters at the turn of the century were less indiscreet than those of today's tabloids!

Another famous resident of the early bungalows in St Mary's Grove was Dame Clara Novello Davies, along with her son, Ivor Novello, the brilliant composer of operetta. Dame Clara taught singing and was the conductor of the Royal Welsh Ladies Choir. One story concerning Dame Clara which caused much amusement is that she positioned her singers individually on various hills in the neighbourhood, their glorious voices echoing round the valley. Young Ivor lived in his own Romany caravan in the grounds of his mother's bungalow. It was at this time (1914) that he composed and published perhaps the most popular song of the Great War, *Keep the home fires burning*.

Until 1913, public transport was literally no more than two horse-power – a carriage being drawn by two equine stalwarts between the Black Horse and the Rising Sun in Bromley via Hayes. A change of horses took place at the Fox, Keston. A similar service ran to Orpington via Downe and Farnborough. At weekends, increasingly, cyclists would be much in evidence, cycling out from surrounding towns and stopping off for refreshment at the tea rooms which seemed to be springing up in some cottage gardens.

In 1902, the go-ahead had been given for a light railway to be built between Green St Green and Tatsfield with a station and level crossing between Aperfield Court and the Fox and Hounds on the Westerham Road, but the necessary capital (£70,000) for the project was never realised and the scheme was abandoned. A row of three-storey houses, Coronation Terrace had already been built in readiness for railway employees to move in but were never used as such. These houses still stand.

During the First World War the wind of change began to blow quite strongly over Biggin Hill. On 2nd January 1917 the first plane, an RE7 landed. The RAF had arrived, and on 13th January a Wireless Testing Park was officially opened. Air to air and air to ground telephony were developed here. In the following year it became a key station, responsible for the North Kent Sector; 141 Squadron was formed and on 18th May brought down its first and only German bomber, a Gotha. This turned out to be the last air raid of that war on London.

Undoubtedly, the greatest impact on the life of Biggin Hill was the opening up of the airfield by the RAF. In 1940, Winston Churchill flew from the airfield to try to persuade the French to remain in the war, but to no avail, and throughout August and September the Germans, greatly superior in number, relentlessly bombed the South East of England. Who will ever forget the Battle of Britain and the part played by the heroic airmen from Biggin Hill airfield? In one early raid around 50 personnel, including civilians, were killed. In all, 453 aircrew were killed whilst serving in the Biggin Hill Sector, but as we all know their sacrifice was not in vain.

From being an obscure rural district in Kent, the name of Biggin Hill echoed around the world in just a few weeks, securing a permanent place in the history books. After the war a memorial chapel was built. Names of the men killed are inscribed on oak panels, while twelve flags representing the allied nations who flew from the Sector and twelve stained glass windows commemorate this memorable period of history. A Hurricane and Spitfire flank the entrance to the chapel.'

SHORNE

'I was born in the village of Shorne near Gravesend in 1911 and over the years the village has changed considerably. I came from a family of twelve and had an idyllic childhood. The village in those days consisted of a few cottages, houses and three small shops – one of which my father owned, "The Bakery". The area was mostly meadows where people kept their sheep and cattle. The remainder of the village was farms and the local nursery. As children we played in the meadows and had picnics which my mother would provide.

We went to the local school in Butchers Lane and when we were older we would walk down the lane to catch the bus to school in Gravesend. There were no buses through the village as there are today.

My parents worked very hard in the bakery. It was kept open until 10 pm every night and half day closing was on a Thursday afternoon. The other shops in the village closed on a Wednesday afternoon so there was always a shop open for the villagers. My father sold corn and the men who delivered it used to carry it up to the loft in the shop and for this they would receive a sixpenny tip. On Saturday night the villagers would bring their joints of meat to put in the baking ovens to cook overnight. Everyone knew, helped and cared for each other.

As a child I lived at Mill Hill House until my father bought nine acres of land and had a farmhouse built on it. The architect at the time told my father not to bother putting electricity cables to the house as it would be a long time coming. This was not so and my father then had the extra expense of having them put in. My mother had a range for cooking and there was a large copper for washing. We all washed in a tin bath. On Monday the copper would go on and all the washing would be done and mangled. On Tuesday the ironing would be done with the old-fashioned black irons. It was around 1960 when we had our first washing machine. In those days there were no fridges and food was kept in pantries and meat safes.

With regard to entertainment, all the family either played an instrument or sang. Everyone used to gather around the piano for a sing-song. There were card games, charades etc which people would play as there was no television. There was the local drama group and choir in the village. Several fêtes were held and these were a great village occasion with everyone helping and joining in.

My grandfather Joseph Houghton donated a plot of land for the new Methodist chapel. People used to go to church up to three times on Sunday. Nearly every family were churchgoers and most families on Sunday would stroll round the village in the early evening. In those days families were large and the congregations full.

During the war Shorne was under fire, and there was the requisition of the aerodromes by the RAF. Several bombs were dropped and the one which fell near Woodlands Lane killed two soldiers stationed there. We had barrage balloons and of course, the formation of the Home Guard. Some soldiers visited the village after the war with their families for several years.

After the war came a complete change in village life. There was a very large expansion of house building and population in the parish. This, of course, changed the whole face of the village. The old school was pulled down and a new one built. In 1911 there were only 932 inhabitants and it was an agricultural village, but by 1960 Shorne had 1,650 inhabitants.'

MAIDSTONE MEMORIES

'My grandfather's father was a Farrier Sergeant in the 7th Dragoons stationed at the cavalry barracks in Maidstone when he met his future wife. She was born and brought up in Maidstone and was, at the time of her marriage, librarian at St Paul's church.

Grandfather moved with the regiment and returned to Maidstone, with his parents, when he was six years old and his father left the army. He went to All Saints school. In those days, the headmaster was very strict and if you "upset the parson, he would tell the headmaster and you were in trouble".

When Maidstone Bridge was opened, all the schoolchildren lined the streets and they were each given a medal to commemorate it. When the town was flooded, horses and carts were used to take the children across the bridge to school.

After school and in the holidays the children would play games in Allington Woods or play around the trees near St Peter's church. He and his brothers and sisters were never allowed to go to any of the fairs that used to come to Fairmeadow. They came three times a year in May, June and October. Thousands of sheep and cattle changed hands and there were also seesaws and swings etc.

He joined the King Street chapel drum and fife band when he was about ten years old. At Christmas time they used to go around all the big houses on the edge of town and play their tunes outside. The occupiers would come to the door and give them money. When they went to Oakwood House, where Wigans the bankers lived, they would be invited indoors. They would be given tea and cakes.

He passed the fifth standard, at school, when he was eleven years old and was allowed to take up freehand drawing. He was very good at this and won a prize of a drawing board and T-square. Sometimes the organist at All Saints church needed two strong lads to pump up the organ. My grandfather was one of the volunteers and for an

34

hour's work they were paid twopence each, but they enjoyed it.

He left school at eleven and went to work in Jacob's store at 12 Week Street. It was a china and hardware store. He was in the office giving change when the money was sent up the chute from the shop floor to the office. He was paid six shillings a week. The crockery was sent to the shop by railway truckload. They had the contract to supply the prison and the village shops used to buy their supplies from them. In the winter they used to hang up ice skates at the front of the shop and when winter was over they would be wrapped up and put away for the next year.

A railway guard came to live next door to my grandfather and he told him that there was a job going on the bookstall at Maidstone West station. The wages were twelve shillings a week so he started work there. He was not very happy there as the manager was always drunk and did not teach him much about the job. The Railway Inspector at the station could see he was not happy and suggested that he join the railway company. He was 16 and wanted to be an engine driver. He asked the foreman if he could do engine cleaning but there were no vacancies at that time so he took a job on the platform and was paid 16 shillings a week. There were ten trains a day. He could earn a little extra money by carrying the luggage of the first class passengers or providing them with foot warmers.

When he was 20 a job as engine fireman became available at Strood. He was then sent up to London to Bricklayer's Arms depot. Before long the railway decided to build a new depot at Slade Green and in 1899 my grandfather moved to the new depot. He was eventually made an engine driver, firstly on the local lines and then on the main lines. When the lines were electrified he became a motorman and ended up a foreman motorman. He retired in 1937 after 49 years on the railway.

In those early days Maidstone was a sleepy, country town. The industry was paper making. At Tovil Mill they made brown paper out of straw; at Springfield Mill banknotes were made and at Turkey Mill they made good quality paper. There was also Hayle paper mill at Loose Valley. There were also several breweries in the town. Market day was on a Thursday. The wealthy people would come into the town in their pony and traps and stay at the Royal Star Hotel. The poorer people would walk in or come by carrier.'
[Extracted from a tape recording made in April 1958]

'I first went to a Michaelmas Fair in Maidstone in 1928. Then, fairs were held in Fairmeadow, on the banks of the river Medway, next to the electricity works and municipal swimming and washing baths.

Simple rides included boat-shaped swings, chair-a-planes, merry-go-rounds and dodgems, coconut shies, hoop-la and darts, all very basic. There were many stalls, mostly selling crockery, household goods, pots and pans etc, fruit and vegetables, but not many clothes as times were hard and money scarce. These stalls continued from Fairmeadow and right up on to the High Street pavements to the Cannon at Middle Row, all lit by smoky flares at night. Carriers' carts were lined up in the centre of the road in the High Street from Middle Row to the bridge and their horses were stabled behind the Rose and Crown Inn. For a small fee the carrier would transport goods from the shops in town to the surrounding villages, a sort of personal postal service. On market days, sheep cattle and pigs were sold in Lockmeadow. The public used the right of way through Smythe and Draysons timber yard which stretched down to the towpath. Barges sailed this far up the river to deliver timber. The animals arrived on foot by road and I hated meeting a herd of cows running through the back streets, as a 14 year old on my way to work. I would dash into a doorway or shop for shelter, really frightened.'

DAME SYBIL THORNDYKE AT AYLESFORD

'The young Sybil and her brother, Russell (the author of *Dr Syn* and other books about smugglers and the Romney Marsh) lived at Aylesford for a while as their father, Reverend Thorndyke, was the vicar. My stepfather, Arthur (Curly) Russell, was the village baker and supplied the vicarage with bread.

Sybil, even in those days, was obviously keen to pursue an acting career and her brother, with her co-operation, used to write plays for her. These were enacted in the old barn next to the vicarage and when the young Curly Russell delivered the bread, he would get dragged in to act in their plays. A more unlikely actor couldn't be imagined. He was a very shy person and a man of few words.

Many years later, when Dame Sybil was famous, she came back to the village to give poetry readings etc at the Friars, which was then the home of the Copley-Hewitt family. Although it was wartime, these were evenings to be treasured, a brief respite when we could forget air raids and rationing and be soothed by the unforgettable voice of Sybil Thorndyke. Money was raised for the war effort and it was remarkable that in a busy career she remembered the village of her youth. She remembered my stepfather too and would always ask about him. In the late 1960s she came again to the church for the dedication of chairs given in memory of her father.

The barn vanished many years ago and the Friars is once again the home of the Carmelite friars.'

FIRE!

'In 1920 a steam-engined tractor went through Swanley village and a spark from it set light to the thatch of May Cottage. The fire brigade was called out. The hose cart, called "The Nellie", was kept at the basketworks in Swanley Lane, Hextable. The horses were stabled at Swanley Junction, a quarter of a mile away. The hose cart was taken to the horses and hitched up but by this time the cottage had burned down. Two new cottages were eventually built in its place. A Fiat car was later purchased, for the sum of £200, for use as a fire engine. On the test run, six men sat in the car and four on the engine with as much hose as could be accommodated!'

'In about 1928 there was a fire in the woodland near Capel and my father took me to see how the fire was dealt with. The appliance pumped water from a large pond to the scene of the fire, but it could only be pumped by a small steam-driven pump standing on the roadside and the water just trickled out of the canvas hose. The fire burnt for days.'

A 'hose cart' was kept at the Hextable basket works for use when fire broke out locally.

'At Crayford the fire appliance was very primitive. Our "fire engine" was a handcart manned by volunteers. This handcart was in a hut which was built in the churchyard wall at the top of the High Street. When in use it would have to be dragged to the fire by the firemen. It contained a large hosepipe and a bucket, but a fire hydrant would have to be found and the hose attached before the fire could be put out.'

THE 1953 FLOODS

'We all know the power of water. Many people who lived near the banks of the Thames at Gravesend can still remember the night of 1st February 1953, when the Thames was whipped into a raging inferno by winds reaching up to 80 miles an hour along the 120 miles of sea and river walls, which caused the banks to give way. In the Gravesend area, shops, houses, public houses and the brewery on West Street were flooded. It was a terrible experience with no lights and the high winds. Everything seemed to be crashing around you. Waterside residents in Gravesend and district considered at the time that these were the worst floods in living memory.

Fortunately, in this area, there were no deaths. Near the river it was tragic to see all the homes that were ruined by the water and the people trying to save some of their belongings. In the Fort Gardens, which is next to the Promenade, there was a large lake. You could not tell gardens from lake as it was all under water. Fortunately most of the goldfish were saved.

Queen Elizabeth II visited Gravesend on 13th February, the first time a reigning monarch had done so for a hundred years. The Queen arrived by ferry from Tilbury to visit distressed areas in Kent. She left later to visit Erith.

In the *Gravesend Reporter* on 14th February it said: "The Minister of Health has announced that all dentures and spectacles lost through the floods are to be replaced free of charge."'

'I worked for Burt, Boulton and Haywood, Timber Importers, at Lower Belvedere. In the 1953 floods the Thames flooded the offices and factory, and the office was transferred to a private house in Upper Belvedere. The office boy (aged about 65) spent three months drying out the files, one page at a time, in front of an electric fire. The smell was horrendous.'

LIFE IN THE WORKHOUSE

The shadow of the workhouse did not disappear with the Victorians, as this account of life in the Maidstone Union Workhouse shows.

'I started work as a seamstress at Maidstone Union Workhouse (later to become Linton Hospital) in December 1923 and during my 23 years of service I saw many changes. The building itself was of great age and was under administration from the Board of Poor Law Guardians. It served many purposes for the Maidstone area and surrounding villages. The chronic sick, the aged and infirm, mental deficients, tuberculosis patients, cancer patients were all accepted for medical treatment and careful nursing.

There was a maternity block in the hospital and a day and night nursery in another part of the building for the mothers in convalescence. If there was any family, the children over two years were placed under care of foster mothers in the Children's Home and those boys and girls over five years had to attend East Farleigh school daily on the Lower Road. It was a very long walk twice daily, in all weathers and some winters were very severe.

The children were called at 7 am and left for school at 8 am taking with them lunch, which consisted of bread and margarine, occasionally cheese, a few biscuits and either an orange, apple or banana, the gift of the Guardians or visiting committee. Home from school at 5 pm there was a hot dinner which was always welcome, of meat, two vegetables and either milk pudding or a suet pudding with syrup or jam, and at 7.30 pm always a cup of hot cocoa. At 8 pm bed, which was much appreciated, especially the travellers' families.

Usually they began to arrive after hop picking was finished and the huts closed for the winter months. There was no alternative for these unfortunate people. No work and no homes meant very little food. Not all these people were vagrants. It was just misfortune or perhaps another baby expected. And so these people were admitted and most of them stayed on through the winter months. The men were allocated work either in the kitchen or potato house, preparing vegetables for the whole of the building. Or in the wood shed chopping wood for fires which were in every ward in those days, no other heating available. The younger men were placed in numbers to prepare the land for vegetable planting as all the vegetables were grown on the grounds surrounding the building. They worked from 8 am to 12 noon and from 1 pm to 4 pm every day except Saturday, when they finished at 12 noon. For their labours they each received 1 oz of tobacco on Saturday morning. The women who were able had to help around the body of the house, making beds, sweeping and cleaning the wards, washing up and any housework required of them. The younger ones worked in the laundry and ironing room, the washing being done by hand. The pregnant mothers had to help with the mending. Unless they were ill, nobody was allowed to be idle and they used to receive a quarter pounds of sweets on Saturday morning.

On Saturday from 2 pm till 4 pm the parents were allowed to have all their children with them in the Board Room and the mother was given a bag of sweets for each of their children. These again were gifts from the House Committee. It was a pathetic picture sometimes to see these little ones greeted by their parents just for two hours in a week, unless either side was ill, then arrangements were made for visiting.

On Sunday they all had to attend Morning Service, the men sitting one side, the women the other and the children in the front pews under the watchful eye of the chaplain, the Reverend B Littlewood. How the children loved him and he loved them.

In those days everything was in short supply and the accommodation was typical Workhouse. For instance, there were only enamel mugs for the men, cups for the women but no saucers. Enamel plates for all meals, leaden forks and spoons and knives which would hardly cut. The dining tables were like long wooden trestles which were kept scrubbed. No tablecloths, no chairs, only long forms which were drawn up to the tables at meal times and placed back around the walls after meals. The floors were just bare boards, no mats or rugs and nobody was allowed to sit around the fires. Although it was cold comfort to the onlooker, you would hear them say: "At least we have got some food and a bed to lay on and we are in the dry." The beds, although spotlessly clean, were only straw mattresses on slatted iron bedsteads – no springs, but they slept. The bedding was in short supply, but each bed had one thick and one thin blanket. As the men used to say: "Better than huddling together on the Embankment."

These conditions lingered on until April 1930 when these old buildings were taken over by various councils and renamed Institutions and the stigma of the Poor Law was abolished. After about three months everything began to change and vast alterations made. All the pots and pans etc were done away with and replaced by crockery. Then the tables went and others arrived. Table linen was rushed from county stores and hurriedly made into tablecloths.

Chairs were sent by the dozens and forms collected and chopped up for firewood. Mats were placed on the floors, curtains made for all the windows and cushions were made for the chairs in the two Infirm wards and armchairs were sent for the really old people. And so it gradually built up to a place which could be called home. All the old cutlery was withdrawn and good serviceable replacements were made. In the main kitchen, all the old pots and pans were condemned and replaced by modern ones. It was a transformation after seeing all the old, dented and discoloured utensils.

After a routine check was made and everything found to be much more comfortable for the inmates, concentration was fixed on the hospital wards. All the old scrubbed wooden lockers, with no doors to hide the patients' belongings, were done away with and replaced by stained wood and tiled tops and doors to close lockers. A chair was provided for each bedside and eventually a bed table. The sister's charge table replaced the old wooden one which used to be scrubbed. The beds were replaced by hair mattresses, a little softer than straw, and the few water beds in use were condemned and replaced by air beds for the completely helpless cases. The old red blankets that served as counterpanes were replaced by white quilts for the main and coloured Alambra ones for the side wards which were used for convalescent patients chiefly. An issue of new blankets was made for hospital use and the old ones were fumigated, laundered and passed by the committee and were used as an extra blanket for the body of the house for winter use. The oldest of them were kept for use in the casual ward for late night admissions, sometimes brought in by the police in such a condition hardly fit for hands to touch through vermin and filth. These were the tramps and usually stayed no longer than 48 hours. They were fed, cleaned and left to sleep until the morning when they were cleaned again, attended to by the barber and then passed by the doctor as fit for discharge. They were given either bread and dripping or cheese and a one shilling wayfarers ticket to travel on. The one shilling was to pay for a bed in a lodging house if they could not reach the next casual ward. Hence all the bedding and also the straw bed was burnt in the big furnace and a new supply awaited the next arrival. It was not easy work for the officers on duty.

In late February or early March, weather permitting, the men were allowed out one day a week to find work for the summer months. Some of them were given a guarantee of work from their late employers so had no difficulty in getting back as soon as the farmers were allowed to open their huts. Others were less fortunate, so remained longer, but usually after 1st April, nearly all these people had left the house and would remain away until 18th October when huts closed again. Then a steady trek back was made again for the winter months. On the morning of their discharge, the fathers were given five shillings and the mothers were given a large bag of provisions to last three or four days for their first work. If there was a young baby, the mothers were given tins of food and milk to last until she got some money. Quite a few of these people were employed locally, so could shop easily. They were all fitted up with suitable clothing and boots and shoes for which they had to sign. And so they made their way. Although they were hard times for these people, there was much happiness in the building and the older people missed their company.'

CHURCH AND CHAPEL

At the heart of town and village life was membership of the church or chapel, in those days when the vicar was a familiar figure and it seemed that everyone went to church on Sunday and every child attended Sunday school. The annual Sunday school outing was often our only holiday away from home and was eagerly anticipated.

VICAR OF THIS PARISH

'There cannot be many people now living in Detling who remember my grandfather, Canon Horsley, who came here as vicar in 1911 until the summer of 1921. He was a great character, very gruff in manner and outstanding in appearance: over six feet in height and very broad shouldered, the latter because he had been a keen oarsman and rowed at Oxford for Pembroke College. He was also a great cricketer and this he kept up when he came to Detling. When I used to spend summer holidays at Detling he was still playing for the village eleven. I can remember watching the matches which, in those days, were played in the vicarage paddock which extended from the side lawns to the garden of The Croft where Mr Richard Cook lived. He used to bowl underarm but I believe got the batsmen out just as well as the more modern method which was just coming in.

The vicar's stipend at that time was about £250 a year. Out of this Canon Horsley paid the gardener Mr Weatherby, the parlourmaid Dolly Curtis, the cook Mabel Curtis (sister to Dolly) and boot boy

Tommy Curtis (brother). I think latterly Tommy went as under-gardener to The Croft where Mr Card was head gardener, but still came to the vicarage part time.

There were no cars of course when the Canon first came and no buses, so he had a rather awful old pony called Gossip who did not like work. It would take half the morning to catch him in the paddock so that he could be harnessed to the trap and be driven to Maidstone. This happened several days a week as the Canon was either at a Chapter meeting or some other business to do with the Rural Deanery of Sutton, of which Mr Lushington of Allington was Rural Dean. Often Canon Horsley had to go by train to Canterbury for meetings, or to see Archbishop Davidson when he and his wife were resident at the Palace.

I remember him as a rather long preacher, but quite interesting although I was only about ten or twelve when I used to hear him at matins and evensong. The only thing was that he would spend a lot of time scolding the congregation who were in church for not coming, which was rather bad luck on them! He was not at all musical and rarely sang the hymns, but there was quite a good choir of men and girls and youngsters – most of them were Browns or Kitneys. Gladys Card could not really manage the organ but she did her best and kept the choir together, even teaching them little anthems to sing.

Canon Horsley was a very good visitor and would walk all round the parish boundaries before lunch! Seven miles, he told my aunt when he arrived back very hungry. I can remember him dragging me and my small sister all up along the woods on the Lynch and across the Fuzzy Field to visit Scragged Oak and Pollhill Farms; also a tiny, but lovely, little cottage the name of which I have unfortunately forgotten. This was a glebe cottage which was sold by the Church Commissioners after Canon Horsley died and the money was added to the stipend which was thus made up to about £350 a year. Not much on which to bring up and educate a family, even in those days, and pay a gardener and a cook general, as well as all the rates and taxes and internal repairs and dilapidations on the old, very large vicarage.'

MOTHER WAS A DEVIL DODGER

'I was born in 1938. My mother was a "devil dodger" – Church of England on Sunday morning and Methodist chapel in the evening. However, it was the chapel that played an important part in our lives throughout the war and into the 1950s.

In the kitchen every Sunday evening my brother and I had a cold flannel whisked around our faces, hands and knees (there was no bathroom or running hot water). A brush and comb would be dragged through my long curly hair and it was then plaited into two pigtails and secured with elastic bands. On Sundays these were concealed with colourful satin bows. My brother and I would then be led by Mother to walk the two miles along a lonely country lane to arrive in time for the commencement of the chapel service at 6.30 pm.

Our chapel was situated on a small plot on the edge of a hamlet surrounded by apple orchards. It was an uninspiring building both outside and inside. There was a central aisle with pews on each side which could accommodate about 100 worshippers. The pulpit was in the centre at the end of the aisle and was approached from the side by several steps. What a view the minister had of his congregation. 'n winter it was lit by eight attractive brass hanging oil lamps. The windows were large and oblong, no stained glass adorned this building. In wartime the chapel windows were blacked out at night y using sacking from the hop pockets.

Every week a different preacher would arrive to conduct the service, often coming by bicycle from the nearest town some eight miles distance. Our pew was two rows from the back. There I could sit swinging my legs backwards and forwards and allocating my extra strong mints to be munched one every quarter of an hour. These had been given to me by my chapel neighbour, Miss Reid, clothed entirely in black and seeming ancient to me. But often the hour would be more than four quarters!

Sitting at the back gave me the opportunity to while away the time surveying the members of the congregation. There was Brother David with his rosy, weatherbeaten face acquired from working on the farm in all weathers. He would be called upon to read the notices and announce the preacher for the following week. Mrs Bridger was tall and thin. She smiled and said "Good evening" and sat at the front. She wore a fur coat like the doctor's wife.

One evening a member made it apparent that he was having trouble digesting the proceedings and finding it difficult to sit upright in the pew, he cupped his hand to rest his chin and supported his elbow on his knee. He drifted into a snooze. When his elbow slipped he almost fell from his seat. He made an audible remark but undeterred the preacher commented that in order to prevent it happening again he would have to raise his voice! An entertaining evening.

An important part of the worship was the music. The singing was led by a lady playing a harmonium. She had a sunny face and wearing her best hat she would be perched on her stool and as she depressed each pedal her whole body swayed to the rhythm. Following along behind her were a cello, two violins, two clarinets and a piccolo. There was no conductor so the music was rather ragged but there was a lot of enthusiasm as they praised God in that small building. There was great relief when the parson said, "We will now join together to sing the last hymn." But we always had to act out a slow polite departure while everybody shook hands with the preacher and with everybody else. There was further relief when Mother did not "stay on". This was when the musicians and some of the congregation remained to play and sing their favourite hymns.

For me the highlight of the year was Harvest Festival. The chapel was overflowing with locally grown produce all lovingly picked and polished, chrysanthemums, dahlias, Michaelmas daisies and not forgetting the hop bines. The pulpit, where the Bible also rested, would be decorated with five bunches of the most perfect black grapes still wearing a misty bloom. I admired the skill of the baker in producing a sheaf of corn from dough, about two feet high, each ear of corn clearly defined. On entering the chapel, an aroma of God's gifts would welcome you. This was an occasion when I knew I would be squeezed up in the pew and extra chairs would be put in the aisle. I also enjoyed singing my favourite hymns. A puzzling event occurred the next evening. We would return for another thanksgiving but this was different. It would be followed by an auction sale of the goods. Suddenly this sacred place would be turned into a market. However, there was always a chance that Mother would buy us a bunch of the grapes I had gazed at so longingly.

As I entered my teenage years, I drifted away from the chapel to Father's domain, the parish church. This was much more interesting – a massive pipe organ pumped at the back by hand, boys in the choir, more boys in the belfry and a youth club.'

EVERYONE WENT TO CHURCH

'I was born in 1897 at St Paul's Cray. That was the age of horse-drawn carriages and long swishing dresses. Earl Sydney was the patron of St Paulinus' church and my mother used to recall seeing his footmen in powdered wigs coming into church with rugs to keep the ladies' feet warm during services. Everyone went to church then and the Sunday school was something we looked forward to.'

'In our house at Crayford in the 1920s, there was not much time for cooking on Sundays. A joint of meat surrounded by potatoes was put into a large tin and taken to the local baker for roasting. It was collected a couple of hours later ready for eating.'

SUNDAY SCHOOL

'I was only three when I first attended the afternoon Sunday school at the local Southborough Baptist Mission in Bromley, clutching my penny for the collection which was made to the sound of our small voices chorusing "Hear the pennies dropping, listen while they fall". I also remember singing "Little modest violet blue, spangled in the morning dew". When I grew older I attended the morning Sunday school. Good attendance was rewarded by joining the annual Sunday school treat to Margate, participated in by many of the local churches.

We met up and walked the mile to Bickley station where we joined the Margate train, filled with excited children all armed with spades, buckets and streamers. The sun always shone and the sand always got into our sandwiches. Most of us wore bright red or orange swimming costumes (our mothers said that they could spot us more easily). We built castles and paddled and splashed in the sea and the day seemed to last for ever. Tea-time came round and we trailed off to Lyons after which we finished the day in Dreamland, where we went on roundabouts and swingboats and screamed throughout our journey on the Ghost Train. Then came the journey back from Margate station to Bickley where we were met by the Dads. We were all very tired but still had the mile walk back home from the station before being tucked into our beds. It never rained on those treats and the memories of those rare outings stayed with us, often revived when, later on, we found sandy pieces of nougat in our blazer pockets or when we inspected the seaweed brought back in our buckets for our personal weather forcasting.

The Band of Hope also played a big part in our social life in those times. A requirement of membership was that we refrain from intoxicating liquor and we signed a pledge that many of us honoured for many years. We used to entertain once a year with songs and poems. There were always prizes for regular attendance and good behaviour which I always treasured and kept.'

A MEMORABLE DAY

'The annual Sunday school outing was the highlight of the year at Chelsfield (though, of course, the Christmas party was also a very special occasion). A week's stay at the seaside was not something that could be considered by the smallholders and farm labourers living in this corner of Kent before the Second World War, so one day at the coast was a real treat. Allegiance to church or chapel tended to waver during early summer depending on which outing was to be first and where it was to be. Hastings was the usual destination, but sometimes Margate was visited.

Chelsfield children off on their Sunday school outing in 1938, the highlight of the year for many of them.

Much preparation was done by the Sunday school superintendent or a deputy. I remember lengthy discussions about the state of the tide on certain dates – would it be coming in or going out? I guess this had some influence on the choice of venue. Letters would be written to find a suitable place for "the tea" – usually a church of the same denomination. Parents were expected to pay the full amount, but the children were subsidised and, of course, "the tea" was included.

Best clothes were usually the order of the day as one didn't want to let the side down. The ladies wore straw hats regardless of the weather, decorated with artificial flowers, fruit or ribbon. The boys were very smart in grey flannel short trousers with matching jackets and knee-length grey socks. Shoes were well polished and hair well brushed. The girls were equally well turned out with pristine cotton socks and well ironed dresses. (It would be a very different story when we returned.)

The A21 was not what we know today with bypasses and dual carriageways, and Penfold's charabanc chugged up hill and down dale hour after hour, or so it seemed to us small children packed three to a seat. There was great relief all round when the Blue Boy came in sight, not least on the part of the driver who would need to top up the radiator before the second leg of the journey.

All eyes would be eager for the first distant glint of the sea. The less adventurous of the smaller children settled on the chosen piece of beach, while the teenagers – a description not then part of our language – would head for the fun-fair or the pier with many instructions about the time and place for tea.

The sight and smell of the steam rising from the tea urns at the end of each long damask-covered table laden with fish-paste and cucumber sandwiches, scones and cakes must be a vision tucked away in the recesses of many minds.

The homeward journey always began at six o'clock and we all tried to get that last glimpse of the sea by kneeling on the seats. It would be almost dark by the time sticky salt and sand-encrusted passengers tumbled out of the "chara" after a very memorable day.'

AFTER SCHOOL ON SUNDAY

' I attended the little chapel for Sunday school at Northfleet in the 1930s. My father used to meet us after Sunday school and take us for a walk across the fields to Springhead Gardens. We would buy a twopenny bunch of watercress, a pint of Gravesend brown shrimps, a pound of freshly picked tomatoes, and a bag of monkey nuts to feed the two monkeys they kept as pets!'

GETTING ABOUT

We relied on horse power to get us about at the beginning of the century, or Shanks's pony! The bicycle gave us greater freedom, then cars began to appear on the roads, though it was only after the 1940s that many of us could hope to have one in the family. The country buses and steam trains have also kept their place in our memories.

HOW TIMES CHANGE

'My very first memory of living in the small village of Ryarsh was the horrid feeling when my mother tipped up the large high pram wheels to get over the edge of the step down the slope to the road.

This was my first recollection of transport, and with my younger sister tucked up safely in one end I perched, legs dangling, at the far end; I was just four and this way Mother walked the three and a half miles to Fairseat where a great friend of hers kept the post office. Miss Hendon was her name and she was a large jolly lady and used to ask for me to be allowed to sit on the very high counter. I loved this and as this post office housed the telephone exchange at that time my mother and her friend would be stopped in their chat by the phone buzzing. This necessitated several plugs being pulled out and changing over and then the bit I loved to see and hear, Miss Hendon took hold of a handle on the side of the switchboard and turned it madly, having said into the mouthpiece, "One moment and I will put you through".

It was a long time before I really grasped what this meant; but at this time there were only two or three people in Stansted with the telephone at home. Because of this we used to hear fairly often the noise of small hooves trotting down Fairseat hill and it was very often while we were sitting in school. We all knew who and what it was but we soon found out if we fidgeted enough and craned our necks the teacher would say in exasperation, "Very well then, if you must go and look at Mr Turble and his donkey cart."

As time went on we journeyed to Fairseat, my sister and I, sharing the back of a fat pony called Kitty. I disliked this very much and I think Mother knew and quite soon I learned to ride a small bike; everyone went everywhere with one of these. My next four-wheeled transport was more to my liking, Grandad's old Model T Ford. My legs were so short and the back seat so high my feet couldn't touch the floor but oh, what bliss and now I could go to school and say, "Yes, I'd ridden in a car." We didn't see many cars at this time, about 1925. Children walked miles morning and night to and from school and those who went on to Wrotham had very long dark walks in winter time. Fortunately in those days it was only the dark that we children feared; how time changes things and folk.'

IT COST A PENNY

'When I was a child at Fordcombe in 1921 we at first had no bus service and my mother would push me the two miles to Langton village to catch a bus. Later we had two buses – the Autocar and the Redcar. When they had a price war we could travel in to Tunbridge Wells for something like a penny.

We often saw the old timber tugs slowly going up Spring Hill, pulled by two shire horses. The timber was stacked on a long trailer at the back and the wheels were fitted with iron shoes which stopped them slipping.

Early Shell petrol pumps at Brenchley in 1937. There were still few cars on the roads.

There was no tarmac on the roads in the early 1920s, and they were surfaced with a fine gravel, which was responsible for many grazed knees. The village roadman, who swept the roads and kept the verges clear, was a friend to all the children walking to and from school and he often chatted to my brother and me as we collected grit from the sides of the road for mixing with the chicken feed – it was supposed to help in the production of hard eggshells.'

'Most houses at Brasted had their own stables and there were very few cars in the village. Lord Philip Stanhope, of Weardale Manor, used to send his Daimler out to pick up and drop people at the station. Harry Hubble had a taxi which would ferry people to the races or sometimes to the seaside.

A major link with neighbouring towns came in 1919 when the first East Surrey bus arrived en route for Sevenoaks and Reigate. Initially it cost a penny to take the gleaming red double-decker bus from The Bull to New Road. It was twopence as far as the White Horse Inn, threepence to Dryhill Lane and fourpence to Chipstead corner. As far as Bessels Green cost a shilling, to Riverhead sixpence, to Sevenoaks station sevenpence, The Vine eightpence, and ninepence to Market Square. The buses had tarpaulin seats so that if it rained you clipped the tarpaulin over your head to keep dry. The drivers were not enclosed either and had to have a tarpaulin cover over them.'

MIND YOUR HEADS!

'In the 1920s an open-topped double-decker bus, number 410, ran through Westerham. If it rained there were tarpaulin covers supplied which you could draw up under your chin, or even hide under completely. When the bus went under a bridge the conductor would come up the stairs and shout "Mind your heads" and we all ducked down low to avoid being decapitated.

Another bus we sometimes travelled by was the single-decker bus up from Crockham Hill. Sometimes this bus just could not manage the steep hill coming up from Crockham Hill to Kent Hatch, and then all the passengers had to get out and walk up the hill and the bus waited for them at the top. One very hot day when we had walked up we found there was a Walls "stop me and buy one" ice cream man at the top with his tricycle. So everyone, including the driver and conductor, bought an ice cream. Good business for the ice cream man!'

'When I was a child at Wilmington, I remember having to get off the bus when it could not make it to the top of Church Hill. When the passengers were all off, the conductor would put a wooden block behind the back wheels to stop the bus running back down the hill. Then the passengers would help to push the bus over the brow of the hill to flatter ground. On occasions the driver would drive off leaving some passengers behind.

At the bottom of the hill the trees growing either side made an archway across the road. In the winter there were just bare branches but in the summer, when the trees were in full leaf, it was a beautiful sight. The only drawback was, as the buses were open-topped, if it was or had been raining, you had to duck to keep from getting wet.'

BUSES, TRAINS AND PLANES

'The West Kent Bus Company moved to the aerodrome at Sundridge in 1929, operating from there for ten years. The hangar was used to garage and maintain the buses. The company was started at the end of 1927, with a circular route which ran in both directions around Sevenoaks. The East Surrey Bus Company also operated in this area, from Sevenoaks to Otford, and Sevenoaks to Seal was served by the Maidstone & District Company. Care had to be taken not to intrude on the others' bus stops and routes. West Kent Company's drivers were supplied with a smart uniform consisting of brown jacket, with yellow piping around the collar and trousers, together with gaiters, the whole uniform resembling a chauffeur's outfit. Later they wore their own clothes, due to financial restrictions.

West Kent buses stopped anywhere when signalled, and ran through all the villages, running all day until 10.30 at night. The bus driver would wait for regular passengers if they were not at the bus stop, and even knock on their front door to see if they were travelling that day. The last bus from Sevenoaks would wait outside the cinema for passengers to come out, and would not go without them. If anyone returned from Sevenoaks with a heavy load of shopping the bus would stop at their house and the conductor would carry the shopping to the door! The last bus from Edenbridge to Chipstead used to stop at every pub, and a great time was had by all! There were no traffic jams to hold them up. Up at Bessels Green there was a clock with a box in it, and the drivers had to check in with it, getting into trouble if they were early, let alone late. They were allowed a few minutes to be late, but had to stand and wait till the exact minute before going on if they were early. The inspector used to wave buses out from the car park in Sevenoaks, so you went out on time. Buses parked in the old Market Place.

Villagers from Chipstead used Chevening Halt to catch the single-track train which ran back and forth from Westerham to Dunton Green, where it connected with the trains going up to London, Charing Cross, or down to Sevenoaks, Tonbridge, Tunbridge Wells and the South Coast. This useful train connected them with Brasted and Sundridge, and is remembered with affection. Drivers and guards were very helpful, waiting for late passengers, helping mothers and babies on and off, and generally providing a service for all.

The airport at Sundridge belonged to a private person, who owned two planes in the First World War. Later, trips were offered to the public at five shillings a time.

The road from Chipstead Common to Chipstead was originally a private road, with a lodge at either end. The Meyersteins of Morants Court were responsible for the bypass not being built for a long time as they would not part with the ground. The A21 bypass was proposed in the late 1920s and it took all those years to get it done. Sevenoaks was snarled up with traffic at weekends, and when children we would go down to Riverhead on a Sunday and sit round to be entertained by the traffic, which used to crawl through the village before the Second World War. We looked forward to Derby Day or Ascot, as the coach passengers would throw coppers out of the windows to the children. Dozens of coaches used to go through and it was quicker to walk to Sevenoaks as the traffic was so held up.'

52

High Street, West Malling and a new motor bus in about 1925.

OUR STEAM TRAINS

'I remember the original plan hatched by builder Richard Durtnell and Colonel William Tippin to link Brasted with mainline railways between London and the Sussex coast. In the end the track only reached as far west as Westerham but they intended to get it as far as Oxted and join up with the London to Brighton line. I used to take the train every day to Tonbridge County school and change at Dunton Green.

The overall journey used to take more than an hour because we would have to wait 40 minutes at Dunton Green. The station was geared to London and people on the Brasted Flyer would cross over and almost immediately be on their way. There were three classes: first for the posh people, second class for season ticket holders, and third for the rest. Schoolchildren and commuters used to go second class and people going out for the day third class. The Flyer was nearly always full because it was such a popular mode of transport.'

'It was in February 1929 that we moved to the village of Green St Green. The road where our house was situated was unmade, very rough with deep ruts which soon filled with water when it rained. When we walked along it we had to constantly cross from one side to the other for somewhere drier to walk. It stayed like that for a number of years.

When I started work later that year I had to cross three fields to

Chelsfield station. In the waiting room in winter there was always a lovely coal fire burning, which was very welcome after the walk over open fields. In those days the trains were all steam.'

'Only four or five houses existed at Badgers Mount in 1923, then more houses were built in the 1930s. The air and smoke vents for the railway, seen on the Mount, were a great source of interest to residents in the 1930s. A bowler hatted man would be stationed beside each one when the Queen's train, carrying her to Dover, passed through in case a missile was thrown down. The stationmaster was suitably attired in his full uniform for when the train passed through Knockholt station.

Transport was scarce and no buses ran until the late 1930s, then only one a week, so many people used the train. In 1937 the season ticket to London cost £4 8s a quarter and as wages were low, many travelled on a "workman's ticket" leaving before 6 am.

A notice to "alight here for Badgers Mount" was displayed at the station until 1940, when for security reasons it was taken down.'

HOUSE & HOME

THE WAY WE
LIVED THEN

The thatched country cottage with roses round the door was reality for many of us in the past – but with large families, low wages and few mod cons they were perhaps not always the good old days!

GRANDMOTHER'S STORY

'I was six years old when, in 1940, my mother and I returned to live with my grandparents. Theirs was an old semi-detached house in the village of Teston, near Maidstone, surrounded then by orchards and hop fields. This is my grandmother's story, how life was for her then as I remember it.

She was a redoubtable lady who had lived through one war and was determined to survive through another. My grandfather was a cricket ball maker and though his was a skilled job, his wages were small so every penny was spent with care. She never bought what she could make herself, using jam and fruit carefully preserved the previous summer. Nothing was wasted; any leftover bread was made into large bread puddings which I remember as being very filling.

Everything was cooked in the old-fashioned kitchen range and it was a work of art stoking the fire up enough to get the correct heat for the oven. It was always in immaculate condition as it was blackleaded every week and regularly on Fridays the dreaded flues had to be cleaned. The kitchen was large with high roof and stone floor. Leading from it was a large pantry with big wire safe where milk, butter and meat were kept. Once a week Gran would scrub the floor and the matting rugs which covered it, then a final scrub would leave the large kitchen table ready again for use. All food preparation was done on that table and we sat round it for meals.

Rain or shine, Monday was washing day. A fire was lit under the copper in the kitchen and clothes were boiled thoroughly, then it was time to put them through the mangle. That was my job. I loved turning the mangle. When it was time for ironing, two flat irons were placed on the range and were used in rotation. My grandfather always wore a white shirt on Sundays so these were always ironed with great care. Sunday was her rest day, that was after she had cooked the dinner and cleared up. In the evening she always went to church; it was her one outing of the week apart from the Women's Union meetings which she always attended. Out would come her best hat, felt with feathers on it for winter, hard black straw with flowers for summer. One never went to church without a hat.

Evening service at that time was well attended and afterwards little groups stood around chatting; all the gossip of the week was related after church on Sundays.

This was my grandmother's life, hard and drab by today's standards but I never once heard her complain and though she had very little I think she was happier than many young women today.'

ONE SHILLING TO RENT

'I was one of nine children, living in Church Row at Plaxtol at the turn of the century. We had one of a row of 18th century weather-boarded cottages west of the church. The cottages had three bedrooms and cost one shilling a week to rent.

The girls slept in one bedroom, boys in the next and Mum and Dad and whoever was the baby in the other. Some families in Plaxtol had round beds with the mattress on the floor and the whole family slept with their feet together in the middle.

I never remember my mother going to bed; she was up when we went to bed and up when we got up. Our upbringing was strict but fair. Our mother was in charge all day, and Father when he came home.'

COLLEGE COTTAGES

'I was born in 1911 and lived in one of College Cottages at Swanley. These were five cottages built in an L-shape, with another that was used as a washhouse. The residents of each cottage had a set day to do their washing.

On entering our cottage you had to go down a steep step to avoid hitting your head on a huge wooden beam just inside the door. The floor of the scullery was cement and there was a long stone sink only six inches deep. In the sitting room there was a fire with three bars and an oven next to it. All food was cooked on the fire.

Each house had an outside toilet. At numbers one and two it was outside the back door, but the others had one at the end of the garden.

I remember my father finding a horseshoe when digging in the garden, which he nailed over the door for luck.'

GROWING UP ON THE ESTATE

'I was born in the 1920s in one of the estate cottages at Southborough as my father was the head gardener of three. Next to our cottage was the stable yard. Although the mounting block was still there, the carriages had given way to cars, but the harness room was still more or less intact. However, the loose boxes and stalls housed lawn mowers, lawn sweepers and similar items.

The chauffeur lived in the other cottage. To the other side of our cottage was the laundry, with large copper and stone sink. It was no longer used as the washing was sent out to a laundry in large wicker baskets. Leading from the laundry was the ironing room, again no longer used, but still with the cast iron stove with the shaped surfaces on which to heat the flat-irons. Above the grass "drying area" was the cart shed, then home to wheelbarrows, handbarrows and miscellaneous items. Next door was the fruit room, housing the ripe fruit on slatted shelves, covered in hay, and root vegetables stored underneath in sand. Behind the tool shed was the frame yard, leading to the potting shed and greenhouses. The three linking houses contained the vinery, tomato house and peach house. The plants that were to furnish the conservatory in the house were raised here and carried down, through the garden on the handbarrow. The other greenhouse had figs, nectarines and a few orchids. The gardens were never short of water for there were two springs in the top field, one of which flowed through the pleasure gardens, starting in the goldfish pond, and the other one flowed into the frame yard supplying three watercress beds.

I think, living in such an environment, I was introduced to fruit such as peaches, nectarines, grapes and figs, which my friends did not have. Admittedly, they were usually specimens that had dropped on to the staging and got bruised, so were not suitable for the "big house".

From the vegetable garden came asparagus, globe artichokes and sea kale. There was also a nut walk and a walnut tree, but the squirrels did not leave many.

We had one horse, Peggy, retired after the First World War, but still needed, very grudgingly, to do a little work occasionally. This was usually rolling the drive or the grass tennis court. For this she had to wear leather shoes strapped to her hooves.

In those days, most tradesmen delivered. The baker came every day with a horse and van, carrying the bread in large wicker baskets. "Charlie" the butcher boy called two or three times a week for orders and delivered them later in the morning, by bike of course. Similarly the grocer on a Friday and the "Oil Man" with paraffin on a Friday afternoon. All the errand boys whistled. The milkman delivered

Thatched cottages were picturesque but before 'mod cons' it was a hard life. Mr and Mrs Mills outside May Cottage, Hextable. Mr Mills was the last man in the village to wear a smock.

twice a day, the milk being measured by the pint and half-pint measure, carried inside the large can. Our milkman had the right to graze his cattle on the common and they would wander down to drink at Halden Pond before going back to Modest Corner and their farm. There were postal deliveries and collections three times a day.

At the top of our road was the smithy, still very much in use then as there were a lot of horses still on the roads. We loved to gather round the doorway, for we were not allowed inside, to watch in the rather murky atmosphere, and the smell, when the hot shoe was put on the hoof, cannot be described or forgotten.

The common was a safe and enjoyable playground for all the children, but how different it looks now. We would fish in the pond, with a cane from the toolshed, string, a bent pin but a *real* bought float. Sometimes, to cast, we would lay the line out behind us across the road, hoping that the occasional car would not appear.

There were two laundries at Modest Corner, one hand and one machine. The large one dried the sheets on lines on its roof, while the hand one had a drying ground on the common. The works hooter was blown at five minutes to the hour and on the hour at 8 am, 1 pm, 2 pm and 5 pm, a very useful timekeeper. Much of the estate is now filled with executive-type houses but I prefer to remember it as it was, ten acres to grow up and be happy in.'

COSTUMES AND LARGE FAMILIES

'There is a great contrast between the lives of older people and the way they live now. They had hardly any social life and never wore bright colours, which would have shocked local opinion. The really old ladies at Chipstead wore shawls, not coats, and flat little hats pinned on with hatpins. The well-to-do wore "costumes", a matching long jacket and skirt, and always a hat and gloves. Dry cleaning was not common so brushing was all the cleaning these garments received. The lady in charge of the nursing home at Riverhead wore the same costume summer and winter, tucking her hands in her sleeves to keep them warm. She had a room at the top of the house where the servants were, with an iron bedstead, and no fire, and only one blanket.

People had larger families then than nowadays. One lady recalls that although there were three children in their small bungalow, they still took in a lodger for a time. Another recalls that her mother and father raised six children in a four-roomed cottage, with mother and father and baby in one small bedroom and five children in the other, in a double bed and a single bed.'

ON A NEW ESTATE

'Our home was on a newly built estate at Dartford and at first had no made up road or footpaths. Four houses along the road the estate finished and there was a fence separating us from farm land. Peering through this fence was a favourite pastime. In season we would see the ploughing, then, when the potato crop was ready, these being lifted and put into sacks. Further up there were raspberry canes, then a public footpath across the fields where, after crossing a stile, we could enjoy the freedom of Dartford Heath where we were often taken for picnics.

The house being new was, for those days, fairly modern. The copper in the kitchen, providing it was kept well fed with coal, gave us hot water which by means of a hand pump was sent up to the bathroom on the landing. This was a job for my father as my mother was neither tall enough or strong enough to cope with it. At Christmas, a board was placed in the bottom of this copper and the puddings were put in for their long boiling. There were three of these, one each for Christmas, New Year and for my birthday in February.

In the living room was the range which had the fire to one side and the oven on the other. It had to be constantly blackleaded but cooked things to perfection. In the summer it was abandoned for the gas cooker in the kitchen. Having lived in Canada for a few years, my mother was used to having an ice box and continued to have one here. The large blocks of ice that went into the zinc container were delivered twice weekly and were a great attraction for all children around who congregated to be given little chips of ice by the delivery man. The drainage tray at the back had to be emptied every day as the ice melted.

The third room on the ground floor was the parlour, where my mother had her beloved piano. At the weekend, when we weren't sent to bed so early, she would play for us to sing or just listen. Then after we were in bed she would play some classical music and providing we hadn't drifted off to sleep in the meantime, when she played her signature tune *Canadian Capers*, we knew that was the end of that evening's concert.

There were other things to look forward to at the weekend – the muffin man with his handbell to announce his arrival; the man in a blue sailor's jersey with a basket of shrimps and winkles; then on Saturday evening the hot pie man. We would listen anxiously to see if my father went out. We knew, if he did, and we were very quiet, we would be allowed to sit up in bed and have a small piece of pie each. On Sunday afternoon in summer, there was the ice cream van. There is nothing to compare now with that cornet of real Italian ice cream.

A yearly event was the fair held in a large field in the centre of the town. Although this was only an annual event the area was always known as the Fairfield. The music, the lights, the various rides were all exciting and at the entrance there was always a crowd watching the stall where toffee and peppermint was thrown over a large hook then pulled. This was repeated time and time again until it turned colour and was made into large humbugs or rock.'

COAL DUST

'We had only a farmworker's cottage at Hextable, with fireplaces in every room. Log fires were common at weekends and coal was kept in the cupboard under the stairs. The coalman would call every week and I well remember having to get up from the kitchen table so he could empty his bag into the coal cellar. If we had a dry spell the dust would fly everywhere. On wet days if the coal sack touched the wallpaper, that had to be cleaned off as best as one could.'

LIGHT AND HEAT

'There was no gas or electricity in the 1920s at Fordcombe, and going to bed in the winter time was accompanied by a lighted candle and a heated brick wrapped in a piece of flannel. Winter evenings were spent in the warm glow of an oil lamp on the dining table, where we sat to play cards, draughts or halma, snakes and ladders, ludo or dominoes, or just to read our books. Mother cooked on a kitchen range in the winter, and on a Valor Perfection stove, which had a portable oven, in the summer. Kettles and irons were heated on the fire, and held by scraps of material to protect our hands.'

BAKED IN THE BRICK OVEN

'My mother-in-law was born in 1882 and was the daughter of a farmer living in Leigh, near Penshurst. She could remember having to fetch their drinking water from a tap in Leigh High Street, set into the wall surrounding Hale Place. The farm had a pump in the yard but in the absence of any sort of drainage system and with the proximity of farmyard and cesspool, it was not fit to drink. Bathing was done in the kitchen with water heated in the old brick copper, after seeing that all five kitchen doors were bolted!

They baked all their bread in a brick oven. This was heated by burning three faggots and when these were reduced to ashes, the oven was swept out with a handful of green twigs, the bricks being so hot that the bristles of a brush would have caught alight. Seven large loaves and three big fruit cakes were placed in the oven and were a week's supply for the family and those farm workers who ate in the kitchen. Cabbage leaves were placed on the top of the loaves to make them shiny.'

NO REFUSE COLLECTION

'The cottages opposite the pub at Betsham had a communal backyard, no gardens and no refuse collection. Every household had to deposit their refuse in the yard. This they did all in one corner and it was cleared about every three months by a local firm. It was taken out to the fields of a farmer and spread over the ground. When the refuse was moved the smell was bad enough, but the rats that came out were as big as young rabbits.'

CANDLES ON THE TABLE

'My father was a champion ploughman when we lived at Eynsford. The night before a ploughing match, we all used to sit round the kitchen table polishing the brasses. Sometimes we sat up all night but the horses looked beautiful; my father loved them. The prizes were often blankets and my father won enough to give each of us a pair when we got married.

My brothers were a lot older than me. They were out courting when I was little. Mother used to leave six candles on the kitchen table at night. They all took one upstairs when they came home and the last one knew to lock the door.'

THE COMING OF ELECTRICITY

'Electricity was not in use until the 1930s. Bigger houses had installed their own generators, but "company electricity" did not appear at Crockham Hill until 1926. This supplied enough to smaller houses and cottages to provide light to the ground floor and one power point that would heat a new-fangled iron or kettle.

With the coming of mains electricity, those with their own generators found the supply did not suit their own gadgets. There was much selling of generators and equipment. Candles and oil lamps were not thrown away though, they were still needed to light your way upstairs.

Until the electricity supply could be guaranteed, the wireless was powered by a heavy accumulator. An intermediary stage was a home charger that plugged into your own electricity supply, and then charged the accumulator that fed the set.'

'Vacuum cleaners were only used on special occasions to begin with, as they were not regarded as being very efficient. Housewives would get their long brooms out, sprinkle the carpet with tea leaves and then brush the dirt away. The electricity company gave house package deals when we were connected to the supply in the 1930s, giving away shades, bulbs etc. Electric irons and kettles could be hired from the company for a penny a week.'

WATER AND WASHDAY

Water was precious, every drop coming from pump or well and carried into the home. There was no running water indoors, and so only the rich had bathrooms – for some of us it was the public baths once a week, or more usually the tin bath in front of the fire! It also meant, of course, no indoor sanitation. Washday was a weekly chore that demanded gallons of water and hours of hard work.

AT THE BOTTOM OF THE GARDEN

'I lived in Wouldham in the 1930s. There was no electricity in the village so we used lamps and candles. Lavatories were sited at the bottom of the garden and the buckets were emptied at midnight by a man with a horse and cart who then took it up to School Lane and emptied on the fields.'

'One of my earliest memories at Halling is of the "lavatory cart". Living in the country, the privy was way up the garden path or across the backyard. It was usually just a piece of wood with a hole in it and a bucket if you were lucky.

Sometimes in the middle of the night we would be woken up by the sound of horses' hooves. A big grey carthorse pulling a very old tanker would trundle up the road and old Mr Norris would go up and down the garden paths emptying the lavatory buckets till daybreak. This must have been the worst job ever.'

ONLY THE RICH HAD BATHROOMS

'Only the rich had bathrooms at Rainham when I lived there just after the First World War. Most of us had outside toilets. Between the toilet and the kitchen was a building that housed a stone copper for boiling up the weekly wash. The water was heated by lighting a fire of wood and coal at the bottom of it. A zinc bath stood on a bench beside it to rinse the wash. There was no piped hot water, it all had to be heated in kettles on the gas stoves.

Bedrooms had washstands with a china basin and a jug of cold water, soap dish, toothbrush jar and, of course, a chamber pot. Some winters I had to break the ice on the water jug before I could wash.

My grandparents lived in an old manor house called Great Kewlands at the foot of Bluebell Hill near Maidstone. The house had been divided into two and an aunt and uncle and their five children had one part, which contained a large wooden wheel twelve feet in diameter. This was intended for a donkey to get inside and tread the wheel round to draw water from the well. We children had great fun racing round it. A tap and running water had been connected so the well water was only required for the thirsty chalk soil in the garden.'

'I was born in 1913 at Well Hill, a hamlet a mile or so above the village of Chelsfield. Water had to be carried from a well a few minutes' walk away (there were said to be 13 wells on Well Hill, hence the name). When I was about ten years old, my parents had a bungalow built on a piece of land where we were fortunate enough to have a natural spring. My father had a large underground water tank built, and from this water could be pumped up by force-pump up to a tank in the loft. There was no electricity or gas and my father had to stand in the kitchen and pump by hand for a length of time each evening, and thus we made history by having "tap drawn" water and a proper bath and washbasin.'

THE MUNICIPAL BATHS

'When I was twelve in 1928, I was a keen swimmer and visited the Maidstone Baths every week. I felt it was very unfair that females were not allowed in the large pool, which had a springboard and chute, as the males sometimes wore the briefest of slips, much too revealing! I remember the fuss and uproar in the press when the council allowed one session of mixed bathing per week, with the proviso that everyone wore regulation swimwear. All females had to wear bathing caps and their pool was quite small. The changing cubicles were on each side of the pool with half doors which showed legs and heads. You undressed, stepped out and could dive right into the water.

Every weekend the baths would be filled with clean, clear water but by Saturday it was so murky one could hardly see the bottom. On Saturday afternoon the water was let into the river and the pools were scrubbed with bast brooms and hosed down ready for refilling with clean water. Charges varied, getting cheaper each day until by Saturday morning it was one penny. By the time I was 16, mixed bathing was allowed most evenings and that was when I met the boy who became my husband.

Not many houses had bathrooms in the 1920s and 1930s so it was usual to visit the public baths once a week. You would be given a rough towel and a small piece of soap, shown to a cubicle and the

Living at Gads Hill, Higham, this typical family of 1910 had a small cottage with no running water or indoor sanitation, heated by a coal fire and lit by oil lamps and candles.

attendant would turn on the taps from the outside with a key. If more hot or cold water was needed you called out. When your allotted time was up the attendant would bang on the door to let you know.'

THE COPPER

'The copper was built in the corner of the washhouse. It was made of brick and covered in cement with the copper inside. The flue went around the copper then there was a metal grate for the fire underneath which was fuelled by wood. A request from Mum for a bundle of dry sticks, to get the water boiling, was a familiar cry on Mondays. The copper was covered with a white, well bleached wooden lid, which made an excellent shield when playing soldiers. Then there was an equally bleached pole to fish the washing out of the copper.

Monday was for the whites and Tuesday for coloured clothes. When we walked home from school at midday on a Monday she would still be busy washing. A quick meal would be prepared with, sometimes, a favourite chocolate pudding which I was allowed to make – cubes of bread covered with hot cocoa. Friday and Saturday were bath nights when the copper water was made hot and carried in a bucket to the tin bath by the kitchen fire. The copper was also used for preserving fruit. The bottles were placed in a half bushel wicker basket. The Christmas puddings were also cooked in the wicker basket. Dad like to sterilise his potting compost in a bucket in the copper – not with Mum's approval.

After emptying the water from the copper, the top was cleaned with hearthstone, the lid scrubbed and the fireplace swept out of ashes. How can a modern washing machine be compared with the many uses of the old fashioned copper?'

WASHDAY

'As a small child, I lived in the same row of houses as my paternal grandmother and Gran had a copper in the corner of the scullery. (I had one, too, when I was first married.)

What a godsend was the copper. On washdays everything went "up the copperhole" to boil the water for the washing. Cardboard, rubber tyres, plimsolls and rags, the copper helped us to get rid of the rubbish and save on fuel. Washday seemed to last a week. The copper was filled with water with a piece of hosepipe fixed to a tap across the yard – or in my Gran's case, a well in the corner of the garden. Half a packet of washing soda was thrown into the copper and the fire was lit.

Then the scrubbing began with yellow Sunlight soap and a scrubbing board. Everything went into the copper – sheets, shirts, pillowcases – everything seemed to be white in those days. A few more bits of rubbish were pushed into the fire and, in no time at all, the copper was boiling like a witch's cauldron. It had to be stodged down with the copper stick and left to its own devices for 15 to 20 minutes while the rinsing water was prepared. The Reckitts blue bag was squeezed into the big galvanised bath of clean water. The blue bag was also used to whiten icing on the cakes in those days. The washing was duly rinsed in the blue water, then through the mangle it went. The mangle was a monster. Two wooden rollers and a handle, everything went through, fingers also if you weren't careful. Buttons popped off shirts, except for the rubber ones on the liberty bodices.

It seldom rained on washing days, or so it seemed, and soon the washing was blowing on the line. If you were lucky you had a pulley to pull the line up high, if not, a clothes prop did the job. Then it was teatime with bubble-and-squeak from Sunday's left-overs.'

A LONG DAY

'On Monday morning, first of all the copper had to be filled and the fire lit. As we all wore so many clothes in those days (I was born in 1908 at Gravesend), there must have been mountains of washing, including all the bed linen, tablecloths etc. After being sorted and washed in a huge zinc bath, the washing was boiled in the copper amid much steam and stirred around with the copper stick, rinsed in fresh water, then in blue water. It was then starched and put through the mangle. This took all day and ended with the bread board, broom handles and all worktops having a good scrub. The lavatory was also given a special do as the seat had to be kept snow white.'

'On washday at our home in Goudhurst, the copper in the corner of the kitchen was filled and the fire lit. My mother was a small lady and she had to stand on a stool. At the end of the washing session there were the ashes to be cleared and the surround of the copper to be cleaned with the hearthstone. I had two sisters and as we got older we turned the mangle for her. The large deal kitchen table had to be scrubbed and the outside loo cleaned.'

'I was born in 1917 at Ide Hill, so things were fairly primitive then. Monday, washday, was a horrible day. We had no water laid on so had to get it from the tank in buckets, and the boys had to collect wood to keep the fire going or the water would quickly go off the boil. We had a large garden so on a good day drying was no problem but on wet days, oh dear! On really frosty days articles froze as they were pegged on the line and literally stood up by themselves. The big old-fashioned mangle with its wooden rollers pinched your fingers if you weren't careful and invariably broke or bent the linen buttons.

Another thing I recall is the feather bed which had to be shaken each day. All the feathers were shaken from the corners to form a huge heap in the centre then kneaded to form an even mattress and left to air. A horrible job, but so cosy to sleep on, especially in the winter.'

'There were several laundries in Bromley, in private houses; some only did shirts and blouses and advertised hand finishing, others did a "bag wash" which I suspect was never taken out of the bag. Most mothers did their own laundry by hand, which usually occupied most of Monday. I loathed washing days as Mum would still be scrubbing the scullery floor late at night, before hearthstoning the copper. If the washing had dried quickly then the kitchen table would be used for ironing, the irons being heated on the kitchen range. The sheets were Mum's pride and joy, their snowy whiteness being her reward for a full day's hard work at the wash tub.'

THE BOX MANGLE

'I lived with my grandparents in Matfield during the First World War and would help with the housework. The house was cleaned with a dustpan and brush until springcleaning, when the carpets were hung on the line and beaten, and then pulled round upside down on the grass to freshen the colours.

After the washing was done it was put through the box mangle. I have seen two of these very solid and heavy contraptions, both in cellars underground (and there were no gas or electric lights then). Their size (seven foot long, three foot high and three foot six inches wide) meant they would have had to be assembled in the cellar itself. They were made of beech, ash or sycamore. The pieces of bed linen were laid at the clear end of the table top, some loose rollers were laid in position on the laundry pieces, then the box was wound over them. This was a box on rollers holding a number of heavy pieces of stone which was wound by a windlass from one end of the table to the other.'

THE FIRST GAS IRON

'I remember washday for the smell of boiling soapy water, and for cold meat and mashed potatoes for dinner.

My mother had one of the first gas irons. It was a big boxy thing with gas jets inside. If you hurried when you lit it, the gas jets flared up, the heat scorching your arm. It was connected to the gas point near the backdoor, and the gas was turned on with a tap. It was a death trap really!

LEISURE AT LAST

'In our rented bungalow at Dartford in the 1930s, the kitchen was very small with not much room to move and my mother found doing the washing rather a trial as there was no copper, only an Ascot water heater which could be temperamental at times. She somehow managed with the aid of several buckets (for wet washing), a washboard and a mangle to get the washing ready to hang on the line. If the fine weather changed to wet and windy the prop might fall to the ground taking the washing with it, so the whole procedure had to be gone through again. If Mother had left the washing out and gone to the shops, our neighbour sometimes took it in for her if the rain started.

Mother used a heavy iron to press the clothes. She heated it on the gas ring. Then when the ironing had been finished the clothes were put on the airer which was placed around the fireplace in the living room in the winter, or in the garden in the summer, so the clothes were properly aired before being worn again.

In the 1950s my father bought firstly a television set, then a washing machine for Mother followed by a refrigerator. At last Mother got some leisure time.'

SHOPPING AND CALLERS
TO THE DOOR

Most villages could supply everyday needs from local shops, and deliveries were made to our doors. There were also other regular callers, such as the muffin man.

FAVOURITE FOODS

'At one time in the 1930s the river Medway was teeming with smelts, which were small grey-green silver fish about the size of a small herring which smelled like cucumbers. Mum would give us sixpence and a clean bucket and send us off to see the ferry man who would fill up the bucket with green fish. They tasted wonderful and added spice to a rather dull diet. Money was very short in the early 1930s and with four children in the family, we often had to share an egg.'

'I was born in 1920 in Gillingham. As a child, I remember that a typical meal would be stew with very little meat and suet pudding afterwards to fill us up. Sometimes Dad would catch a wild rabbit and Mum and I would have to skin it and chop it up to make a stew or pie. On Fridays I went to the local fish and chip shop to buy fish for twopence and chips for a penny. On Sundays Mum would cook a roast dinner, usually one of our own chickens.'

'My father's favourite tea was a large onion and a hunk of cheese eaten with a slice or two of bread and butter and a cup or two of tea. He also liked onions cooked on a cold winter's night before going to bed, with plenty of pepper on them.'

SHOPPING EVERY DAY

'Mother had to shop every day because there were no means then of keeping food fresh (no refrigerators or freezers in the homes then, they cost too much), so she went to the local shops in the main road at Dartford. You could get all the necessities of life in those shops but you could only get oranges at Christmas and nuts in the autumn. However, you could buy a halfpenny worth of sweets and get quite a lot for your money – liquorice bootlaces (in black or red), gobstoppers, sherbet dabs, jelly babies, dolly mixture and pretend cigarettes and other delightful things!

If Mother wanted butter though she went in to the town to the United Dairies shop where an assistant would cut some off a big slab and weigh it and then pat it into an oblong shape; then he would wrap it in a UD wrapper. Quite a lot of effort went into a half pound of butter. The UD delivered our milk in a float drawn by a horse. There was actually a privately run dairy in our road but we only used that if we had unexpected guests at the weekend when I might be sent to get a pint or two or some cream. There was another milk roundsman but the milk came in a churn-like contraption out of which the roundsman ladled milk into his customers' jugs. We also had bread delivered by a horse-drawn van; but Mother made all the pies, puddings and cakes herself.

We either walked to the shops or used horse power in the early years of the century, as here at Bearsted.

The coal merchant brought our supply of coal or coke in a horse-drawn dray and he would heave the sacks up onto his shoulder (one at a time) and carry them into our garden where there was a coal shed, while Mother stood at the window and counted to make sure he gave us the right total of sacks. He naturally looked very dirty.'

FAVOURITE SHOPS

'Miss Lester's was our favourite shop. It was only small but she used to sell all sorts of sweets. "Kiss me quicks" were all pretty colours but got very sticky if we kept them too long. "Cupid's whispers" had writing on them – I Love You or Will You Be My Sweetheart? Halfpenny turnovers were shaped like a horseshoe with a lid and inside was a little present. Farthing prize packets had presents too. There were sherbet suckers, bulls eyes, coconut chips, Spanish bootlaces and lots more in jars. Miss Lester was very patient with us and while we were choosing what to buy with our farthing, she would make a cone-shaped bag to put them in.

The Bonnet Box was a different kind of shop. That was where Mother bought our hats, coats, gloves and material for making clothes. I used to like choosing a hat. If it was a summer hat, the lady in the shop would bring out a box of artificial flowers for trimming. Winter hats were usually trimmed with satin ribbons. We could never bring the hats home with us because the flowers and ribbons had to be stitched on to them as well as a piece of elastic, which went under our chins so that our hats would not blow off in the wind. They would be sent up to our house wrapped in lots of tissue paper and in a round cardboard box with "Bonnet Box" printed on the lid.

Mrs Lane kept the fancy shop. She always wore a black dress, mittens and a lace cap. She and her daughter made a lot of the things that were sold in the shop – table centres, doilies, pin cushions. I used to go there to buy a new thimble.

Of course, there were the grocers' shops and butchers, but one shop I liked, because of the smell, was the corn shop. I would have to go there to get corn for the chickens or a bag of flour for Mother.

The milkman called twice a day at about nine o'clock in the morning and four o'clock in the afternoon. He came round with two cans of milk and measured it into our jug with a steel pint pot.

Sometimes the muffin man would come down our road. He would carry his muffins and crumpets in a tray on his head, ring a handbell and shout "Muffins to sell".'

'My father was manager in the 1920s of quite a high class butcher's shop on the Pantiles at Tunbridge Wells where all the gentry used to shop, driving up in their chauffeur-driven Rolls. Part of my father's wages was a ration of meat, so needless to say we had a fair share – meat for breakfast, dinner and supper. In the winter instead of an early morning cup of tea we had beef tea or mutton broth. It certainly kept out the cold.

It was fun going shopping with Mother. The grocer's near where we lived had rows and rows of small drawers where every imaginable thing was kept, including sugar, tea, coffee, rice, lentils and semolina, all of which was weighed and put into blue bags. Butter came in large blocks and it was fascinating to watch the grocer pat the butter into one pound portions with a pattern on the top.

Another lovely shop was the Bon Marche where the bill and your money was put into a container, fixed on to a railway-type contraption and sent flying around the store to the office where it was dealt with and any change and the receipt came winging its way back to you. A likely purchase would be 2¾ yards of material at 1s 11¾d per yard. No calculators in those days. On Saturdays there was a street market in Calverley Road where bananas were 13 for one shilling, Mrs Andrews sold her home-made boiled sweets, which were delicious, and in the winter there was a hot chestnut stall, among many others, all lit by acetylene lamps.'

'Chatterton Road in Bromley is still a bustling community retaining several of the original shops that I knew as a child. The baker, the butcher and the chemist are all reminders of a quieter, more stable age. The Co-op still stands where my mother bought her groceries, which were individually parcelled up and her payment for the goods was put into a cup by the assistant and conveyed along wires to the cashier who checked it and sent back any change by the same means. My mother was a member and always ensured that her number (661) had been credited with the value of her purchases. The corner shop of Cook and Biggs sold all haberdashery, sheets, wool and corsets. Mum always bought things "on appro". In addition, there were small businesses in private houses. Mrs Hornegold sold milk, and Miss Copus walked round with bread in a funny box on wheels.'

VILLAGE SHOPS

'Marlpit Hill, a village on the outskirts of Edenbridge, was very different in the 1930s. The village, separated from Edenbridge by fields and pastures, boasted several thriving shops. A corner grocery store had its own bakehouse delivering newly baked bread and cakes for miles around by horse and cart, later by trade bicycle and van. One day a certain errand boy was delivering a loaded basket of loaves on the rather heavy and unwieldy trade bike. Zooming downhill he lost control, ending up in a pond with all the loaves of bread floating round him. This shop also had a butcher's section where home-killed meat was sold. The owner raised sheep, pigs and chickens on a nearby plot of land and he had his own slaughterhouse which was kept extremely busy around Christmas time getting the poultry ready.

Also in the village was another general store with post office, bakers and butchers. Both shops sold ironmongery and all sorts of groceries and paraffin. There were other shops, a newsagent's selling tobacco and sweets, a haberdasher's and shoemender's and a bicycle shop. Other amenities were two pubs, one actually a hotel, a working men's club, three builders' yards all in one road and a wood yard that made hurdles among other things.'

'Wouldham in the 1930s had four public houses, all of which did a roaring trade. There were nine grocers and sweet shops, at least three of which sold everything including clothing and oil. One incorporated the post office and another was the newsagent. There were at least two greengrocers. One went round the village in a lorry and the other a horse and cart – the one with the lorry also delivered coal and had a fish and chip shop. The other coal merchant was also a general carrier and took people to work in a bus. There were two butcher's shops and animals used to be driven through the street to

The Leaver family outside their shop opposite Snodland railway station in the 1920s. Small local shops provided nearly all our needs.

the abattoir at the back of one of the shops. Bread was delivered by the baker from the next village.

EVERYTHING LOCAL

'In the 1930s, most household requirements were obtained locally, or at the most within a radius of three or four miles. Crockham Hill had a general store selling groceries and vegetables, medicines, paraffin, working boots and wellingtons, candles, pots and pans, maids' caps and aprons, white stockings for confirmations, hurricane lamps and a wide range of wicks for oil lamps and cookers, rubber heels for shoe repairs, mouse traps and rabbit snares. You name it, it was there, either on the mahogany shelves, or stored in the cellar below the shop. The coffee grinder was kept in the cellar, a dry, stone walled, brick floored room, with an equable temperature that changed very little. The smelly things, like the paraffin and carbolic soap, stayed in the stone building behind the shop.

The butcher, almost next door, supplied meat for most of the households and would make deliveries in his car, one of the few in the neighbourhood at that time. The ice for his store room came each week in a dripping, closed truck from Hays Wharf, London. The same truck left blocks of ice at the shop, to be kept in a straw-lined hole in the ground until needed for the ice cream churn. The post office, further up the village, also had a range of sweets and groceries.

Mr Clifton, a one time coachman, was the local carrier, between station and village. He drove a flat waggon, pulled by one large horse. His waggon and horse had a large barn at the bottom of the garden for accommodation, one of a range of buildings behind the row of cottages in the village. There always seemed to be rats down there, after the horse's feed and living in the straw. One of his regular deliveries was the weekly box of assorted cakes, sent by rail from Lyons of Cadby Hall. The most expensive item in it was the Fresh Cream Sandwich at one shilling and two pence.

Bread was delivered in a small motor van about three times a week from the bakery two miles away. Fish and vegetables came from Edenbridge, three miles away. This was another horse-drawn flat waggon, with buckets of herrings and cod hanging from hooks at the back.'

MILK TO THE DOOR

'At Barnehurst in the 1930s, the milkman would come twice a day, taking orders in the morning for the midday delivery and at midday for the next morning. The milk came in a horse-drawn float, and if the horse also left a "delivery" it was recognised that it belonged to the household outside which it had been deposited – always welcome for the garden or allotment.

My parents had no refrigerator until 1959. The milk would be put in a cool place in the house or even a hole in the garden on hot days. It stood in a bowl with a wet cloth over it with the ends in the bowl. I suppose it helped, but it still went off very quickly.'

'Over 50 years ago I was born in a small town surrounded by several farms. During his school holidays, and at the weekends, my brother used to do a milk delivery round for one of the local farmers. The farmer's name was Mr Mortimer. He was a small man who sported a very large moustache. Always dressed the same, clad in glossy knee-length gaiters and a brown leather waistcoat, he looked a formidable figure; however, despite his stern appearance we quite liked him.

The milk from Mr Mortimer's cows was poured into very large milk churns, which were placed on a pony and trap in order to visit his customers around the town. On Saturdays I was allowed to climb on to the cart and help deliver the milk on our estate. I would have been about seven or eight at the time. Being a small person I had a great deal of difficulty reaching the step into the trap, but somehow, much to the amusement of onlookers, I always made it! It was very interesting visiting the various kitchens to collect the milk jugs, and what an assortment they were. China, earthenware, patterned and plain, most of them sadly chipped by the continuous banging of the metal ladles that carefully measured the required quota of milk. What a comical sight it was, for these long-handled measures and the churns were taller than I, and as I held the jugs high above me, the milk splashed all over my face. When full, each jug was carefully returned to its owner. (No locked doors in those days.)

When the round was finished, Mr Mortimer would drive the trap back to his farm about half a mile away. I went as well, but there were no seats so I had to stand all the way; I was just like a mini Boadicea as I held on to the empty milk churns. What excitement!'

REGULAR CALLERS

'We lived on a farm a mile and a half from the village of Frittenden. My mother did not drive a car. The butcher delivered the meat, the baker delivered the bread, the milkman brought the milk, measuring it out of a churn and always giving the cats some in their saucer – when it was the "girl" she always gave them a generous portion. Once a week the groceries were delivered from the village shop – and once a week Freddy would call and sit down in the kitchen with my mother and write down her order. I can still hear him saying, "Any jellies, custard powder or blancmange?"

During the war the fish man always called once a week. It completely put me off cod as that was all he seemed to have.'

'Our milkman at Ryarsh, Bob Hayden, called every morning with our milk which he ladled into our jug from the cans hooked on chains suspended from the carved wooden yoke over his broad shoulders; later we did have a horse and cart to bring the milk and the wretched animal would wander along eating grass from the verge and leave the milk lady far behind. The butcher delivered twice weekly, and what a to-do in summer to cook everything so that it would keep and then cover it with a fine wire meat cover and place it in the coolest part of the larder.

The groceries came from a branch of International Stores in nearby West Malling, but the poor man who cycled round taking down orders must have earned his wage after going all round our village. The large green van that delivered on Saturdays was always well received.'

'In the 1930s all the tradesmen delivered. The milkman at West Wickham came twice a day on his horse-drawn float and the coal was delivered by horse-drawn carts. The baker pulled his cart, and

HIGH STREET

FRITTENDEN

Jan 194*6*

Mr J Honess

F. WARD

Family Butcher

PURVEYOR OF FINEST QUALITY MEAT ONLY

Oct 6	Chops	2 . 9½
13	Liver Chops & meat	4 . 11½
20	Sth & Kidney Suet	2 . 4½
27	Lamb	4 . 4
Nov 17	Beef	4 . 8
Dec 1	Mutton	6 . 5
15	Lamb Cheef	3 . 11
		1 . 9 . 3½
	Killing two Sheep	5 . 0
		£ 1 - 14 . 3½

Paid

With Thanks

(Ward)

A bill for meat from Ward's butcher's shop in Frittenden 1946. It includes 'killing two sheep' for five shillings!

meat and groceries were delivered by errand boys on bicycles. The muffin man came round once a week ringing a bell and carrying the muffins in a tray on his head. Occasionally the Wall's ice cream man came round on his tricycle.'

'Regular callers at Golden Green were the rag and bone man, the knife grinder on his converted bicycle, the fish man who provided Sunday tea, and the chop man who came every Thursday evening and gave Mum a welcome rest from cooking. The baker and the butcher delivered twice a week.'

'At Goudhurst the grocer called for his order on Tuesdays, and delivered on Thursdays. The butcher came daily for his order. On Saturdays a little man called with his basket of wares – bootlaces, matches, cottons, mending silks and penny bars of chocolate. Sometimes we were allowed to have a bar of chocolate each.'

FROM THE CRADLE
TO THE GRAVE

We were much more likely to be born, to suffer our illnesses and to die in our own homes in the past – sometimes even to have minor operations on the kitchen table! Families passed on home cures, often relied on in the days when the doctor had to be paid for, but the district nurse was a welcome and familiar figure in many households.

SETTING UP HOME

'I was married on 25th October 1930 at the little church in the fields at Ifield near Singlewell. Two of my sisters and my husband's sister were bridesmaids. There was quite a fuss about the hemlines of the dresses. My sisters had handkerchief hems, which were very fashionable, but my sister-in-law's was plain. They wore big black velvet hats underlined with blue. One of my sisters was a florist and she and her employers made the bouquets. The cost of the cake, flowers, photographs and items of furniture etc are set out below:

	£	s	d
Two tier cake	2	12	9
Cupid standing			6½
4 cupids sitting @ 3½d each		1	2
Hire of stand		2	6
	2	16	11½
Bride's bouquet		5	0
3 bridesmaid's bouquets		15	0
Gents' buttonholes		1	0
Ladies' buttonholes		1	6
6 photographs of wedding group	1	1	0
4ft oak sideboard	4	10	0
4ft oak bedroom suite	21	0	0
4ft 6in bed	6	0	0
Spiral spring	3	0	0
Hair mattress	5	10	0
3 piece velvet suite	26	10	0
Gate leg table	2	15	0
Clothes basket		3	6
Pail		1	3
Washing board		1	2
Poker			6
Shovel			7½
Kettle		2	9
Chopper		1	9

I had been married six years when our daughter was born. Like everyone else, I had made the baby's layette – nightgowns and daygowns with the sleeves scalloped and slotted with ribbon, the bodice tucked and the necks trimmed with lace; flannel and cambric petticoats, all scalloped at the hems and a binder which was wound round and pinned to keep the navel flat; also shawls, jackets and bonnets. Two dozen terry nappies at least plus one dozen muslin squares were needed. All these had to be displayed to various visitors. The pram was always selected but it was considered unlucky for it to be delivered before the event.'

DELIVERED BY THE DISTRICT NURSE

'Any babies born in the Chelsfield area were delivered by the district nurse, who travelled round the neighbourhood on a bicycle, with a

Edmund Higgins and Eliza Hickmott, both in service at the vicarage, were married at Bearsted in the early 1900s. The bride 'wore a pretty grey dress trimmed with white moire', reported the local newspaper.

large Gladstone-type bag strapped on the back.

Another baby was due at about the same time as me, and I understand there was some concern at the time that we might arrive on the same day, and Nurse Hardy would be hard put to be in two places at once. A further difficulty was that her special scales had to be passed from one family to another in order to record the baby's weight at birth.'

HOME CURES

'Minor illnesses had to be treated at home with remedies that seem a little strange to us. When she had an earache, my mother-in-law as a child at the turn of the the the century at Leigh, had a "pepper pill" placed in her ear. This consisted of ground pepper in a screw of muslin, which had been dipped in the brandy bottle. This was also considered good for toothache.

She could even remember, as a small child, having a piece of leather hung round her neck for her to chew on when her gums were sore from teething.

There was also the practice of taking the rather fleshy petals of Madonna lilies, steeping them in brandy and using them for dressing cuts sustained on the farm. Perhaps this was to counter tetanus.'

'I remember lying on the rug in front of the coal fire (which, in the chilly months, was host to daily sessions of toast or crumpets cooked on the long-handled brass toasting fork), with a brown bag half filled with hot salt and pressed against a troublesome aching ear; it helped a great deal. Getting a boil in an unfortunate place meant having it treated by a hot linseed poultice kept in place by a "ladies' diaper" as ordered by old Dr Strouts, who puffed, wore dark suits, starched wing collars on his shirts and a bow tie. Pains in the chest were relieved by sloppy bread poultices fashioned in father's large handkerchief or bits of old sheeting. These were changed and reheated every four hours or so. Cotton wool soaked in diluted iodine was always dabbed over grazed knees.'

THE HOSPITAL CLUB

'In the 1920s we belonged to a hospital club at Ide Hill, for free treatment at the hospital. Members paid twopence a week, which was entered in a book and the money sent in at regular intervals. Mum did the collecting as she was at home during the day. We had lots of visitors. Some members got in arrears and then there was a panic if any of the family should fall ill or have an accident.'

BAD MEMORIES

'One bitterly cold day in 1929, I arrived at the Maidstone Ophthalmic Hospital in Marsham Street to have my tonsils removed. My Mum came with me into a large room, with lots of much younger children and I was told to take off my clothes except for my vest and navy blue knickers. All the other children did the same, helped by their mothers, who then had to go and leave us.

One by one, the smallest first, they were taken away by a nurse and I was getting more and more frightened, then they were brought back on trolleys. When they came to they cried and cried, and a harassed nurse plonked a screaming child in my arms and told me to hold her for a minute. Although I was used to babies, having a very young brother and sister, I didn't want to look after this one and started crying myself. At 13 I was the oldest child there so was last to go, eventually had long white woollen stockings put on me and was helped onto a trolley.

I remember so clearly going into the operating theatre, being lifted onto a table and having a gauze mask put over my nose and mouth and something dripping through. I started screaming so loudly my mother heard me way down the long corridor and nearly fainted.

When I came to, I was back in the big room, children still crying, and told I must wait until I'd brought up clots of blood and then I could go home.

My mother couldn't afford a taxi, so I was wrapped in a long woollen shawl and had to walk home very slowly in the bitter cold.'

'In January 1950 I went into Maidstone hospital with rheumatic fever. They found a shadow on my lung and diagnosed tuberculosis. I was in hospital for six months, but they tried streptomycin on me and it worked. I was sent to a convalescent home for three months. It was an awful place and very strict. We were in dormitories of six or eight and if you talked in bed you were sent to an isolation room. We had no lessons and had to go for long walks in the cold. The food was terrible – lots of porridge and junket and a spoonful of cod liver oil every day after dinner.'

'In 1938 it was discovered that both my brother and I were diphtheria carriers. We were carried off in an ambulance to the fever hospital at East Malling. To an eight year old it was a million miles from home. We had to spend two months there, which included Christmas, until our swabs were clear.

It was one of the worst winters in my memory. My parents trudged to East Malling on foot through deep snow to visit us. They were not allowed inside the hospital, they stood on little wooden ladders outside the windows and talked to us.'

'Along the footpath at Loose, known locally as the Rainbow, which runs from Kirkdale cottages skirting the stream, was Little Ivy, our grandfather's home and his father's before him. They were undertakers for the village. All the coffins were made by hand as there was no electricity for machinery. A handsomely painted bier had to be used at funerals as the streets of Loose were too narrow for a hearse and horses. At a funeral, Grandfather Harris would don his top hat and walk in front of the bier and his pall bearers pushed the bier from the house to the church, and to the cemetery in the village.

Every girl who married in Loose church received a hand-turned rolling pin and board from Grandfather Harris, many of which still exist.'

'Quite often when there was illness in the large houses in Gravesend in the 1920s, straw was laid in the road to deaden the sound of the horses' hooves.

After a death among the neighbours, the same person was always sent for to perform something mysterious to us called laying out. Later, of course, we came to know all about it as in those days there were no funeral parlours. The body was kept at home until the funeral, with friends and relations in and out.

I remember some of the grand funerals with a glass hearse drawn by black horses with black plumes on their heads and horse-drawn carriages led by men in black with top hats. It was impossible to see the women mourners' faces as they were covered in black, right down to their feet. If a widow, the woman wore widow's weeds – a long black veil which covered her almost completely. After a few months of mourning, mauve and then grey could be worn. Men and children often wore a black band or diamond on one sleeve.'

A BORN ROMANY

For the Romanies, home was not to be found within four walls. This is the story of one woman, a born Romany.

'I'd like to say that I've been asked to do a survey on my life as a born Romany. I was born at Horsmonden in 1921 in a caravan; the house dwellers call them caravans but we call them waggons. The life of a Romany is, when you are brought up you have no schooling, go to school or anything like this, but you know everything that goes on earth really because if you're born of a Romany person you see all things the house dwellers read in books. You see it, so you're educated that way. You see what goes on along the country lanes when you are travelling as children. You see the fields where there are animals, lambs being born, all through the seasons, you see the fruit growing every season because you do the farm work as from children. You go along and you see flowers growing along each side of the roads, along the old lanes, primroses and you see the dogroses. They were the travellers' gardens, the Romany's gardens because although we never had any ground to turn round and make our own gardens, we had plenty of country lanes.

So I had a very pleasant upbringing, until I got older and realised there was more to life than just our Romany life. I could never understand why the house dwelling people, the Goldies as we called them, in Romany tongue, didn't like us until my mother said one day, "Well, we never have been liked", because before Jesus was on earth, she said, we used to be slaves until he set us free. When we come through life, it's not an easy life, you are always chastised over something with the house dwelling people but when I look at them as through my eyes I can't see any difference, because we are all brothers and sisters.

I was brought up to cook at five years old. At ten years old I had my mother's family to look after. I had no school so it's always been a hard life, because that is necessary, the reading and writing, but God didn't give us that. He sent us on earth to forage as a way of living. We have to be contented for what He did for us. The life of a Romany person is not dull, because there's always something going on. There were the horse fairs. There's the china they like collecting. They like collecting lace and things like that. China is the most precious thing to them. They like buying china. Where English people go on holiday for the sun, English gypsies stay at home, go to the fair, and buy china to put round their waggons. Crown Derby is greatly collected.

We weren't allowed to wear any make-up at all, which occasionally we did, if we got up the road and put our lipstick on, or powder. You weren't allowed to use any rouge. You had to go up the road if you wanted to put on any make-up. You had to wash your face in coconut oil or olive oil, that was your moisturising cream. You had lots of soaps, olive oil to wash your hair. You had lots of rules laid down by your parents. You didn't dare speak out of turn to your elders. While this is all going on you're wondering when you see the house dwellers what they're doing. You think why can't we live like that? Perhaps when you see the taps in the houses you used to wonder why you never had a tap to go and turn on.

The waggons were nice because they would sleep about six and you did have the stove in the waggon and you would cook as you went along. You'd have a meat pudding in an iron pot, cooking it as you rolled along the roads. Nowadays I suppose you'd call them "meals on wheels" but they were waggon meals. When you set down by the side of the road, the meat pudding would come out of the cloth into our china. That's why we always like nice china to put our food on. That wasn't too bad because that's the way we were brought up. We would do our washing alongside of a river in tubs. To boil our clothes we would get some bricks each side of the tub, fill the tub with water, and put our whites in one tub; you'd never see shirts boiled with women's clothes. They were always boiled on their own. Also the tea towels and tablecloths would be boiled in different water. They were very strict about that. Romany people would never put all the clothes mixed up together in a washing machine like in the launderette. I saw one woman put all the tea towels with her husband's shirts and bits and pieces and I thought I don't think I would like that, because I think tea towels are very special things, so should be kept to one side. That's the way I was brought up, to wash the tea towels in separate tubs.

On Sunday morning, that was our leisure day. You would see the waggons all around the field and the women sitting on a big tarpaulin embroidering the pillowcases, sewing lace on the bottom of the sheets. The children always had long hair, they would be washing and doing the children's hair and plaiting it. You would see the very old ladies doing the cooking on the open fires and rolling the dough out on the table to put the meat puddings into the pots. Sometimes you'd have plum pudding, they would be put into a cloth, there would be that, half a bacon and meat pudding all in the one pot. It was huge. The currant pudding would go into a different pot with, say, an apple pudding in a cloth. So all this would be done. Little knuckles of bacon would be cooked on the open fire on Sunday. So you imagine all this food being cooked in 20 or 30 waggons all on open fires. Of a night-time when the food was cooked, you would see the travelling people at a huge table, and they would all sit and eat around that. There were some very posh travelling people and they would have the best. Unfortunately we weren't one of them. We weren't rough and dirty. We've always been brought up clean and respectable but when you really got down to seeing the rich people, they would even have silver plates and silver cutlery. They would have about three tablecloths on one table, and a cloth from the waggon would be brought out to protect them from the smoke. So we do know what it is to have manners when you are sitting round a table. You wouldn't dare to speak around a table when you were having your food.

We had nine children in our family, and had all home-cooked food, because we couldn't afford fish and chips etc. They were a luxury. Even a doughnut was luxury to us. If we had a bar of chocolate a week, that was luxury. Our main treat was jelly babies, mother bought and gave us three each. Also sugar knobs, with melted chocolate on, we called it chocolate cubes. Sometimes I go and visit the old ladies who are still living in the same way. A girl could marry at 16 but had to have her parents' permission. The head of the gypsies also gave his/her consent. If you became engaged to a boy, you didn't have an engagement ring, but either his tie or scarf he wore round his neck. This was called a cunie. When you got married you had to have a 22 carat gold wedding ring, or 9 carat if not, very heavy, very wide so people could see it. The bride's father bought the waggon and the bridegroom's father the horses.

There's quite a lot things I would have liked to have done. I would have liked to have gone to school because that's the only thing that's in my way now. You do miss out on that. We did want to know what a bath was, like the house dwellers had. We used to get a tin bath in the floor of the waggon, two people washing our back. It was a very tiny bath but we managed and we used to do this every other night, especially if we were working out in the fields. We always had three waggons in my family, one for the boys, one for Mum and Dad and one for the girls. We all had separate waggons. We wasn't all brought up together. The beds would be feathered beds, and pillows. Five of you could sleep in a waggon. There was a top and bottom bed. There would be a stove in there, in the winter we would listen to a wireless, or we would tell one another stories, or one of the old women would come and tell us about her days, when she was young. So that was our entertainment. Most of these old women have now passed on. If it was a nice night we would sit out by the fires and they would tell us how they met their husbands. They would go to a horse fair each year, and maybe meet someone they would like.

Every Romany woman has a waggon given to her. They used to burn the waggon, when she died, so no one else could have it. They used to burn it so her spirit could rest in peace. Her clothes would also be burnt so no one else could wear them. China would be broken, so they couldn't be used by anyone else. It may seem cruel but it's carried out up to today. That's why gypsies don't have many possessions. They don't pass things on when they die. When I lost my mother I managed to keep something of hers back, which I feel guilty about but look back with loving memory. The same thing will happen to me when I die. I don't approve of it but it's tradition.

In 1939, when the war started, that's when the waggons started disappearing. I was called up for the Land Army along with about 100 more of us. We were billeted on the Lead Front in Kent, along Romney Marsh, and we had to go to do the farmwork so we were more or less in the front line. We had to go and pick potatoes even with all the aeroplanes flying over the top of us during the war. We all did our share of work because we worked for the country as we were told, which we know we did. People don't think we did anything. We lost cousins in the war. They went out to France and got killed over there. I think we lost around 20 young men, in my personal family. We had different ways of looking at things, I suppose, because we thought what a waste of life. We were put anywhere because anything the Land Army women wouldn't do, we had to go and do. They didn't care where they shoved us.

Now it comes to my way of looking at life, as I have grown up and I have been here about 50 years. I'm a native someone might say, but I'm not really because although I know these people round here, farmers and others, we are still classed as gypsies. My mother used to say that you'd never be able to fit in, you take people as you find them, don't take any notice. I'm pleased I took her advice because if you took notice you wouldn't have any homes at all. The house dwelling people are no different to us, especially when you get to know of them and you think why can't they understand us. Well I know now they have not been taught about us. They just take us as old gypsy people. We've stood back and taken it so long, it doesn't hurt us anymore. I have ignored all of it.'

CHILDHOOD & SCHOOLDAYS

GROWING UP IN WEST KENT

Looking back, we grew up in a different world. A world where the roads were our playgrounds, we could wander on our own where we pleased without our parents worrying, and we kept our childish innocence well into our teens. Perhaps the summers were not always long and sunny, but they seemed so! .

BORN ON CANDLEMAS DAY

'I was born on Candlemas Day 1907, the youngest of eleven children – three boys and eight girls. Two children died in infancy, the rest of us grew up strong and healthy.

My father worked for Squerryes Court. He was one of the upper ten amongst the servants. These included the butler, the bailiff of the farm, the head carpenter and head gardener. My father was responsible for house maintenance – he was painter, decorator and jack-of-all-trades. Later he was trained to run the electricity generator. He didn't have a very big wage – I think he earned about 24 shillings a week. He used to lay his money on the mantelpiece on a Saturday, and I can remember the shining gold sovereign. The upper ten stood apart from the other servants (or thought they did), and we were brought up to imagine that we were better class than the rest of the children. Mother made us keep up a very high standard.

We lived in Lodge Lane, where several of the houses were occupied by the estate hands. We all had to mind what we did, in case we offended the Squire or his Lady. When they drove up the lane we were supposed to bow or curtsey. We got very good at hearing the horses' hooves in time to disappear.

On Saturday nights we all used to go into town. Mother would do the shopping and pay the bills. We had a general store, and a greengrocer where we often got an orange. Of all the shops only Evendens (the ironmongers) is still as it was. We had two bakers who delivered by horse and cart, a fishmonger who got fresh supplies every day, a chemist, a baby-clothes shop, a tuppence a week library, and a Swedish masseur who shocked the town by running away with the vicar's daughter. The great thing was the town brass band, that used to play in the square every Saturday night, whatever the weather. We braved the elements and listened to the only kind of music we had.

Of course, we had church music – we all went to church once or twice every Sunday. Before that we children went to Sunday school, and then we were marched up to the church. We had to behave ourselves and do as we were told.

The two eldest children were boys. They both went to Hosey school and did very well. One ended up as stationmaster at Herne Bay, and the other was well known for his skills as a plumber and decorator. The girls went to school in the town, where we received a very good education. One of my sisters gained a scholarship to Tonbridge. She went there on the train. The war prevented us younger ones from getting there. One of my sisters was apprenticed to a dressmaker – she was an excellent seamstress. The others went into service. When I was 14 I decided I was not going into service, so I went into a shop. I don't know if it raised or lowered my status, but at least I didn't go into service.

Westerham Hall wasn't built until the end of the 1914-1918 war. There was very little building in the London Road. There were two houses and the almshouses on the right, then fields and a nursery until you came to the railway station. On the left was the school and the Crown hotel. In those days Westerham was a very quiet place, and Croydon Road was nothing but a dirt track. My grandmother lived in Cathedral Cottage in Croydon Road, and we were sent there after school, looking just right. But, by the time we had gone up the mud track, had a dabble in the puddles, and looked in hedges for bird's nests, I was usually a pretty sight. I had no regard for my grandmother at all. She was an old cat, and always picked on me because I didn't come up to the standard of the family at all. But we did have a happy childhood. We could go up on Farley Common, which was a mass of bluebells in the spring and blackberries later. The children played football on a beautiful pitch, kept cut fine by the rabbits and the occasional tethered goat.

In September we always had school holidays to go hop picking. We all wore our oldest clothes. There were five or six girls big enough to help pick with our mother and make sure no leaves went in the big bin. Our father was most aggrieved – he considered hop picking beneath us. But Mother liked to earn the extra money to pay for winter clothes and shoes, and I think it was the only holiday she ever had. It was a long day out, and we had to walk quite a long way to get there.

One big event stands out in my memory, when the Squire's daughter was married. All the elite came on the day of the wedding. The tradesmen of the town came the next day. The next day we were invited to luncheon. I thought we were going to have something special. There was a big marquee, where we were served boiled beef and carrots! I pushed mine away, and my sisters were so ashamed they said they would never take me anywhere again. I said, "We have this at home – I thought we were going to have something special." We did get some treats when the Squire and his Lady were away from home. The horses still had to be exercised, so the coachman took us for rides in the coach.

My father did not go to the public houses. He had a barrel of beer in the house, which he drank with his breakfast and dinner – just as we would have a cup of tea. Although he worked very long hours he found time to be a keen gardener. He had an allotment on Farley Common, and often won prizes for his vegetables. During the 1914-1918 war we did not go hungry – Mother kept chickens, and Father kept pigs. There was sugar only for jam making, no butter, and we had to queue for a little bit of margarine. My father was also in the horse-drawn fire brigade. The horses would rush to the gate of their field when they heard the fire bell. The men all turned out very quickly, and wore heavy brass helmets.

My mother belonged to a coal club and a clothes club, which were run by the ladies of the church every Monday. She paid one shilling to the coal club, and sixpence to the clothes club. This paid for a well stocked coal cellar, and good calico sheets and pillowcases, as well as a penny handkerchief which we found in our stocking every Christmas. We had to earn pocket money, and even then it went in the slit of an old treacle tin with the lid soldered down. The girls collected milk from Squerryes dairy for local old people. My brother went round Westerham on his bicycle, lighting the gas lamps and putting them out later. We also collected wood for an old lady who took in laundry, but I don't think we did that for money.

This wonderful childhood changed suddenly when my father caught pneumonia, and died within 24 hours. We were all devastated – I was only 13 at the time. What really stands out in my memory was what happened a night or two after he died. There was a knock at the door and two old working people, dressed from head to toe in black, stood there. They said they had come to view the body. Apparently this was an old custom. They were taken upstairs so they could make sure he really had died. Life altered a great deal for us after that.'

VILLAGE LIFE IN THE 1920s

'I was born during a Zeppelin raid in 1916 in Keston where my mother and father were living while waiting for living accommodation at Warren House, Coney Hill (now the Police Sports Ground) where he had been taken on as a chauffeur to Lady Laidlaw, a member of the Guinness family. They had come over from Ireland where my father had been chauffeur to the Iveaghs.

The car he drove was covered in brass and he wore a white livery.

My brother and sister had been born on the Guinness estate at Raheny just outside Dublin. We eventually moved into the lodge at Warren House, a beautiful cottage overlooking Coney Hill. My granny, aged 70, had come to live with us to help my mother when I was born as my sister was two and a half and my brother 14 months.

We had a happy uninhibited childhood playing in the extensive grounds of the estate or on Hayes Common. Every Saturday morning we had to be dressed up in our best clothes and line up by the garages to receive a bag of sweets from Lady Laidlaw for which we had to curtsey and say "Thank you, your ladyship". She was a very imposing figure with a large hat and sunshade. My brother was so nervous of her he bowed and curtsied!

My father later left Lady Laidlaw and went to work for Mr and Mrs Campbell of Pickhurst Manor. While my father was chauffeur at the "big house" my mother would cycle to Bromley to do needlework for the Wright family who owned a big family business in Bromley. She also made the staff uniforms for the "big house". My sister was the first of us to go to Hayes school in the village, but when my brother was due to start school, he wouldn't go without me, so we were allowed to start together. I was just four and it meant a walk four times a day across the common to the school in the village.

It was a Church of England school and we were periodically examined in the catechism by the rector. The whole school stood round the hall and we didn't know where he would start, but hoped to be asked the question "What is your name?" With what pride we would answer "N or M" and receive sixpence. We learned to write in sand trays first and then on slates with scraps of squeaky pencils. I don't remember learning to read; I seemed to be always able to read and while the reading lesson was in progress I was sent to tidy up the book cupboard – how I loved this task. Counting was learnt by using cowrie shells. In other lessons, when we had finished our work and were waiting for the others to catch up, we would be given small squares of material which we frayed out and put the threads into little recesses in the desk top. I think the teacher must have been stuffing cushions as a hobby. I never learned much from music lessons. We learnt the Tonic Solfa and I never did understand what it had to do with music. In Geography we learnt all about Eskimos, Pygmies, Red Indians and the Chinese but I never really knew where they lived and we never learnt about Europeans or Americans.

The school had three classes – infants, juniors and seniors. There were two teachers and the headmistress, who lived in the adjoining school house. There were 70 children aged five to 14, all from the village, mostly from the shops and some from the estates like ours.

We had a general stores, butchers, blacksmiths, post office, public house, church and rectory. On the way to school we always stopped to watch the blacksmith at work – the sparks flying, the huge bellows blowing and the unforgettable smell of burning hooves.

If it rained we made dams of twigs and stones to flood the road on our way home to dinner and rushed back to school to see if they were still there. We bowled our hoops and whipped our tops and skipped in the road as we made our way to and from school. There was very little traffic and no kerbs – just tufts of grass to mark the edge of the path.

On Sundays we attended Children's Eucharist in the mornings and Sunday school in the afternoons. After tea, if it was still fine, still dressed in our Sunday clothes, we went for walks with Mother and Father across the fields, past the pig farm at West Wickham where we stopped to scratch the pigs' backs with oyster shells, then on to the New Inn by Hayes station where we sat outside and waited for Father to bring us an arrowroot biscuit or a twopenny bag of Smith's crisps.

One of my earliest recollections was of the Peace Celebration in 1919 when we all received a china mug filled with toffees and tied with red, white and blue ribbon. I still have the mug. But one of the high spots in village life was the Rectory fête in the summer when we wore white dresses, bows in our hair and white socks. There were stalls, ice cream, sweets and sports. The school took a very active part in the May Day celebrations on Hayes Common and we practised maypole and country dancing in school for weeks beforehand. The greatest thrill was to be chosen as May Queen. My sister was chosen as an attendant one year but I never reached such heights. After the main celebrations we would drift away on the common looking for empty lemonade bottles which we could exchange at the post office sweetshop for a few pennies.

Most of the village was owned by Sir Everard Hambro and it was a big event to see him wheeled across the road and through two wooden doors. What stories we made up about what was behind those doors! Many of the Hambro family are buried in a massive memorial area at the end of the churchyard. We lived in a tied cottage in Hayes until I was about ten years old. We had a very happy home life although there was little money to spare. We had three toys – a tricycle, a doll's pram and a wheelbarrow, which Father made for us. We had very few books and I would read them over and over again. I still have an annual, a Christmas present, which I can recite from cover to cover. I loved writing and doing sums and would sit for hours just copying anything from a book on any scrap of paper I could find. Paper and pencils were very scarce and we saved bags, bills and old envelopes. Someone gave me a book of sums without answers and I worked at it every evening until I had finished, then I started again.

When Father was at home in the evenings, we played card games, dominoes and board games. On Saturday nights we bathed in a big tin bath by the kitchen range and afterwards we sat in a row on the table for Father to cut our nails. Our cottage was covered in ivy which father cleared now and again. Once he found a nest with five eggs and Mother broke them into a rice pudding the following day. We grew all our own vegetables and Father worked in the garden whenever he could. A favourite of mine was lettuce cut up with salt, pepper and vinegar. Father grew mustard and cress in the shape of our initials and pricked our names in marrows so the letters got bigger as the marrows grew. An aunt had given us a big high pram and Father took it apart and made us a swinging boat – it was very popular with our school friends. He fitted a board on the chassis and that was our "chariot". Our favourite games were funerals – carried out with all due pomp and ceremony using dead mice, a clockwork train and holy communion. Mother used to be very cross when we did this, so we only played it when she was out.

At the end of each day, my brother and I were sent down the garden with a candle to the closet. It took a long time because we stopped on the way to put the candle flame under the hawthorn shoots and wait for them to explode. Then, having arrived, we rolled up the toilet paper (old newspaper) to make cigarettes which we smoked with relish, filling the closet with acrid yellow smoke. A call from the back door brought us hurrying back indoors.'

A WONDERFUL CHILDHOOD

'I was born in Erith in 1920, the youngest of four. Noisy Erith trams ran in front and trains behind our home which was near the old church (St John the Baptist) and much of our life centred around the church. We went to Sunday school, Children's Guild, Girls' Friendly Society, Brownies, Guides, etc. These activities were held either in West Street in the old church school building, where my father was educated before the West Street Board of Education school opposite the church opened in 1901, or in Corinthian Manorway, at the GFS hut, which was on stilts because of its proximity to the river bank – sometimes during Guide meetings boys would push sticks up between the floorboards from underneath – The Erith Yacht Club building was close by. The river bank was one of our play areas, and we saw liners on their way to dock at Woolwich, and red-sailed barges.

Frank's Park was another playground and a third was Church

Five Bearsted children on the rocks at Hastings in the 1900s. Hats were essential wear whenever we went out.

Manorway, opposite our home in Lower Road, which led to Callender's Cable Works, Erith Oil Works and other factories. We spent a lot of time playing in the Manorway which was quiet except when the men went to and from work. At the end of a shift cyclists came first, then we played hide-and-seek behind the rows of men walking up the Manorway. There were apple trees behind the railings and some of the local lads would go scrumping if they could bend the railings and get through. Wild roses bloomed in summer giving a splash of colour. There were also ditches in those days. I got a foot and leg in one when trying to walk across on a narrow pipe. Once my brother fell right in and came home dripping slimy, smelly ditchwater. My mother heard his cries before he reached our door – perhaps he thought he would get into less trouble if he cried. My mother's first action was to pour water over him, clothes and all, in a tin bath in the yard to clean off the worst of the muck. Doultons came from Lambeth to Church Manorway in 1927 and had cottages built off Valley Road to house workmen they brought with them.

I remember going to the Firemen's Tournament at Callender's grounds when brigades gathered from all around the South East. My father was in Vickers Erith's works brigade. I liked to put on his brass helmet, but it was very heavy. Teams competed to be the first to fix a hose to a hydrant, unroll it, turn on the water and knock down the target with the jet. Some firemen climbed the practice apparatus to rescue a dummy, and a clown delighted us children with his antics on the apparatus.

Local factories apart from the four already mentioned were Fraser and Chalmers, Borax, Corys, etc. We had clocks, but the different sounding factory hooters/sirens gave us the time in the mornings at 7.25, 7.30, 7.55 and 8.00, at lunchtime, and when the workers downed tools for the day. When attending West Street school my mother expected us to be up when the 8 am blower went, and later the school bell called us to lessons. There was no truancy in those days. If you missed school one afternoon, the School Board Man was at your door the next morning, even if you had returned.

Empire Day was a great occasion in the school year. When fine we were in the playground, wearing red, white and blue ribbon wherever possible, daisy chains round our necks and daisies in our hair. We sang the National Anthem, a song for each of Australia, Canada, New Zealand and Africa; the Welsh National Anthem in Welsh, *God bless the Prince of Wales, Flag of Britain,* a Scottish song and an Irish one, and there was an Irish dance, a Scottish dance and English maypole dancing. The afternoon was usually declared a holiday.

We played outdoors when it was fine. In summer we sat on the ground playing Jackie Fivestones, or bounced a ball under our legs or against a wall. There were seasons for whips and tops, hoops (ours were wooden, but some boys had metal ones with skids), skipping ropes. If someone had a long rope several girls would skip together, singing, "All in together, never mind the weather". We always sang when skipping or doing "bumps". We also played hopscotch and a game using cigarette cards – "fag pictures" as they were called.

In the autumn, in Frank's Park, we gathered conkers for conker fights, and also sweet chestnuts to eat raw, boiled or roasted. My father showed us how to make tin can fires: perhaps a Libby's milk tin, with a wire handle and a thick cloth and an old glove to hold it with, We put in paper, small pieces of wood and coal, lit it and swung it in a circle backwards over our shoulder to keep it going till the chestnuts were roasted.

Having an elder sister and brothers I could go with them "down the Manorway", "up the bank", or "up the park". Sometimes we spent the afternoon in the park and my mother would bring us a picnic tea. On Friday or Saturday evening my mother and perhaps two of us would walk "up the town" to Erith town centre, and return by tram if we had heavy shopping. As well as the shops there were stalls in the High Street lit by flares or naphtha lamps. Shops and stalls were open till nine o'clock on Saturday. A neighbour made boiled sweets in his garden workshop and sold them from home and from a stall. I used to take supplies to the governess at the infants' school. On Fridays children who'd had a birthday that week each chose a sweet in turn, one for each year of their age.

I had my tonsils out during the General Strike. My mother and I walked to the children's clinic in Avenue Road, where we used to go to have teeth extracted. I was only five and had watched hungrily as the rest of the family ate midday dinner. I was undressed and put into a blue rubber hat and apron before being given gas. When I came round my mother dressed me in my best red velvet dress trimmed with brown fur. She was told to go home and I would arrive later by ambulance. There being no trams because of the strike she had to walk home and was dismayed on turning the church corner to see the ambulance go past. She ran the rest of the way home and arrived panting a few minutes later. She had bought *Briar Rose* (Sleeping Beauty) to read to me whilst I was in bed. My throat was very sore and I had to gargle with Condy's Fluid, a purple solution of permanganate of potash crystals.

The Thames burst its banks in January 1928. Warned of high tides, people had put sandbags in front of their doors. I was seven and my family did not wake me. I was cross because I did not see the river flowing along the road. Houses between us and the church were flooded, but we were lucky as the water turned and ran down Church Manorway to the factories. There was only a tidemark on the footpath to be seen in the morning. Erith Regatta was held on the first Monday in August, the Bank Holiday then. Factories, the council and others entered crews in races on the river. My uncle rowed for the Urban District Council. There was a carnival parade through the town and events in the park and recreation ground during the afternoon and evening, ending with fireworks. During the week there was a shop window display competition and other events in the town.

In the 1920s even families with men in work could ill afford to pay for the doctor, who came only when someone was really ill, as when my brother had rheumatic fever and when I had bronchitis as a baby. Home remedies were used: boracic lint for boils and whitlows – bread or linseed poultices were also used. We were given cod liver oil and malt from a 7lb jar to help resist colds, and were rubbed with camphorated oil if we had a cough. For coughs at night a teaspoon of butter and sugar worked like a charm. We were given liquorice powder in water (ugh!) on Friday nights, had a good wash each evening and a bath in a galvanised tub on Saturday night ready for Sunday school.

We had gaslight downstairs, but candles, oil lamps or nightlights to light us to bed, and stone hot water bottles slipped into old woollen socks. My mother saved during the year to give us a Christmas party and we all helped in the preparations. To make holders for coloured candles my father enlarged the holes in cotton reels with a red hot poker. A candle was put by each child's place at table. The gaslight was put out during tea. After tea the Christmas tree candles, in clip-on holders, were lit and little presents given out. We made our own Christmas hats. Once the point of my brother's tall red and green hat poked into the gas mantle, ruined the mantle and set fire to his hat. Quite a disaster as gas mantles were not cheap.

My elder brother said on his 70th birthday what a wonderful childhood we had compared with children today. Some food for thought there I think!'

LIFE AT MILL HALL

'We moved to Mill Hall at Aylesford when I was six months old and one of my earliest memories was the sound of lions roaring early in the morning which came from Maidstone Zoo, at Cobtree Manor, owned by Sir Tyrwhitt Drake. At Easter, all the family would walk to the zoo and we were there when two elephants were christened "Gert and Daisy" by Elsie and Doris Waters. One day while taking the elephants for a walk over Aylesford Bridge, the keeper almost lost one which decided to follow a policeman. The local bobby at that time was Mr Stan Jenner and when dressed in his uniform with gloves, boots, goggles and helmet on his motor-bike, he was a force to be reckoned with.

At four and a half I started school in the Brassey Rooms with Miss Bethel. The older children were taught by Miss Smith, who stayed there long enough to teach her pupils' children and grandchildren (my son being one of them). Christmas at school was exciting because we went home in the dark after a party (our parents met us, of course). Guest of honour was Father Christmas; we all knew it was Mr Wilson of the "big" school who rang sleigh bells before coming in.

Journeys to and from school were walked mostly on my own with two main hazards – Mr Kemsley's cows (from Preston Hall Farm) coming out of the fields to be milked (I had a red hat and coat), and gypsy caravans all painted and full of children and dogs – I had been told that they would run off with naughty children.

When I was older I had to take my younger sisters to Sunday school in Aylesford church with Canon Everett. For Sunday tea we had either shrimps or winkles, depending on the time of year, purchased from a man who came on Sunday mornings. Our Sunday school treat in the summer was usually a picnic at the Friars, then a private residence, either outside by the fish pond or, if wet, in the refectory.

The river Medway was near to us. It seemed to be much wider then because large sea-going boats carrying coal came up to the wharf at Mill Hall and turned around there. One of the boats was home to a Dutch family called Smythe and I used to wait for their little girl, Betsy. Betsy had a younger sister who had been born in Japan. Often I used to go on board for tea. The river from New Hythe to Mill Hall was called "the cut" and the piece of land left in the middle, when it was straightened, was called "the island". In those days, the island was covered in blackberry bushes and my brother and I would go with Dad to pick some for Mum. Our rowing boat was old and leaked so I had to bale out with a cocoa tin. Before Allington sluice gates were built (in 1937) the road by us was often flooded and the rowing boat was used to "go up the street".'

HOME FROM INDIA

'My parents were on Army holiday leave from India, when I was born at Chatham Military Hospital. On my birth certificate in my father's handwriting is: 10 am, Thursday 10th December 1936. A memorable time for Britain and her people – not because I was born, but because this was precisely when Edward VIII broadcast his Abdication Speech. My mother said that most of the nurses abandoned her in the delivery room, and went off to gather around the radio to listen to the momentous news.

Six weeks after my birth my parents, five sisters and brother and I, sailed for India. Sadly my Dad died in 1942 and in 1946 after Indian Independence we returned to England. That winter was most severe, with snow from October to March. It was so cold and my growing teenage brother was often hungry. Ration books were new to us, and in any case the landlady of our boarding house took them all off us. She gave us a few coupons back. We went shopping and ate heartily thinking, "This is not too bad." It wasn't until later that we realised we had used up a month's coupons in a week!

Now what do I remember from those days? The incredible snowy beauty of everything, especially the hoar frost on the branches. Trying to avoid standing on the cold lino on my bedroom floor. Scraping the frost off the inside of the windows to peer at the icicles hanging from the shed. The world seemed beautiful and full of marvels.

A vivid memory is meekly submitting to the Saturday morning dose of ghastly castor oil – to keep me regular! Fortunately Saturday was also Children's Cinema Club, when hundreds of us noisily, but harmlessly, participated in the adventures of Laurel and Hardy, Abbot and Costello, Roy Rogers and Trigger, Lassie, Charlie Chaplin, Ma and Pa Kettle, Doris Day etc. One Christmas I remember being intrigued when we children were entertained in our sitting room by a tiny Charlie Chaplin, who danced in the space between the armchairs. I must have been a young teenager, yet I didn't realise it was a paper puppet and the adults were working the strings. Nowadays I doubt that a seven year old would be mystified.

Where food was concerned nothing was wasted. Vegetable peelings were boiled up to feed the chickens and my pet rabbit. My foot still bears the scar where I dropped the scalding mess. One day my dear Fluffy died, and I nearly threw up when I found out that my mother had cooked him. Irish stew, made with half a crown's worth of breast of lamb and pearl barley, was one of our favourite meals.

All my sisters and my brother married and left home. As Mum was a widow, naturally my duties included many household chores such as cleaning, going to the launderette and library, gardening, lawn mowing and hedge cutting. I couldn't have minded doing any of this, as neighbours have since told me that I usually sang the latest songs, or I whistled. One of my sisters taught me to whistle and I was always very proud of this skill. Apparently *To be a farmer's boy* was a frequent rendition of mine. The only thing I did dislike was being sent back if I returned from shopping with short change. A small amount like a penny made me feel so embarrassed.

Mum smoked a lot, and she also had a cheeky sense of humour. If she ran out of Woodbine cigarettes, she would put a "Woodies" packet in the window as a signal for our neighbour that she needed some ciggies. On one occasion she put a picture of Errol Flynn in the window!'

BORN DURING THE WAR

'For most of my 55 years I have lived in the village of Bearsted. I have vivid memories of when I was a child and I put this down to the Second World War. The first recollection I have is of the soldiers and the army tanks going through the village. I used to stand at the gate, half scared because of the awful noise they made, but excited at the same time. The soldiers would always wave and some would make a special effort of passing our gate in the street and if I was there, giving me some chocolate. Now chocolate was a thing you did not have very often!'

At an early age I must have been interested in anything to do with the stage, as I can remember several occasions when my mother was frantic because she could not find me and there I would be sitting at the side door of the Women's Institute hall watching the soldiers from Bartie House rehearsing for one of their many shows.

My mother was involved in helping with providing the food for the soldiers who would be given their meals at the Men's Working Club. She would sometimes have to peel enough potatoes to fill a tin bath, and then carry them to the club. One day I was helping her and dropped my end of the tin bath. The street was covered with not so clean peeled potatoes.

There were many old characters who lived in the street and around the village green. There was one old gentleman who would stand at his gate every day and talk to the children. Another old lady who did not like children would sometimes throw something at you out of the window. Cross Keys estate and Trapfield were not there until the early 1950s so there were not many village children. There were the children from the village, the Ware Street children and the ones from the posh side – the other side of the Ashford Road. Trapfield was a smallholding where you could buy vegetables and fruit. A stream used to run behind the Royal Oak and the houses in the street through to Trapfield, and became flooded on many occasions.

There was also the excitement every day of waiting at the gate for the cows to come down from Foster's farm at Sandy Mount to be taken to the fields up Watery Lane. The village children used to have their own "cow stick" and help drive the cattle; we all had our own cow and you knew which one was yours every day. Milk was brought round from Foster's farm on a pony and cart.

My bedroom overlooked the oast houses and every September it was comforting to hear the sound of the kilns starting up and inhale the lovely smell of hops and sulphur. My mother did not go hop picking but I did go with my friend's mother and it was good fun – up at 5.30 am, the mist all around and we would wait for the lorry to pick us up at the White Horse then take us to Betts Farm at Otham. The worst part was the first vine pulled in the morning as it was wet with mist and you would get covered with dew. The evenings in the village at this time of the year were filled with the Londoners. Hop picking went on up until the middle 1950s and then the oast houses were closed down. I feel that a part of the village was lost when this happened and I very much missed the sound and smell of the oast houses.

I started school during the last year of the war. My first day at Thurnham school is quite clear in my mind as one boy started to cry – he later became the school bully. All the children used to love to hear the sound of the planes going over, and we would stand in the playground and wave. We also had a monitor who would sit on the step outside the school during the summer listening for the doodlebugs. In the winter they would have to sit just inside the cloakroom. As soon as one was heard we were hurriedly taken into the air raid shelter where we would sing songs.

My days at Bearsted school were happy. We used to have sports on the green once a year, and folk dancing at Captain Litchfield's. Our PT lessons were held in the memorial hall and we had to walk up, then back down Yeomans Lane once a week during all weathers. Sports days was quite an event – we did manage to win small prizes and always points for our House; there were two houses then – Barty and Fludd – named after previous well known families of Bearsted. Swimming lessons were quite an outing and exciting for us all as it meant a bus ride to Maidstone swimming baths. When we returned and if it was a summer's day we would put our swimming costumes and towels on top of the air raid shelter to dry.'

LIFE WITH MY GRANDMOTHER

'When the war came the children started to be evacuated from London, and as my mother did not want us to go right away, we went to my grandmother in Kent, at Roughway near Plaxtol.

This started one of the happiest times of my life. Of course I missed my parents, but I was allowed much more freedom than ever before, mainly because Grannie couldn't run after us. Apart from the fact that I was expected to take my brother everywhere, life was great.

He was rather a nervous child and wouldn't stand up for himself. Consequently he got picked on by the other children, and the fact that we were newcomers didn't help either. He was terrified of cows, and always had a thing about cows until he grew up. He frequently woke up and said there was a cow under his bed, which had to be driven out and down the stairs, and then he would go to sleep. When the other kids chased him, Grannie would get her walking stick and shake it at them, but they knew she couldn't do much about it.

Children nowadays will never know the freedom we enjoyed. We used to wander for miles to collect bluebells, primroses, frogspawn or tiddlers in a jar, and later on in the year blackberries. One of our favourite places was called "Black Cottages". It was a wood behind the cottages on the Maidstone/Hadlow road, about four miles from the village. There were simply masses of bluebells there, and we used to pick armfuls of them. We would catch the bus one way and walk back or vice versa, perhaps being gone for hours.

We were also allowed to walk along the edge of the hayfields, so long as we kept to the path, which we mostly did, apart from small forays into the hay to pick toddling grass or poppies, whichever took our fancy.

The Bourne stream meanders all round the village of Hadlow, and passed through the mill. At the back of the mill it swelled out into a small lake, called locally "The Cut". This was forbidden to me, as I could not swim and it was quite deep. We used to content ourselves with taking our socks and shoes off, and paddling along the stream where it thinned down again, getting out when it went under the bridges where it was deeper and looked a bit more menacing. The White Bridge was one of these places, and we said there were whirlpools you might get sucked into (we had vivid imaginations, as children do).

Another thing we used to do was to play rounders in the summer evenings after school. This was played in a field up Court Lane. The long summer evenings seemed endless in those days, with swifts screaming overhead, and I recall that there were all ages, boys and girls who used to play. When we got tired of this, we played rolling down the bank until we made ourselves feel sick. Just past this field was the dung heap, all steaming and smelly.

There seemed to be seasons for games in those days, bouncing balls, marbles, throwing cigarette cards, hoops, whips and tops, hopscotch and skipping. When we skipped we used to sing:

> Nebuchadnezzar the King of the Jews,
> Bought his wife a pair of shoes –
> When the shoes began to wear
> Nebuchadnezzar began to swear,
> When the swear began to stop
> Nebuchadnezzar bought a shop.

Grannie's house was a detached cottage right on the path, with a concrete yard at the side, entered through a large wooden gate, with a wall over it. This was shared with three other cottages the other side of the gate, although it was mainly only used by the people next door.

I used to spend hours playing ball against the wall. We also played a game called "corner to wall" outside. The garden across the road was much higher than the road, and was supported by a wall. The game was that one said "corner", and the other "wall"; the one who said corner went to the kerb first, and then across the road and back to the wall. The other did it the other way, and the first one back won. We also had iron hoops which we used to knock up and down the road with a piece of wood, as there was hardly any traffic then.

The milkman was Bill Warren, and he used to come round in a pony and trap, with the milk in a churn with a handle on it, like a covered bucket, and the top half opened to get the milk out. This was ladled into a jug, lovely creamy stuff it was too. It was so creamy that in the hot weather it often went off, and then Grannie would make butter with it, but it was always too rancid for me.

Of course there were no fridges then, and the milk was kept in a metal safe, or in a basin of cold water on the scullery table in hot weather with a net with beads round the edge to keep the flies off. All the meat, bacon or cheese was kept in this, but there wasn't usually too much. The butter ration was only two ounces, and what meat we had was eaten on Sunday. We often made a meal of potatoes and gravy, or a bowl of Grannie's soup in the winter.

We also had no running water in the house. The pump was at the top of the gardens against a high wall, and was shared by all of the houses. One of my jobs when I got older was to see there was enough water for the day by filling two buckets and a stone crock, which was covered with a board to stop the mice falling into it.

All the lighting was by gas, and although there were lights upstairs these were not used unless you were ill. You had to take a candle to light you to bed, and it was creepy with all the shadows and the flame dancing in the breeze. My imagination worked overtime, I always thought there was a lion waiting upstairs for me.

My brother and I hated thunderstorms, and used to cover ourselves with newspapers and scream and cry until the storm was over. Grannie was very superstitious, and when there was a storm all mirrors were covered, and knives and forks put away, even hair grips were suspect. Knives were never left crossed, as Grannie said there would be a row between those using them. You shouldn't use the same water when washing your hands, for the same reason; you had to spit three times when you saw a dappled horse (a thing which still amuses me today) and you threw a pinch of salt over your shoulder to ward off the devil. It always amazed me that Grannie had these foibles, as she was a good Christian woman, but I think it was more a case of not tempting providence.

She must have been a very good looking woman when she was young, as even in old age she had a nice face. She was married at 21, and left a widow at 37 with seven children.

She had to work very hard to bring up her family, and worked in the fields, or did housework. There was no social security then, and they used to walk miles to get a bowl of soup. She was a very good cook, having been in service, and could make a meal from next to nothing. Her soup was made from bones and it was delicious, mostly vegetables with an Oxo or some Bovril or Marmite in it. I have never tasted soup as good since, and I pride myself on being a good cook. We had lots of suet puddings and of course fruit was nearly always available. The farmer at Castle Farm then, a Mr

Pearsen I believe, would dump his surplus apples and anyone was allowed to take what they wanted.

Grannie also made a delicious pudding called Well Pudding. This was a basin lined with suet pastry, and filled with layers of currants and brown sugar. This had a lid put on it, and was boiled in a saucepan for a couple of hours. When it was turned out all the sugar had turned to syrup, and it was lovely. Sometimes Grannie made currant buns, but we used to say that she stood at the top of the stairs and threw the currants in, as there was so few.'

WHEN SUMMERS WERE LONG AND SUNNY

'I was born in Rainham in 1944 and my family have lived there for generations. In his youth my father used to cross the river on a Thames barge with a friend's father to load mud, using a large flat shovel, for the making of cement; they then had to wait for the high tide to float the heavy barge back. My grandfather owned one of the very first Model T Fords in the area and he taught people to drive in the field next to the house. My father spent the war making the wooden patterns for the Sterling bombers at Rochester airport and his toolchest had a piece of shrapnel embedded in it from one of the times the factory was bombed.

The highlight of our year as children was the Gillingham Park fête when there would be a travelling fair and our next door neighbour would take us there in his car and give us half a crown to spend – on the way home he'd treat us to pease pudding and faggots from a shop in the high street. We cycled most places or walked, at weekends down Boxley Hill to Penenden Heath to play on the swings while our parents had a drink in The Bull.

My grandmother lived in Sittingbourne in a little two up, two down house with an outside toilet and washhouse and when we visited her on Sundays we would go down in the evening to listen to the Salvation Army band and have winkles for tea using her hatpins. She made wonderful suet puddings wrapped in a cloth and always used soda in the vegetables to keep the colour.

I went to school with my sister at the convent in Sittingbourne. In those days you could get a detention for having the wrong hat with the wrong coat, and you never ate or ran in uniform (it wasn't ladylike) – the local M&D bus driver would wait for us at the bottom of the field to save us walking to the bus stop! We went on school trips to London to visit the art galleries and attend lectures, to visit the Houses of Parliament, and best of all to go to the Old Vic to see whatever the 'O' level play was.

The local bobby was well known to all of us and a great friend. I remember leaving my Brownie uniform at the bus stop and he

106

dropped it off with Brown Owl for me. On the way home from school I would buy a pennyworth of stale iced buns from the local bakery and feed them to the sheep as I walked through the church path and fields to get home (no houses anywhere, just sheep and rabbits and quite safe).

My father worked at Parhams in Gillingham when we were small and brought home discarded offcuts of wood which he chopped into kindling and we tied into bundles for sale to the local shop. We also pickled onions by the score for sale and made cherry brandy (to drink) from morello cherries growing in the garden. The house was alive with fruit flies while it fermented.

Money was short and mostly the rule was if we didn't grow it we didn't eat it. Sweets were a luxury and when Dad got paid he would buy three tubes for us on his way home and we would dive into his pockets as he came in. Barter was common – my father was a carpenter and he was paid in fruit, vegetables and eggs for all sorts of little jobs. We used to donate our cod liver oil from the clinic to a friend to fatten his chickens and at Christmas we'd get one cheap. We'd go chestnut hunting and eat them roasted from the fire and we'd toast bread and have it with cinnamon or beef dripping. I was often sent to the butcher to get the dripping as he was more likely to be generous with the portion to a small girl.

I saw Rainham change from a smallish village where you couldn't walk down the street without meeting and greeting nearly every other person, surrounded by green fields, farms, fruit trees, sheep and woods where we slid down haystacks, scrumped plums, fished for eels in the creek and found bee orchids and adders in the woods, to a great sprawling dormitory town where there are no fields, no farms and certainly no sheep. The fence maker has disappeared, the oast houses are a community centre, the Royal cinema where we went to Saturday morning pictures has gone and the woods are restricted to little parcels where people dump their litter and you certainly wouldn't let small children roam unattended.

Summer always seemed long and sunny then, and we were never bored. We carved chalk, made itching pips from rose hips, pea shooters from cow parsley, we cooked dampers in camp fires, made kites, camped in the garden, dressed up, swung from trees, fed the chickens, helped with the sick lambs, kept rabbits . . .'

GROWING UP AND THE NEW LOOK

'In 1946 I bought a pair of "Joyce" shoes. They were red leather with three-inch platform soles, sling-back, with peep-toes. They were very comfortable and were worn for years. They cost £4 – very expensive!

107

In 1947 came the New Look. My first long New Look dress was reseda green overchecked in black. I bought it in Gravesend for £4 2s 6d. The first time I wore it, I can remember walking down Military Road in Chatham and all heads seemed to turn in my direction. After a few similar outings, I shortened the dress by making a deep hem and waited until the New Look became more popular.'

'In 1947 I had just become a teenager and to me Christian Dior's New Look was marvellous. It was swingy, smart and sensational. My first flirtation with this fabulous fashion style was a navy ballerina-length skirt which I wore with a short red tartan jacket edged with velvet and a natty velour hat trimmed with a saucy feather. I really felt the "bee's knees". When on a visit to London, wearing this outfit, a policeman outside the Houses of Parliament thought I was French. I thought I had attained the "Parisian Elegance".

I was educated at Notre Dame Convent, where our needlework mistress was also impressed with Christian Dior but who was unable to do much about wearing it as she was a nun, but she encouraged us to alter our existing clothes (not our school uniform). We lengthened our skirts by adding to the hems and making insertions with contrasting material. We made our jackets and blouses fashionable by adding a peplum to them and put two petticoats together to make the skirts stand out.

My only regret was that I wasn't old enough to wear high heels but the ballerina shoes were cute so I made do with these.'

OUT AND ABOUT

We walked everywhere, sometimes miles every day. There were few cars before the Second World War, and bicycles were our usual means of transport.

LATE FOR SCHOOL

'We lived in a cottage at the back of The Man of Kent at Little Mill, a hamlet of East Peckham. I started school in 1905 aged five years, and walked with my sisters Emily and Mabel to East Peckham primary school – we mostly walked home again for dinner, but sometimes took food with us. Once I got caned for being late for school – it was probably because I'd had to run across the fields to the butcher in Snoll Hatch for the daily pennyworth of suet. Mother made a suet pudding every day – my father loved them – in the summer they were fruity. On Wednesdays I had to buy three pennyworth of pieces and that day we had meat pudding, enough for the family of six, with vegetables from the garden. Bread and milk were delivered to the cottages by horse and cart. We kept rabbits and they provided our weekend meals. We had to collect food for them: dandelions, hogweed and young cow parsley. It was aginst the law to snare wild rabbits.

We bowled our hoops to school. The lanes were mud with stones rolled in by steam rollers from Arnolds. The stones came from the quarry which was between the Bush and what is now known as Seven Mile Lane (at that time there was a track from Roydon Hall to the Harp public house known as New Road). We used to play football (with an old tennis ball) in the playground at school, but one day a boy fell and broke his leg, so games in the playground were stopped.'

WALKING FOR MILES

'I was born in October 1908 in Gravesend. Our father was a thatcher and his work took him to various farms in the area, some of them miles away. In those days all farms had a stack yard, the harvest being carried in and stacked in one place as a rule.

When our father was working within walking distance of home we children would take him a can of tea. One of our walks took us over the fields and lanes to Thong, a hamlet quite near to what became known as Laughing Water. Imagine us, if you can, none more than nine or ten years old, walking a distance of two or three miles from the top of Sun Lane where we lived. There were no houses until we saw the isolation hospital on our right after going down Whitehill Lane which was then called Sanatorium Hill, and past the gypsies' camp at the entrance to the Warren called Palmer's Meadow, then across the fields to Thong. I can't remember if there was ever anything left in the can for Dad after all our many stops and starts on the way. Then, of course, we had to walk the same distance all the way back. I shall always remember the great variety of wild flowers we picked in Palmer's Meadow and all the wild weeds and grasses.

Our paternal grandparents lived at Camer near Meopham where Grandfather was farm bailiff to Smithmasters Farm. At times Mother would set out to visit them for the day. It must have been at least four miles or more. My sister Flossie and I walked with Kath in the pram. We walked across the fields to Singlewell, then we had to wait at the kissing-gate for someone on the farm to help us get the pram over the gate. Then we went past Ifield church to Round Street and Sole Street and through Camer Gardens to The Street and Granny's house. Then at the end of the day we had to walk all the way back. As the eldest I had to keep walking but the others had a ride on the old pram now and then. Poor Mother must have been worn out at the end.'

SCHOOL AND SHOPPING

'I was born in 1913 at Ash near Wrotham as it was then. Later the postal address was moved to Sevenoaks. The postman cycled four miles, up Wrotham Hill, to deliver and collect letters and parcels to the surrounding villages. We always had a delivery on Christmas morning, and as we were near the end of his round he was always merry by the time he arrived. My father always had a drink ready for him. Later he had a motor cycle with a box sidecar.

At twelve years old I went to Gravesend county school for girls (now the grammar school). There were no buses then, so I had to cycle four miles to Longfield Halt to catch the train to Gravesend. This line is now closed. It was downhill all the way and on cold frosty mornings we were frozen by the time we got to Longfield. The lady where we left our bicycles always had a good fire going to warm us, and our fingers ached as they thawed out. In winter it was dark when we returned, with paraffin lamps on our bicycles.

We had a free time as children, able to play in the fields and woods with no thought of being molested, and thought nothing of walking a few miles to visit friends.

Most everyday shopping was done locally, with the baker calling three times a week and hot cross buns were delivered on Good Friday morning, hot. Our milk we fetched from the White Swan pub; they had a small farm and kept a few cows. If a new coat or shoes were needed it meant a journey to Gravesend, walking to Longfield to catch the train. Mother pushing my younger sister in the pram, which was put on the train. I was about six years old then, and we were expected to walk the four miles.

The summer holidays at the village school began after Mr George Day, the local farmer, said fruit picking was starting. He grew strawberries, raspberries, blackcurrants and gooseberries on the fields where New Ash Green is now built. The fruit was taken each day to Fawkham (now Longfield) station to be put on the fruit train to London markets. The summer always seemed sunny then. In winter we had some heavy falls of snow, and the village was cut off for days. In 1928 we had such a heavy fall that the snow built up

110

On the beach at Margate in the 1930s. We were well covered at all times – but how we loved those rare treats at the seaside.

over our front windows and we had to be dug out at the back. We had fun then walking on the top of the hedges. Some of the village men got together and dug passageways to walk through the snowdrifts. My mother was a wine maker and every morning we took them a can of hot elderberry or ginger wine to warm them. No doubt they dug better after that. At that time a bus service had started and one bus was stuck for a week in a snowdrift.'

HUNDREDS OF MILES!

I was born in Barming at the beginning of the First World War. One of my earliest recollections is of being picked up by my mother whilst she pointed to something in the sky she called an airship.

Just after the end of that war, when I was about five or six, I was playing in our garden with a friend, a boy around the same age as myself. He suggested that we might go to visit his uncle, who owned a shop in the town (Maidstone) and who might give us a drink of lemonade. Also, if we took a bag, we might be able to gather some "green meat" for my friend's pet rabbit. The possibility of the drink of lemonade won the day and off we trotted. I was wearing my old, bright red garden coat which had one or two buttons missing and

111

my friend was carrying a sack, much too large for the handful of green leaves we were eventually able to find. We seemed to be walking "hundreds" of miles before we came to the town and hundreds more miles before we found his uncle's shop.

Sad to say, his uncle didn't seem overjoyed to see us, which was, we felt, surprising. He did, however, give us a drink of lemonade which was a great thirst quencher. Then he took off my garden coat, bundled it into the sack (I wondered why) and in no time at all, we three were seated on a tram bound for home. Needless to say, my mother gave me a lecture on the perils of walking so far from home without getting permission. She also told me that if it hadn't been for Grace, a young telegram girl who lived near us, and had seen us walking townwards, we might easily have been lost and have needed the police to find us.'

WANDERING AROUND MAIDSTONE

'I was born in Salisbury Road, Maidstone in the 1920s and the playground for all the children around was Penenden Heath. We would walk there through "The Hedges". This was a fairly narrow lane about half a mile long with tall hedges on both sides. The walk would take a long time because there was so much of interest – birds and their nests, hedgehogs and all kinds of insects. There would be a group of us and often we would take our lunch; it was always safe and no worry to our parents.

Once on the heath we would play or watch cricket or football, then drift to the top end of the heath, an area covered in gorse and known as the "fuzzies". Sometimes we would go down the hill to the rabbit warren. This was a wonderful place for children. One side was woodland and the other an open space with hundreds of rabbits everywhere you looked. Other times we would go down the other hill towards Boxley. Just a short way and on the left we crossed a stile and we were in the "Sheep Wash". Usually there were cows or sheep grazing – they took no notice of us – and in springtime there were masses of primroses and cowslips. At the end of the Sheep Wash was a stream, always crystal clear, where we paddled and looked for tadpoles and minnows.

Sometimes we would wander through Cuckoo Woods, often full of bluebells and wood anemones. We would then make our way home through Peel Street Hedges and into Granville Road. We loved this because at the far end of the road was an old shack where Nanti Bill lived with his donkey.

He was a well known character – more like a tramp – always unshaven and with a battered grey trilby on his head. I believe he made a living making ladders. The donkey pulled a cart full of wood.

It was well known that on his way home he called in at The Rose public house in Wheeler Street for a drink. The donkey would not move on until he, too, had a pint of beer.

On the right-hand side of The Hedges was a large field and every year St Luke's Sunday school children had the Sunday school treat there. We marched from the church and spent the afternoon competing in all kinds of races, then had tea under a huge oak tree. My brothers were good athletes and always came home with three or four John Bull Printing Outfits – the prize for the winners. The girls usually received a skipping rope.

Another well known figure in this area was Mrs Fremlin, of the brewery family. She was very old, dressed from head to toe in black, always wearing a black bonnet when out riding in a carriage drawn by two black horses. Another familiar sight was the warders going home to lunch from the prison. All would be carrying a white cotton bag with a drawstring top. This contained loaves of bread, made by the prisoners, and the smell when passing was delicious.

Every Sunday, our family went for a walk, during the afternoon in winter and the evening in summer. My delight was to get on a tram at Mill Street and go to Loose Valley. On the way, in Upper Stone Street, we would pass the lodging houses on the left-hand side and we always sat upstairs on the tram so we could see inside. It was full of elderly men, usually lying on their small beds, in a row and covered with a grey blanket. This held a great fascination for children.'

WE WALKED EVERYWHERE

'As children we walked everywhere whether into Bromley to do some shopping or to visit the Library Gardens ("Keep off the Grass" and "No children under 14 unaccompanied by an adult" and certainly no running about!), or to visit our grandparents who lived at Green Street Green, some five miles from Bromley. We knew all the footpaths to the surrounding villages like Hayes, Keston, Farnborough and Chislehurst and used them regularly.

As a treat we might go on the bus to visit the shops in Catford or Lewisham. We all had bikes as we got older, reconstructed from spare parts by our father, but before we were allowed out on them on our own we had to prove that we could look after them, pump tyres and mend punctures. Then came the joy of going off on our own for the day with our sandwiches, drinks, pump and puncture outfit safely stowed away in our saddlebags. We could ride around all day and never see a car or van in the lanes. Mind you, we had to be home by a certain time or there was trouble.

There was a recreation ground near our home where all the local children played rounders, cricket, football or just chased about. The keeper's word was law. Woe betide any child who was rude to him; he knew all our parents and would certainly report any misbehaviour. In spite of this and the names we called him under our breath we all had a lot of respect for him. When the war came the railings went, it was never the same "rec" and now there is no keeper to watch over the children.'

A LONELY PATH

'Those of you who live at Orpington may know the area where St John's Road meets Crofton Lane. It was there I was brought up. At the age of six or seven it was decided that I should join others of my age and go to the big school. As this emporium of learning was two stations away it entailed quite a journey, for there were no buses and Pett's Wood was still one vast farm apart from the wood itself. So wet or fine, we children had to walk along Crofton Lane to the railway bridge and then follow the railway along the cinder path to the station. I believe this footpath still exists in spite of estates being built over the fields. In summer it was fun but in winter those two miles seemed endless. Especially coming home, quite often on one's own.

One day I was very late and missed the usual gang. I ran and hopped until I was exhausted and then found I could walk much more quickly with my eyes shut! I suppose I was a bit odd as a child. While the path was straight all was well, but as some of you may know, at one point the path branches on to a footbridge while the main route bends to the right. Well, I went slap into an iron post. When I arrived at the station (in time for the Bromley train) I was covered in blood, mostly from my nose. The porters were most considerate and two school prefects grabbed me and lay me on the carriage seat. As I had a "pash" on one (unmentionable these days I believe!) I just let them get on with the mopping up operations.

Somehow the situation was passed on to my mother. Maybe the policeman we all loved had to come pedalling up from the village or maybe we had a phone by then. One of those standing ones with a hook at the side. At any rate she eventually arrived driving our motorcycle and sidecar. When mounting this monster my mother used to dress up in sort of oilskin trousers and an old leather coat. I was rather ashamed of this outfit but couldn't help admiring the way she managed this iron steed. I was duly shoved into the sidecar and driven home with not much sympathy as she had had to leave my brother with a neighbour.

That was 1923 and I just wonder what mother these days would dare to let her child walk alone along a rather desolate path without an adult. A rather sad reflection on our society.'

COMPLETE FREEDOM

'I was born at Castle Hill, Brenchley in 1931. My brother, John, arrived some 18 months later and for our early childhood years we played and started to grow up together in our own small world. We did not have a car so if we went out anywhere, it had to be on foot, bicycle, or on rare occasions by bus to Tunbridge Wells with our mother. An early memory was being taken in our pram to Horsmonden to its Jubilee Celebrations (King George V in 1935) and waving a Union Jack flag, though I think our visit to the Furnace Pond en route was more exciting with its footbridge over the river which had frightening slats through which the water could be observed. The seat overlooking the valley on the road between Brenchley crossroads and Castle Hill was erected at this time and we always knew it as the "Jubilee Seat".

In such quiet and generally peaceful and uneventful surroundings, we were consequently both rather shy children, unlike today's confident youngsters, and when the day came for me to start school, it was a terrifying experience when my mother left me in the classroom.

Meanwhile, at weekends and any other opportunity, John and I would play, roaming the fields and woods in the vicinity with complete freedom. We enjoyed birds' nesting, noting down the position of nests and guessing the variety of bird – we never took eggs, the excitement of finding a nest was sufficient for us; "exploring", "camps" in the wood, "spying" on the few people and vehicles that passed along the road, sometimes taking car numbers – but that became boring as there were often very long waits between motors; more often we crouched in our vantage place watching a farm horse and cart lumber by leaving bits of its load of hay, straw or manure caught on hedges and tree branches.

At hop picking time, the countryside was invaded by the hop pickers who came from London's East End and lived in huts in the wood. The local general shop at Castle Hill would put up its barriers for the duration of hop picking to keep these somewhat alien loud groups of people from actually entering the shop and overwhelming the gentle little elderly lady who ran it. She had jars of sweets I remember and one could buy a pennyworth! The local bus which took me to school charged one penny to go from Castle Hill to the school and the conductor wore a silver coloured small machine over his shoulder into which he would insert a yellow ticket and wind a handle at the side which would print the date etc on the ticket. Children boarding the bus at Pearson's Green paid a penny halfpenny and had a blue ticket issued to them. We would collect tickets and join them together concertina fashion by folding.

We also collected milk bottle tops – bigger than those used today and made of cardboad with a perforated small hole in the centre. The girls used them to make fluffy wool balls by winding wool round using the centre hole; the boys used them to skim in competition with each other. Our milk came from Mr A.T. Spencer who had a farm and herd of Black Dexter cows at Palmers' Green Lane. He delivered the milk each day himself in pint and half-pint bottles. At school those who wanted to could have one-third pint bottles of milk costing a halfpenny and nearly everyone had school dinners at one shilling and threepence a week – no choice and we had to eat it all up!'

GAMES, TREATS AND CHORES

Games went by seasons, and we all knew when to leave off playing tops and start playing with hoops! We played in the road, and toys were scarce in many families so we used our imaginations to make our fun. Organised groups such as the Scouts and Guides were often our gateway to a wider world and camp was a great adventure, as was any holiday away from home. But we all had our chores to do as well, and pocket money often had to be earned.

A GREAT ADVENTURE

'I was born in Maidstone in 1935. In those days it was considered a great adventure to rent a house by the sea and for our family it was always Westgate-on-Sea. My father had an old Austin car with a grid on the back which let down and all the suitcases were piled one on top of the other and firmly secured with a leather strap.

My grandparents and aunt always came too, following in another old Austin. One of us kept looking backwards in case they broke down on Detling Hill. In the middle of the back seat, with me firmly on her lap and my brother and sister either side, sat "Nurse", a forbidding figure all in grey and never without her round grey felt hat. She was a real martinette. I recall many a whack with the hairbrush. Every night she would roll up my hair into cherry bobbles with bits of rag. I was considered really naughty if the curls disappeared next day, regardless of the weather.

The highlight of the holidays for me was the donkeys. Sometimes we would go into Margate and walk to the end of the pier to watch the *Royal Daffodil*, a big white day cruiser, and the *Royal Sovereign* but we never went on them, that would have been too adventurous. We paddled in thick red woollen swimsuits.'

OFF TO CAMP

'The early part of my life was lived through the Second World War in Dartford, all very exciting for me as a child. Two things stand out at the end of the war. The first was that organisations were allowed to "parade" so, with great excitement, we in the 4th Dartford Guides hunted in our church cupboard for the flag which hadn't seen daylight since the war began. There was to be a grand parade to include Guides and Scouts from all over Dartford at Christ Church. Well, we found our flag, unrolled it and shock, horror, no one had told the moths about rationing – the flag was full of large holes! On the Sunday of the parade, while all the other company flags were flying in the wind, ours had to be held with a firm hand on the pole so as not to let everyone see our large moth holes.

The second memory is also linked with Guiding. We were allowed to go to camp; my friend Phyllis and I were selected to join with the Rangers for a week's camp at Nurstead Court Farm. It seemed miles away (in fact it is about a mile from where I now live). We had to have a "camp dress" for this holiday and as money and coupons were scarce Mum made mine out of an old sheet and dyed it blue. It was smashing. We set off, sitting on top of the camping equipment on an open top lorry. When we arrived we were to share the field with a cow and a horse, both of which kept getting caught in our guy ropes during the night. We slept in a large round tent, toes to middle; the "lats" (toilets to the uninitiated) were situated at the far side of the field. Between them and us were large blackberry bushes. Our Captain, wanting to make sure we were kept "regular", provided prunes for breakfast and a tiny tablet for each of us before going to bed. After the first night we found the best place for the "tiny tablet" was not to be swallowed but hidden somewhere under the grass. I sometimes wonder if the cow and the horse had problems after we left.

One of our daily chores was to get the water. The tap was situated on the far side of the field and you had to take buckets to fill, then tip the water into a large dustbin. When it was our group's time we thought of a better plan – take the dustbin to the water, fill it up – we couldn't move it. We had to tip most of the water out, bring it back and fill it properly, so much for shortcuts! I think the one thing that will always remain with me from this camp was the smell of

117

LONGFORD
SWIMMING POOL

DUNTON GREEN   **NEAR SEVENOAKS**

A unique feature, fresh running filtered water

BATHING
Admission 4d.
BOATING

8d. ALL DAY   **JOIN OUR CLUB**   1/- PER HOUR
(Membership 7/6)

PUTTING
AND ENJOY THESE
RECREATIONS
TENNIS

18 HOLES 6d.   **AT HALF PRICE**   2/- PER HOUR

SPACIOUS LAWN FOR SUN-BATHING

TEAS BY THE RIVER, Devonshire Cream, Home-made Cakes, etc.

Season, May 1st—September 30th

---

*An advertisement for Longford Swimming Pool in the 1930s. If we could afford it,
a day at the pool was an exciting treat.*

burnt stew. To this day it brings back memories of my first camp. Whilst writing this I wondered why I couldn't remember the next year's camp. Then it came back to me. I should have gone, it was all arranged, then one very distraught mother – a visit to the doctor, no way could I go. I had nits!'

POOLS AND PICNICS

'As a youngster I lived in Orpington, and if we wanted to go swimming the nearest indoor pool was a bus ride away at Eltham. I attended St Philomena's Catholic school and we had Ascension Day off, when an outing to the outdoor pool at Bickley was arranged for the hardy, as the water in mid May always seemed very cold. If the sun shone you could lay your towel out on the terraces above the changing rooms.

In summer we sometimes took a picnic and drove to Hilden Manor in Hildenborough. This pool had a waterfall and tables and chairs set out on the grass. We also went to Woodsgate at Pembury. The changing cubicles formed the outside wall, there was grass to sit on and a fountain.

Guide camp was the highlight of the year. Our clothes were packed in a kit bag and blankets were pinned together to form a sleeping bag. Everything was loaded into a covered lorry and we all got in and sat on the tents or anything else soft. What fun waving to the cars behind us, and of course singing all the Guide songs.'

WAX DOLLS

'I liked playing with the little girl next door, because she had lots of toys – a big doll's pram, a doll's house and lots of dolls. I would stay for tea and we had it at a little table of our own. This was very different from home, where we had to sit up to a big table, very close together and keep our elbows close to our sides.

I had a favourite doll. She was made of wax. She had lovely flaxen hair tied with blue ribbon and clothes of pink silk. I made her a bed from a shoe box. One day, I left her in a chair by the fire when I went out to play. When I got back she had started to melt, but I still played with her even though she wasn't pretty any more, because it was all my fault.

After wax dolls, they were made of celluloid, but they used to crack and break easily. The next ones were of china. They had to be handled carefully and we had lots of dolls without heads.'

TOYS WERE SCARCE

'Toys were in short supply during the war and I can remember having a doll whose body was filled with hard straw. I called her Ginger Rogers as she had ginger hair that I curled up with Mum's dinky curlers. She cost Mum seven shillings and sixpence at the village post office at Wilmington.

At the age of seven I went to Ensworth for a holiday. What fun when the milkman came in his horse and cart. I would take the jug and see him dip the measuring container into the churn then fill our jug. This was all new to me as our milk came in bottles with a cardboard top. You would push out the middle to form a small hole, use two tops together and wind wool round them between the two and the end result was a fluffy ball.'

'I was born in 1914, the youngest of three girls, at Westerham. Our father was killed during the war but we had a wonderful mother who loved and cared for us.

We had an old shed at the top of the garden where we played with our friends for hours. There was a curtain up at the window and the shed was swept out every day. I used to be the "milkman" and made the milk from chalk and water in an old white enamel bucket. Eggs were made from mud with a dessert spoon and dried in the sun. Cakes were also made from dried mud and runner bean flowers were used as cherries on the top.

We played games in their seasons. Hopscotch, spinning tops, hoops, five stones, and skipping. We also went on lovely picnics, and after tea we would have treasure hunts to find different leaves, nuts, flowers etc. Lots of fun and it cost nothing.'

STREET GAMES

'I was born in 1915 in Chatham. After school and during the holidays street games were our entertainment, with no cars to worry us. We played football, cricket, street skipping, hopscotch and a game called "jump diddy wacko" – there were two teams of four children. One team stood facing away from a wall and got into a leapfrog position with hands on knees. The other team would leap on, to see how many children they could leap at a time and if they could reach the wall at the back.

The girls played with wooden hoops, the boys with iron ones. We had spinning tops, marbles and many more games. Most children had to do their chores before being allowed out.'

'Games seemed to come in seasons. Every spring out came the skipping ropes. Sometimes we skipped alone and sometimes with a long rope between friends. We juggled with two, three or four balls, both in the air and up against a house wall. Sometimes we were in trouble for making dirty marks on the wall. Hopscotch was fun too and paving stones made a splendid place for this. Five stones was another game, played with five coloured stones and a small ball. You had to pick up different numbers of stones while the ball was in the air.'

'Out of school we spun our tops, bowled our hoops, or skipped with our ropes across the main road. There was no public transport and very few people at Fordcombe owned a car, so the roads were very peaceful. I have often wondered since how we knew when it was no longer top-time and became hoop-time, or when hoop-time changed to skipping-time – these activities just seemed to happen at about the same time each year! On summer evenings in the cricket field we played stoolball, using two oak trees as our wickets. The ladies of the Women's Institute had started playing this game during their social half hour, and we learned by watching them, and sometimes even being allowed to field a ball.'

'In Old Bexley village, when one stands by the post office bus stop and takes note of the traffic that goes by it doesn't seem possible that it was once quiet and peaceful there, when one could look along Bourne Road and not see any form of vehicle for several minutes at a time.

It was along the gutters, on the way to school, that several games of marbles would take place, one set following a few yards behind the other. This was what we called travelling – one bowled his marble along the gutter for a few feet and his opponent tried to hit it with his. If he succeeded he picked it up and the other fellow would have to bring a fresh marble out and start again. The crisis came when a drain appeared, someone had to go ahead to stop the marbles going down! This game soon got children to school where they were promptly rebuked for having dirty hands. The second version was played in the school playground. A chalk ring was drawn and an equal number of marbles were placed inside and then they were bowled at in turn, all those you knocked outside the ring you won.

All games seemed to have their season and spring days brought out skipping ropes and tops. The usual venue for these was Victoria Road, now named Albert Road. The council houses on the one side did not exist, the site was entirely allotments up as far as the slight bend in the road and enclosed by an iron railing. This railing served to tie one end of the skipping rope to and such was the amount of traffic that a rope could reach right across the road without any interference. Skipping was usually done by the girls although it was supplemented at times by whip-tops which were spun by winding the thong of the whip round the top and then jerked loose thus making the top spin and it was kept going by lashing. The whips were mostly improvised affairs, any old stick about 18 inches long would do whilst the thong could be a piece of string or tape or even a boot lace made of leather or cotton as long as it was pliable. The boys usually used peg tops which had a long metal peg protruding from the case of the top. These were wound up by a piece of cord and thrown to the ground at an angle thus causing them to spin. Competitions were held to see which girl could skip the longest and which boy could spin his top the longest.

The top part of the recreation ground was privately owned up to the 1914-18 war and during the summer months it was occupied by cattle grazing contentedly – when milking time came they were tied up in turn to the enclosing fence and if fun was made of the milkman whilst he was working he made the most of his handy "ammunition" and you had to duck pretty quickly! The recreation ground proper, at the bottom by the stream, was a popular place for picnics during the summer months – the grass was only cut once a year so it served as a hay field and parents with picnic baskets would meet their children from school and go there. During the First World War the whole lot was ploughed up and used for allotments.'

HOPPING TIME

'Hopping time brings back many happy memories, even though we had to pick so many hops before we were allowed out to play. If our mothers said we had to pick so many hops we did so, nobody thought of disobeying. I do not remember any Londoners in the Southfleet area over 75 years ago. The locals from Gravesend, Northfleet, Swanscombe and other villages would come and at six o'clock in the mornings the roads would be crowded and the dust that came up had to be seen to be believed. No roads were tarred, only Kentish ragstone or granite rolled in and that was it.

The highlight of the day for us boys was when the man came round with his handcart full of sweets and iced cakes. A cake was a halfpenny and it was delicious. Another highlight for us children was when the Fried Fish man came round. It was cold, mind you, but you would get a big piece for threepence, and if Mother had a meat sandwich as well we were in heaven. All this was washed down with tea brewed over a wood fire and with the smell of hops all around, it is something I have never forgotten.'

Hop picking was a family occupation, even the youngest going along for the ride! This family were picking at Brenchley in 1940, Battle of Britain year.

EVERY MISTAKE

'I lived on a small farm on a quiet back lane in Otham and one of my earliest memories is of the time after tea on winter evenings. Father and Mother would sit either side of a big log fire in their armchairs and I sat in the middle on a stool made for my father by his mother's father, who was a wheelwright. My father was born in 1894.

The reason that I remember it so well and why I sat in the middle by my father's side was that he was teaching me my multiplication tables. He always held in his hand a long wooden ruler and if I got them wrong I got rapped on my knuckles. I was told that I would get the same again for every mistake I made.'

EARNING POCKET MONEY

'I did not have pocket money until I was 14 years of age. I had to earn this money on Saturday mornings, working on our local farm at Southfleet from 9 am to noon. We used to do bean nipping, and pulling rhubarb and spring onions ready for market. We were paid sixpence a row which seemed endless. At 14 we were also allowed to go fruit picking. We picked raspberries, gooseberries, black and red currants, plums, damsons and apples. The money I earned in the school holidays was used to buy me a new school blazer and socks to go back to school in September. I was very proud that I bought these clothes myself.'

GAMES AND CHORES

'We had a lovely time playing with tops and hoops (my brother had an iron one which I much preferred to my girl's wooden one). We made ourselves trolleys from wooden boxes and four pram wheels or whatever we could get hold of. We had great fun racing down the church hill at Ide Hill, which is fairly steep, or seeing who could go fastest.

I often think what a hard time our parents had. The men worked from early till late and the women struggled to make ends meet, often with a large family and no modern appliances to ease the work. We had linoleum on the floor and two long strips of coconut matting which covered most but not all of it (we played "fag cards" for hours, they skimmed a treat on the lino). It was my job on Saturday mornings to take the matting up, shake it and wash the floor, how I hated it. Why were girls always expected to do the domestic chores while the boys could go out to play?'

SCHOOLDAYS: THE BEST YEARS OF OUR LIVES?

Most of us attended small village schools, little changed since the time of our grandparents. All ages at one small school, wet clothes drying by the classroom fire, learning to write on a slate – memories we all share. Discipline was strict, yet many of us have cause to be grateful to those teachers who instilled a basic education with little equipment and few resources.

THE VILLAGE SCHOOL IN 1917

'These are the memories of two villagers from the Swanley area who attended their village Church of England school, which served as a school during the week and after a few alterations, as a church on Sunday. The following account is by a lady who was seven years old in 1917.

"We lived near the school, in fact we could see it from our house as there were only fields which have long since been built upon between us and the school so there was no excuse for being late. The first bell rang at five to nine and the second at nine o'clock when we had to be in the playground. When it was fine we lined up in the playground before being sent inside. School was from nine until twelve and again from one thirty until three thirty, and I went home for dinner as we lived so near. The first lesson was always the scripture lesson and we had a service in Lent taken by the local vicar. Part of the original iron building was still beside the school and the chairs were stacked in it for the church service on Sunday.

"Every Wednesday we walked one and a half miles to the local village high street where we had domestic science lessons in a large room above the fire station. These lessons were part cookery and part laundry which gave us a good grounding for being a housewife. We had needlework lessons in the school. When you had a cookery lesson you were given the money and had to go to the local butchers to buy the meat that was needed, then it had to be cooked and we had it for our dinner so there was no waste. You learnt how to keep a store cupboard which was useful in later life. When you were given some laundry to do it had to be washed and ironed then the bath and buckets had to be cleaned before your work was marked. We had to wash and iron and fold correctly handkerchiefs or teacloths, I still fold them this way even today. We always worked with a friend in twos and I remember when we were washing a roller towel we were wringing it out and as we worked down the towel to the end it filled up with water and air so I gave it a great squeeze and we were covered with water and so was the floor and I ended up with a low mark.

"The marks were put in the register and this was taken back to the school and given to the headmaster the following day so that he could see how well you were doing or if you had misbehaved. These marks were read out in front of the boys which I found rather embarrassing, especially if they were low marks. We had a separate playground from the boys and the playground surface was like cinders so if you fell over and cut yourself it caused a nasty mark. In the playground we played rounders and ball games, skipping and playing with a top and whip."

The following account is by a gentleman who was four when he began school in 1919. "The children sat on small chairs in separate lines behind one another in front of the teacher. The lady teacher was very strict and she sat in front facing the class on a high chair. She would hold a card against her knee with a letter of the alphabet on it and we would repeat the letter after her, then she would hold up two or three cards and we would repeat the word and this was the way we were taught to recognise our letters and words. We used tin trays filled with silver sand. The sand was flattened out and we would write or draw in it. The trays were collected each day and stacked together until they were needed the next day and this flattened the sand so they were ready for use.

"Most of the children went home at lunchtime but those who had to walk a long way brought their lunch with them and had it at the school. The headmaster was a good teacher, and at lunchtime he would play marbles with the boys in the playground and if you had been naughty it was all forgotten until you returned inside the school, he always left his bad moods behind in the school and enjoyed lunchtime in the playground.

"The boys went every week for a woodwork lesson to the local village about a mile and a half away. They would go by bike or else they had to walk there and back again. The boys were taught the basics of carpentry by the woodwork teacher and if you misbehaved he would throw small off-cuts of wood at you.

"At Christmas time a local farmer and nurseryman would give the school a Christmas tree and a case of oranges so that all the children could have an orange for Christmas. The Christmas tree was placed in the headmaster's room and could be admired by all the children." '

HARTLEY SCHOOL

'When I attended Hartley school from 1912 to 1917 the old school was no longer in use, which had been built in 1841 for the education of the labouring, manufacturing and poorer classes of Hartley, Fawkham and Longfield. A small room had been added in 1876 and a much larger room in 1907. These latter two rooms provided the accommodation when I attended the school.

The small room was occupied by the infants, and presided over by one teacher, Miss White. In the large room all the older children from nine to 14 were taught, for which purpose the pupils were divided into standards one to six according to age. The three upper classes were taken by the headmistress and the other three by her assistant and separated by a gap between the desks. Between the two rooms was a sliding screen which could be opened should the occasion demand. If the teacher was rash enough to ask for assistance in moving the screen, half a dozen of the larger boys would immediately leap to their feet and push and shove at it with such gusto that often the rollers came off the track and the whole thing became hopelessly jammed halfway across. The process then had to be reversed and a fresh start made.

The school was heated in winter by two coal fires, one in each room. When the weather was particularly cold, the children were allowed, in turn, to warm themselves at the fire. Lighting was by oil lamps suspended from the ceiling. All the children had to walk to school, so those who did not live within easy reach brought sandwiches for their dinner which they ate in the school.

The summer vacation was in two spells of three weeks each. One was during late June and early July, to allow for the soft fruit picking and the second in September for the hop picking season. When not in school, the children congregated or played in the gravel-covered playgrounds; the one on the north side being allocated to the infants and girls, while the boys were restricted to the one on the other side. At 9 am and 1 pm the children assembled in their places, having been summoned by the ringing, by the headmistress, of the bell suspended above the entrance way. From time to time a more daring boy would climb up on the roof from where, unobserved, he could ring the bell. However he would eventually be caught and he paid for his bravado by being caned on the hands in front of the school.

Writing was one of the subjects taught. For this, wooden pens with steel nibs were supplied and the desks had holes into which ink wells fitted. These were filled from a large bottle of ink made up from water and ink powder. These ink wells provided the basis for another prank, when a boy would obtain some calcium carbide, a substance used for acetylene cycle and motor lamps. As he walked to his desk, usually at the back of the room, he would drop pieces of carbide into the ink wells he passed. This immediately caused the ink to bubble up over the desks and, at the same time, the strong smelling gas was given off. Again the culprit was usually caught and punished.

As Hartley was a Church of England school, it was customary for the rector, Rev Bancks, to look in from time to time. I recall that he did no more than pass the time of day with the headmistress and sign the register. However, on his appearance at the door, everyone stood up and remained so until told to sit down and the same procedure was repeated on his departure.

One of the high spots of the year was Empire Day, 24th May. The flagpole, with the Union Jack, was erected on the school, and a maypole was set up in the playground. The boys were dressed in military style uniforms and the girls in their Sunday best. There was dancing round the maypole and marching, followed by a few well chosen words from Lady Emmett of Fairby Grange who came to lend dignity to the occasion, which ended with a request to Miss Fiddis to grant a holiday for the rest of the day. This was graciously conceded and then the whole school marched round the yard and saluted the flag. Then out on to the village green to scramble for the sticky sweets which Lady Emmett's older children were allowed to scatter on the ground.

Mrs Peek ran a small confectionery shop using the front room of her wooden house for the purpose. Here, on the rare occasions when we had a penny or even less to spend, it was possible to buy sherbet suckers, liquorice bootlaces or aniseed balls at a farthing each. For a penny one could buy a bar of chocolate cream or a bottle of ginger beer or lemonade.'

SLATES AND PENCILS

'I started school when I was five, at Rainham in 1905. We sat on long forms with long tables in front of us. We started the day with a hymn then the teacher read a story from the Bible, then the lessons began. We were each given a slate and pencil and were shown how to do letters. At the end of the lesson we had to rub it out with a piece of rag so we had a clean slate for another day. When we had learned to write properly, we were given an exercise book and a lead pencil.'

SEDLEY SCHOOL

'Sedley school at Southfleet was very different in my day (I was five in 1909) – you went in one end at five years old and came out at the other at 14 years, the finished article, or should have been. It didn't always work out like that but the teachers did their best. The classes were too big, there's no doubt about that. There was a board on the wall opposite the headmaster's table, much the same as a hymn board in church. The number of children at school was put up there every day. It could range from 280 to 320 children, so you can imagine what the six teachers had to put up with.

At this time the playground was divided down the middle by a high and solid wall, boys one side and girls the other. All we had at that time was a small lobby to hang our coats and scarves and the smell of damp clothes hung about all day. At dinner time the school was locked up, no meals in those days. All the teachers went home to dinner so the unfortunate children who had come a distance had to eat their sandwiches in the lobby or anywhere else, so long as they could keep dry. No wonder so many caught colds.

The most popular games in the playground were tops, marbles

and bowling hoops. Another game the boys enjoyed was with cigarette cards. The cards were flicked with thumb and forefinger across the playground. If your card landed on top of another you were the winner. Another game was to press your card against the wall about five feet up and let it float to the ground. If the breeze caught it, it could float well away. The first boy to get his on another was the winner. Of course, leapfrog was always popular, but there were always plenty of scraped knees as no one wore long trousers.'

IN THE MIDDLE OF THE WOOD

'I shall never forget the school in which I began my school life. A small wooden building, it stood in the middle of ancient woodland in Chiddingstone Hoath.

I was taken to school on my first day by my elder brother. The war was over and peace reigned once again. Teaching must have been difficult for Mrs Townsend, the senior teacher, and Miss Coomber as there were only two classrooms divided by folding doors. It was not unusual for us to be practising our reading whilst the older children were singing their tonic sol-fa on the other side of the screen. Both teachers were very dedicated and cared so much for us all. I can remember receiving a doll at Christmas. Miss Coomber had made one for every little girl in her class. I cannot remember what presents the boys received but each boy had one. Miss Coomber must have worked the whole year to get the presents finished in time.

The summer days were lovely and we spent some afternoons country dancing under the trees. The music for the Circassian Circle and Sir Roger de Coverley was provided by a wind-up gramophone balanced on a tree stump. We had a large school garden and Mrs Townsend kept bees. In winter the open fires were wonderful and we were able to stand our bottles of milk round the guard to warm. As every child walked to school, the fires were most welcome. The playground was anywhere in the wood, there were natural outcrops of sandstone to play on. We all knew when playtime was over because a hand bell would be rung loudly from the school steps.

There was no running water so any water needed for drinking had to be brought from neighbouring houses in large enamel jugs by the older boys. As there was no water we therefore had earth closets situated on the boundaries of the play area, quite a long way should it be raining. Although we had no "mod cons" the freedom of that lovely place was worth everything. The building still stands but is now a dwelling.'

Keston schoolchildren in the 1920s. Schools were to change very little in the years between the wars.

MAIDSTONE GIRLS' GRAMMAR SCHOOL 1926

'I started at Maidstone Girls' Grammar school in 1926, just after the General Strike had ended, luckily for me, as there were no trains during the strike. One of my school friends had to travel in the carrier's van or any other vehicle manned by public spirited volunteers. I travelled to Maidstone West station, then walked to the other end of the town to the school, then situated in Albion Place, Sittingbourne Road. It was a quarter of an hour's walk, not very pleasant in the winter wind and rain, arriving at school with dripping felt hat and gabardine, trying to dry them out on inadequately heated radiators. The summer uniform was panama hat and blazer. Anyone seen without a hat was liable to detention on Wednesday afternoon instead of sports. To be seen speaking to a boy, or even worse, sitting next to one in the train, was more than one dared do.

We were allowed to have an annual dance in the gym and some of us thought it would be nice to invite some boys from the boys' grammar school. Some of the girls had brothers there. Needless to say, this idea was immediately squashed by the headmistress, so we had to dance with each other, or as a special honour, might be asked to dance with one of the staff.

A bright spot in the morning break was the arrival of the "bun man" with a basket loaded with sticky buns at a penny halfpenny and doughnuts at twopence halfpenny which helped to take away the taste of the mugs of boiled milk with skin in it which I loathed. The school dinner cost sevenpence when I first started. It was cooked by the caretaker and his wife in a kitchen that would have horrified the Health Inspectors of today. However, I can't recall any cases of food poisoning in the time that I was there. The food itself, if wholesome, was hardly appetising. The pastry we called "tiles", an apt description. These were served with a little watered down golden syrup. Blancmange was a white cornflour mixture with little or no sugar or flavour, and rice, a solid lump cooked in water. The meat was tough with fat and gristle and I found it difficult to leave a clean plate as was expected. At least it taught me how to appreciate good home cooked food.

The staff were all single women as they did not remain in employment after marriage. They were usually dedicated teachers who stayed in the same job until retirement. We had to work hard if we wanted to get matriculation, which required passes in at least five subjects, which had to include English literature, English composition, history or geography, chemistry or biology, French (oral, essay and translation), Latin or German, mathematics (separate papers for arithmetic, algebra, and geometry). If one failed in one of the essential subjects then the whole lot had to be resat the following year. We had some respite from these serious subjects in art, music, gym and domestic science (which included scrubbing down the tables and cleaning up after we had finished cooking).

Once a year we had a sports day at which not only races were run, but a drill display was performed by the whole school, accompanied by the town band playing Sousa marches, usually "King Cotton". The gym lessons became a lot more fun with the arrival of climbing ropes, ribstalls and vaulting horse. We were allowed to take off our gym slips and do our exercises in blouse and knickers, though some girls were too bashful to do so. Our gym mistress always wore a short gym slip even though she was quite a mature lady, just like Joyce Grenfell in the film *Happiest Days of your Life.'*

HIGHLIGHTS OF OUR YEAR

'One of the highlights of our school year at Fordcombe was Empire Day, which was on 24th May. It seems strange now to remember that the British Empire encompassed, in addition to the British Isles, the whole of Canada, Australia, New Zealand, India, South Africa and several others of the African Continent – all of these countries being coloured pink on our world maps. The Union Jack flew from all public buildings in towns and villages, and many also from private houses. We always flew ours from a bedroom window – this, I must tell you, was not only for Empire Day, but also to celebrate my brother's birthday!

At school for weeks beforehand we practised patriotic songs, and when the day came we were dressed up to represent the various countries in the British Empire. I remember particularly representing Wales, with a plaid shawl thrown round my shoulders and the most wonderful tall Welsh hat. I had to sing by myself *O Land of my Fathers*, with the refrain "O but my heart is with thee; as long as the sea thy bulwarks shall be, to Cymru my heart shall be true". This I happily chanted in spite of the fact that beyond being able to indicate Wales on the map I really knew very little about it. One of the bigger girls was Britannia, in a long white dress and with a Union Jack draped around her. Her crowning glory was a shining helmet, on loan from the Tunbridge Wells Fire Brigade. With all the countries dressed as far as possible in something resembling a national costume, we must have presented quite an inspiring sight! Many of the parents, together with the vicar and the school managers, and any other village folk who were free, all came to listen to our singing and reciting, and a feeling of patriotism enveloped us all. Our family day was not yet complete – we still had my brother's birthday tea to look forward to!

So one progressed through the various school classes. When I first moved into the senior classroom in 1924 the enormous photograph of Queen Victoria still had pride of place on the wall above the fireplace. This same year our elderly headmaster retired, and he was replaced by a young married headmistress. This caused some interest in the village, as married women seldom worked outside their homes. I was now between nine and ten years old, and quick to notice little changes from the old regime. Queen Victoria soon disappeared, and for some time we had a picture of "The Laughing Cavalier", eventually to be replaced by a photograph of Princess Elizabeth when she was about two years old. Our painting lessons no longer consisted of the green spray of privet or ivy, with only green paint squeezed out of a huge tube on to the saucers we shared – one between two. Now we were encouraged to paint brightly coloured patterns and pictures of our own imagination. The painting lesson was now called "Brushwork".

In sewing lessons we were no longer spending hours "running and felling" long seams, perhaps on a nightdress we were making. A sewing machine appeared, and as a result we found that we had time to learn embroidery stitches, smocking, etc. Reading lessons became more interesting with a greater variety of books, and because the headmistress took her turn with the rest of us when we were

Stansted infants in 1926. Some children were still wearing the boots common in earlier decades.

reading aloud we all were encouraged to read as well as she did.

During the summer term we were taken for nature walks, usually through the fields by the river, collecting sticklebacks, caddis worms and various other unidentifiable creatures. If you have never seen a field of flax growing alongside a river you have missed one of the countryside's loveliest sights! Educational outings by coach to London were also arranged. Changes in the teaching staff also took place – notably "Governess", our infants mistress, retired. This provided the opportunity for the headmistress to move her class into what had been for some years the infants classroom. This was one of our biggest changes, and meant that I spent my later years in the same room that I had entered with trepidation – but also excitement – at the age of four and a half years.'

A GREAT ADVENTURE

'We came to Crayford in 1927 when I was five years old and just about to start school. The first schooldays were a great adventure. I was escorted by a neighbour's daughter who seemed grown up to me, but in reality must have been about twelve. We went to the tiny Catholic school in Old Road. This had only three classrooms.

There was a big cast iron stove on one side of the room and in the winter the crates of milk we were given at lunch time were placed near this to get warm. I detested milk and being lukewarm only made it worse. On a slate by the door each morning there was chalked the number of pupils in attendance that day. The school board man always glanced at this when he came to check the register and make a note of absentees who hadn't had a letter sent by their mother.'

THE KINDNESS OF TEACHERS

'The old church school at Plaxtol had 100 pupils, taught by only two teachers. The kindness of the teachers is still remembered. One used her own money to buy socks and plimsolls from the village shop for the poorer children, many of whom had to walk long distances to school.

The playground was divided into two, half for the boys and half for the girls. In frosty weather, the funloving headmaster would throw buckets of water on to them to make slides for the children.'

BACK IN MY OLD SCHOOL

'I had a dream recently, and in the dream, I was back in my old school. I smelt the wet cane that was soaking in the wash basin in the cloakroom which later on, we would be making baskets from. I awoke and my mind went back 50 plus years ago to when I was a school girl.

My village school was made of Kentish flint stones, and consisted of three classes, but only two rooms, the smaller one being for the infants, and a large room for two classes for seven to fourteen year olds, all girls. These two classes were partly separated by a large blackboard, and a large open coal fire, that was constantly fed with coal by the headmistress who taught the top class. During the cold winter months she would stand the small bottles of milk round the large fire, for those of us who brought our halfpennies to buy, and were allowed to drink with a straw provided at lunch time.

When we reached the age of twelve, we had to spend each Tuesday at a school in the next village a mile away, where we were taught a subject called "Domestic Science", which consisted of being divided into pairs, and each pair taking turns weekly to cook a meal for the staff of the school, or launder and iron garments, clean a room, or occasionally, sweep the chimney. This latter usually brought letters of complaint from the parents of the girls who were allocated, as they would arrive at their homes covered in soot, looking like chimney sweeps.

When the school governors visited the school, we treated them with awe and would stand up when they entered the room, and we were often asked to sing one of our school songs to them. Before we broke up for Christmas, one of the governors would dress up as Santa Claus and would give each one of us a shiny threepenny bit, with which we could buy a bar of chocolate for two pence and ten Sharps toffees for one penny.

My last year at school was mostly spent teaching the infants, as the infants teacher was often away sick, and the Head used to ask me if I would take over, which was a great joy to me. The very small children would draw with their fingers in trays of sand, and I taught the older ones the three R's. This training helped me later on when I became an infants teacher, and what a difference in behaviour from children of yesteryear compared to children of today! Can you imagine a 13 year old being able to control a class of 16 small children as I easily did 50 years ago?'

ASH VILLAGE SCHOOL

'When I went to college to train as a teacher, I had a grant and loan from Kent County Council and one of the conditions was that I had to agree to teach in Kent if required to do so until the loan was repaid. Due to wartime difficulties the Education Authority would allocate you to the school in need that was nearest to your home, so one day in mid August 1944 I arrived on the doorstep of Ash village school to take over the infants. It was at the tail end of the buzz-bomb campaign and the beginning of rocket attacks. I used to think, as I cycled the back lanes to work, that if one landed on me no one would know for hours.

I started teaching at the school in mid August because school holidays were geared to the needs of the farms. While the main harvest of hay and corn was the concern of the farmers and their men only, when it came to fruit and potatoes it was the women of the village who bore the main burden and so the summer holiday was shorter than that of town schools and the autumn half term was extended to two weeks to cover potato picking when the hands of the older children were a welcome addition to their mothers' labour in the field.

There were four shops in the village, all run by elderly women. The two main shops were in The Street selling most daily necessities and one was also the post office, built as an addition to a row of old cottages. Of the other two shops, one was in a converted room in a house near the council houses and the other was a small annexe to the Anchor and Hope pub. Traffic through the village was almost nil. Petrol restrictions were partly responsible for this but also, of course, the cost. Opposite the school playground lived a family who owned a large black dog. On warm summer days, Bess's favourite spot was in the centre of the road in the sun. Any stray car using the road had either to drive round her or hoot repeatedly until she decided to shift. She was never hit by a car. As I cycled out of the village every afternoon, I did not get to know many of the villagers. Mothers seldom brought their children to school, that was a job for older brothers and sisters. Consquently my memories for the most part are of the school. It was a three class school comprising of infants and seniors in the school building and juniors in the adjacent village hall. The hall was also used for school dinners which arrived in aluminium containers from another school kitchen. In spite of everyone's belief that school dinners were horrible, this was not the case with us. It is true that they were geared to filling the children, but there were strict rules to ensure a good balanced diet and they were well cooked and arrived piping hot.

The hall was heated by a barrel-shaped coke stove which often became red hot. The classrooms in the school building had open fires. In winter, when the school milk was frozen soon after delivery, some of the children liked it icy. Others preferred it hot and just before playtime, a row of milk bottles stood just inside the fireguard and sometimes got too hot to hold. In those days the milk bottles had wide necks with cardboard lids inset. In each lid was a small round area with a semi-perforated edge. The theory was that each child used its thumbnail to complete the perforation and pushed in the small circle of card to insert the straw. In practice there was always one who pushed in the whole lid sending milk splashing over everyone and everything.

Later the milk became free but in the late 1940s the parents paid a halfpenny a bottle and some children had one in the afternoon as well as the morning. Monday morning of each week was the time for getting in the money. First the register was marked and then the dinner money collected, a ritual that was interrupted continually as children from the junior and senior classes brought in the dinner money for their young brothers and sisters. Then the milk money was collected and, of course, both dinner and milk money had to be recorded, totalled and physically counted. Then it was the turn of the National Savings. As the newest and of least account, the collecting of savings money was my job. Once again the juniors and seniors trooped in to pay over their cash, I collected from the infants and when the books tallied, took the money to the post office. Luckily in those days children were a lot more controllable.

Many of the younger children had never been out of the village (although some had been evacuated for a time). A year or two after the end of the war, we decided to take the whole school out for a trip to the sea. We went to a small bay near Wye. The effect of so much water on the move stunned the little ones to a very nervous silence, but with a little coaxing they did all eventually manage to paddle. No bathing suits – that needed clothing coupons – but a good time was had by all.

With the passing of the first post war Education Act, the pace of change began to quicken. The senior children were now bussed to Swanscombe and what a fuss that caused. The fumes and cement dust that had for years plagued the unfortunate inhabitants of that region, came as a physical shock to children used to unpolluted country air and led to an epidemic of minor chest complaints. Happily this ceased when, in answer to many protests, the children were switched to Northfleet schools on the edge of town. The village hall was no longer needed for a classroom but KEC continued to rent it for PE and school dinners.

The doctor who for many years had a weekly surgery in one of the houses now used the hall one afternoon a week with, at the same time, a clinic held by the district nurse for new mothers.

Special events and happenings seem to be mostly to do with the weather. There were the big "snows". I think the first one was in the late 1940s or early 1950s. The village was entirely cut off. The school was closed for over a week. I used to phone in to see if I was needed. When the school was reopened I had to walk in. A body-wide footpath had been dug from the village to the A20 and you had to walk through an above-head high passage all the way. It was too deep for the snow ploughs for a long time but the throughway was gradually widened and then enough dug away to allow traffic to restart.

Happy events? There was always (and still is) the summer fête. Families would return to the village visiting relations so they could be at the fête on the second Saturday in June. Everyone attended and caught up on the news. And there was the Christmas Fair in the village hall. Again, everyone turned up and the gossip over the teacups was as important as the buying and selling. It was the centre of much of village life where you could meet everyone you wanted to because, of course, they would all be there.'

THE WORLD
OF WORK

ON THE LAND

Generations of West Kent men worked on the land, and whole communities depended on the farming world. It was a hard life, but often satisfying, particularly in the days when horses worked the land alongside the men.

A FARMING COMMUNITY

'Chelsfield was very largely a farming community in the early years of the century. Apart from the general stores, post office, bakery, harnessmaker and blacksmith, all of which were run by their owners, there were few openings that might offer employment other than farming.

My father and grandfather were fruit, vegetable and grain farmers. Their farm had on it a small row of tiny huts and with the advent of the soft fruit season these would be occupied by families of travellers who would stay until the end of the season and then pass on further down into Kent for the hop picking season. They were paid daily for the fruit they picked, with little metal discs commonly known as "funny money". These were cashed at the end of the week for real money. Then followed a general rush off to the two local pubs where, sadly, much of it was spent by Saturday evening. My early memories are of hearing either much singing and merriment, or shouting and drunken brawls as the inebriated fruit pickers tried to get themselves home late at night.

Up to the time of the Second World War all the work was done by horse-drawn implements. The land was ploughed, raked and harrowed in preparation for the seed driller and roller, although after the war some seed was still sown by hand broadcasting just as it had been through the centuries. During the war years all this was taken over by the newly acquired tractors. The first was a Fordson, with iron wheels, but later came the Fergusons – much lighter and more manoeuvrable, with rubber tyres.

Corn harvesting was carried out by a reaper and binder which cut the corn and tied it into sheaves. The sheaves were stooked by hand, and then stacked until later in the year when the threshing machine, driven by a steam tractor, was hired for the occasion. Later in the 1950s combine harvesters arrived to eliminate most of the hard work, but we kept one cart horse called Punch, partly for odd jobs and partly out of sentiment. Time came when the local newspapers

Arthur Stanbridge and Punch, the last cart horse on Henry Foreman's farm at Chelsfield. The land behind is now beneath the M25.

carried an item headed "Punch is dead", and the last cart horse for miles around had left this life.'

IN ALL WEATHERS

'At Capel the shoe and boot repairer was quite a busy man, as often people had only one pair of boots. The boots had to be dried by the fire in wet weather and dressed with a water repellant ready for the next day's work. Wellingtons were rarely seen.

Very few farm workers possessed any kind of waterproof coat and it was quite common to see a worker draped in a hessian sack – one for apron and skirt combined and one over the shoulders for a cape, with a corner of the sack tucked in at the top to form a hood over the head.

While working away from home a midday meal most likely consisted of bread and cheese washed down with cold tea carried in an enamel bottle. If a man became ill and unable to work he received no payment from his employer, and pensions were so small that it was not unusual to see quite elderly people still at work, out in all weather conditions. Most people had a plot of garden in which they

141

Getting in the last cartload of hay at Highlands Hill Farm, Swanley in the early years of the century.

grew vegetables, and it was said that farm workers only had one day's holiday a year – Good Friday, so that they could plant their potatoes to provide them with plenty of food. No wonder they did a lot of rabbit catching to make ends meet. On estates the gamekeepers were employed in the springtime in hatching pheasants' eggs under broody hens, and afterwards the hens no longer required were sold as boiling hens for about two or three shillings each.'

I WAS NEEDED ON THE FARM

'I was born at Little Cockshot Farm at Hawkhurst at the turn of the century. I left school at 14, the normal age then, and as the First World War was on my brother joined the forces and I stayed and helped on the farm. All went well and I took on more and more jobs, until in 1928 my father was taken ill and I had to carry on. I was 28 then.

We had five cows, 30 sheep, pigs and fowls, a horse and pony. I was up at 5.30 am to do the milking. This was a twice a day job. The milk was sold at the door to customers who came either morning or afternoon for the fresh milk with their jug or can. Any not sold would be put through the separator, a machine which, by turning the handle at a certain rate, would separate the cream from the milk. The cream would be made into butter in a few days.

The horse (Prince) and the pony (Ruby) had their separate jobs but were used together sometimes. The pony cart was used to take pigs or lambs to market and I enjoyed those journeys to Robertsbridge or Northiam.

Of course, I had help. A permanent part timer and others when needed, as well as a man with a machine to cut the grass for haymaking and a man for sheep shearing. We had no gas or electricity and water had to be fetched from a spring across the field. I kept the farm going until my father died in 1930.'

WORKING WITH HORSES

'My first regular job was at Manor Farm, Betsham in 1917. My father could not afford to apprentice me to a trade so the foreman at Manor Farm took me on and put me with one of the horse men on the farm. We were out of the yard by 6 am in the summer and 7 am in winter and when we returned at night we were not finished. There was all the old bedding to take out from the previous night, fresh bedding to put down, besides feeding and watering the horses, followed by brushing and grooming them and racking them up with hay for the night. All this for seven shillings a week.'

'My father left Gordon Road school, Strood at the age of 14. The family doctor advised his mother to put him to outside work as it would be good for his lungs because he had been a sickly child. His uncle was, at that time, bailiff for William Ballard at Temple Farm, Strood. He found a job in the stables for my father.

The care of horses meant starting work at 4 am. So that he could be near the job his aunt found a room for him at Temple Manor, the farmhouse. To start with, the job involved mucking out the horses, cleaning and sweeping the stable and stable yard, and cleaning the waggoner's vast collection of horse brasses and regalia.

As time went on, the old waggoner taught him how to look after the horses, how to groom and harness, how to recognise illnesses, sprains and hoof problems, how and when to administer medicine and massage muscles after a long day in the winter wet.

At that time, William Ballard worked three farms. He owned two but Temple Farm was rented from the Darnley estate. The then Lord Darnley decided to sell the Temple Farm (which was named after the Knights Templar, who had previously built and occupied the Temple Manor House, where his uncle and aunt lived). The money raised was needed to keep the rest of the estate running. My father was transferred to Grange Farm, London Road, Strood. He was now able to move back with his parents. He was taken on as assistant waggoner, the waggoner being William Swaffer. Now he helped run the team of shires, the governor's riding horses and the cobs and ponies used in the various carts and waggons. He was introduced to the art of ploughing a straight furrow, coupling up and guiding the horses while pulling the reaper, potato spinner, harrow and rollers. In due course, after winning a county ploughing match, he was declared a fully fledged waggoner.

He courted and married the shepherd's youngest daughter and moved in with his wife's family in the shepherd's cottage where eventually I was born. In due course, the old waggoner retired and moved away and the job was given to my father, together with the waggoner's house. We were so near the stables that we could hear the horses moving and stomping in their stalls. Too much movement in the night and my father would get up and climb the iron steps from our garden to the farmyard to see what was making the horses restless.

At the start of the Second World War, the order of the day was "Dig for Victory". The governor decided to dispense with the old team of black shires and replace them with a new team of partly broken Welsh shires. They were dispatched from Wales by train to Strood goods depot a day earlier than expected. The governor called my father on the Sunday morning to go with him to fetch them home. My father always wore traditional waggoner's attire – corded knee breeches, leather leggings and stout boots. This day, he was about to tend his garden and had on his gardening clothes. This would not have mattered except, on their return to the farm, a photographer was waiting to take their pictures and to my father's everlasting disgust, he was photographed in his gardening clothes with his new team of shires.

The new horses were only half broken and were a lively bunch and we didn't see much of my father for he had to tend them more or less constantly to get them into the ways of working the farm. Everyone stopped to look when my father took the young prancing horses down Strood Hill to Skinner's Forge, where Arthur Rose the blacksmith was to put on some heavier shoes. The care of farm horses was a 24 hour, seven days a week job and my father now considered me old enough to help with certain things. I was not allowed too near the horses for they towered over me. My father would say, "Always stand where they can see you then they will not knock you down." It was all the tedious jobs he involved me with, such as the endless cleaning of the brasses, making my fingers black and having to scrub them clean with soft soap, which left your hands smelling horrible. I had to rinse out and rewind into rolls, the green and red webbing which he used to plait the manes and tails for working. There were always ropes to splice, harness to mend and leather work to repair. After the mending came the polishing with saddle soap. It had to be just right, he didn't want any smears of soap on the leather.

On cold winter nights, after a day's work in the wet, we would mix bran mash. I would line up all the buckets in Mother's kitchen and scoop out the bran, two scoops per bucket, while Father boiled the kettles of water on the stove. He would pour the water over the bran which gave off that hot bready smell. We stirred it round with wooden paddles until it absorbed the water and swelled up inside the buckets. Sometimes he would mix in conditioning powders, which were supplied by Mr Ebbits, the vet, from Rochester High Street. I would be handed the hurricane lamp, with strict instructions not to swing it about, and off we would go to the stables, to and fro, until all the buckets had been taken to the stables and each horse had been bedded down for the night. By this time, it was my bed time and there was not time left to read, or draw, or sew by the fire as I would have liked.

During the Battle of Britain and the night time bombing, my father and the other farm hands were on permanent fire watching. They had to be on hand in case of fire at the stables, so that the horses could be got out quickly. As the bombers came over, the guns from Dillywood Camp would fire directly over the farm, disturbing the horses. As soon as the warning went, my father would leave Mother and me, in the shelter at the bottom of the garden, and go and stand in the stable with the horses. During lulls, we would hear him shouting the horses' names and calming them down.

After the war, the tractor and the lorry took over from the horse. With great sadness, the horses were sold and my father became yard hand, for the governor's son, at N & T Cutler, Cattle Transporters, until he retired.'

CHANGES ON THE FARM

'Just a few doors up the road from my home at Otford there was a dairy farm where we got our milk in the jug. In the late 1940s I was allowed to go on the milk round on Saturdays. This entailed a ride on the horse-drawn milk float with the churns of milk and the pint and quart measures hanging from their sides. My job was to run up the paths to the houses and collect the milk jugs so that the milkman could fill them with however much milk was ordered. How times changed after the war – hand milking changed to machine milking and milk floats changed to being power driven and milk came in bottles more and more. Over the years farm-bottled milk became

Harvesting at Chelsfield before combine harvesters changed the face of farming.

scarcer as milk was collected from more farms and taken to the dairies for pasteurisation and distribution.

Other changes took place too. Harvesting in the 1940s and early 1950s was still a fairly labour-intensive job. The corn was cut and bound into sheaves which then had to be stood ears up to dry before being loaded onto a waggon and taken to the stackyard. Here the sheaves were stacked to await the arrival of the threshing gang – a group who toured the countryside visiting the farms to get the corn ready for use. There were always some ears of corn left standing after the field was cut and we used to go up in the evenings and "glean" these ears to supplement the kitchen waste, such as boiled potato peelings for the hens.

I can't remember any fertiliser being used during the war, just good old fashioned farmyard manure and also some foul smelling stuff which I was told was cotton waste which came down from the mills in Lancashire – I could never understand how it came to have such a smell nor why it invariably seemed to be black or blue!

Gradually combine harvesters came in, which gobbled up the fields of corn and threshed them at the same time, spewing straw and chaff out behind them. This led to the advent of the baler, firstly rectangular bales, and then small round ones. So stacks of hay pitched up by hand with a pitchfork and cut out with a hay knife for winter feed became things of the past and elevators were used to stack the wire-tied bales, later to become tied with jute string and then plastic string.

Other changes took place too – cattle feeding habits changed to dried grass, alfalfa (a member of the clover family) and silage. All were tried and the old hay knives were used once again, this time for cutting the silage out of the clamps. The old-fashioned cowsheds where the animals were tied up for the winter were discarded in favour of large yards – covered or part covered – where the animals were loose housed. The cattle may have been more comfortable but it made mucking out much more difficult!'

HOP PICKING

As well as the regular visitors from London, many local families went hop picking, finding the money a welcome addition to the budget for the coming winter. Hop picking has very special memories, of smells and tastes and sounds that still hold their excitement.

QUITE AN EVENT

'My memories of farming when I was a child (born 1909) centred mainly on hop growing. In the 1920s there were about 20 growers of hops in Marden. Hop picking in September was quite an event. The farms housed hundreds of Londoners in rather poor huts, by today's standards, to pick hops. They arrived by rail in special trains from the dock areas. It was a paid holiday and all the family would join in, picking the hops into bins or baskets which were then measured out into sacks (called pokes). The rate of pay varied according to the crop, generally the average pay was five or six bushels for one shilling. A good picker would pick about 20 bushels a day.

Most of the pickers would return to the same farms for many years and nearly always wanted their old huts. It was a holiday for the children and the country air and sunshine did wonders for their health after living in the slums of London. They were generally a happy crowd with plenty of Cockney humour. We were pleased to see them come and pleased to see them go.'

TWO WEEKS' HOLIDAY!

'At the beginning of September we looked forward to (not a holiday) but two weeks' hard work in the hop fields. Some people hated it, but it was a wonderful atmosphere.

The hop fields were about three miles walk away from my home at Allington with a very steep hill either way to negotiate. At 6.30 am you would see people with prams and boxes on wheels, all heading the same way; the young children in prams hemmed in with food, kettle, bottled drink etc for the day. I loved that early morning walk, with the good fresh air, along lanes edged with wild flowers and apple, pear and cherry orchards. Now all houses, alas. We were of course tired by the time we arrived but a fire was our first job, and the kettle was soon singing for our first cuppa of the day.

The fields look lovely before being invaded by pickers. Hops were grown over the rows like a canopy, and when there had been rain or heavy dew, when the bines were pulled we got showered, but soon dried. The rows had bins in each one and you had your own, bines were thrown over the bins and the hops stripped off taking care not to put too many leaves in. There was always the drone of people laughing, talking and many times singing the current songs. The bins were about eight feet long, made of wood and hessian, and the measure and tally man would come round about three times a day to measure the hops with a big bushel basket, into big pokes ready for the kilns. The pay was six bushels for a shilling (hard work). Children used to like to have a few branches and pick into an upturned umbrella to earn a penny. The Lollyman came round selling boiled sweets, toffee apples, etc and his call was a regular event of the day.

The only thing I hated was the state of your hands; the juice of the hops forms a black coating which is only removed by wet leaves, but we all got so hungry that food still had to be eaten. We usually had half to an hour's break for lunch but of course again a fire had to be lit for a cuppa (most welcome by then).

Children had a high time swinging on the empty wires, jumping all over the pokes, if not caught, and if they were lucky having rides on the tractor. The last call was about 3.30 pm then the long trek home and those three miles seemed to have stretched to six when you were tired, hungry and dirty, but we were very lucky. My Dad was always home before us and had the kettle boiling and new potatoes, runner beans and carrots and bacon or sausages all cooking and smelling delicious, all vegetables fresh from his allotment. Bedtime was usually about nine, ready for the early morning start. When I was 14 I had half a bin to myself and worked very hard to keep up with my mother. After a fortnight came the great pay-out day, and I proudly received a big white note value £10. Yes, I know what it feels like to be a millionaire. This bought me my winter coat and shoes.

I am in my eighties now but I can still remember the pungent smell of the hops mingled with the smoke from little fires and marvel at how we relished slices of cold spotted dick in such conditions.

The last day the song would be heard,

> Now that hopping's over
> The money is all spent,
> How I wish I'd never gone,
> A-hopping down in Kent.'

HOP PICKING STORIES

'When we moved to a farm at Boughton Monchelsea in 1947, we had no experience with hops at all, but with advice and help from friends and neighbours we soon got into the swing of things.

Hop picking started when the pickers, from the East End of London, arrived to occupy the huts they had booked the previous winter. Approximately a week before this, the huts were all cleaned out, whitewashed and supplied with clean straw for filling their mattress cases and a load of wood for cooking – later on most had paraffin stoves. Then we sat down and waited for the families to arrive, when they did in lorries with their pots and pans, clothes etc. It was the most exciting time for our girls who stood at the dining room window shouting "Here they come". From then until the end of September or beginning of October it was all go.

As food rationing was still on, we had to see they were supplied with groceries and meat, from the butcher in Marden, which was delivered twice a week. The local grocer set up shop in our larder, which used to be the dairy and had an outside door. He did a roaring trade from 6 to 8.30 every evening. We sold paraffin from the back door for lamps etc. I remember one day, a boy was sent to have a can filled and, finding no one about, thought he would help himself and let several gallons run away into the garden. It was a few years before that part grew anything again.

On the first day everyone turned up for work at 6.30 am. The rules had to be read before they could start picking. There were three sets of twelve bins and a binman who dealt with any problems or helped the measurer, who started to measure at eleven o'clock and again at five o'clock. The hops were put into large sacks, called pokes, weighing approximately 56 pounds. The hops were then taken to the oast to be dried. The measurer had to see the hops were picked cleanly with no leaves. All sorts of things fell into the bins – watches, cutlery, sandwiches and one lady lost her radio which was fortunately retrieved before reaching the oast.

Some of the pickers were real characters. One lady I remember was called Bella, because she used to shout so much. She was a really good hearted person, always ready to help her friends. There was also a very formidable lady who was on East Ham council (later on she was mayor), she had a large family and she used to bring her grandchildren down. One boy was sitting on the fence outside our house, talking to my daughter. He asked her where she went to school and she replied, "Maidstone Technical School for Girls". He looked most surprised and said, "Do they have Technical Schools in the country?"

One Sunday morning there was such a commotion at the back door. Bella had been cooking the dinner. She had a large pot of stew on an oil stove next to the bed on which her small puppy was playing. All at once it slipped into the pot. Poor little thing, it was so badly hurt that my husband had to destroy and bury it. I never found out if they ate the stew.

Another very sad thing happened. A picker was sitting outside her hut, entertaining her visitors, when she was stung by a wasp and collapsed. She was rushed to hospital but died soon after being admitted. It really upset everyone and her family did not come again to pick.

In Coronation year they had a tea party, outside the huts, for the children. Our girls were invited and had a lovely time.

On the Saturday before they went home, they had a glorious bonfire and sing-song. They burnt all the rubbish and left-over wood. Also on that Saturday they were paid for their labours. Some families had a considerable amount, some less as they had already drawn quite a bit. The local police attended, I do not know why as we had never had any trouble. We always had a barrel of beer or cider in the shed opposite the back door and the binmen used to help themselves. One year it was a young policeman on duty and he also joined in and had to spend the afternoon in the hay shed sleeping it off.

As a family we all loved hop picking. I used to do the booking from 1948 until we began machine picking and later my husband did the measuring. I must say that I might not have liked it so much if I did not have my parents come to take over the housework for me. My eldest daughter was a good picker but the younger ones were not so good.

Hop picking near Bearsted in the 1900s, and time for a brief rest on the hop bin.

We gave up growing hops in 1991. We still see some of the pickers as some spend a few weeks a year in the huts which are so different with calor gas stoves, battery televisions and wall-to-wall carpeting.

Life is a lot quieter now but I would not have missed the happy times we had.'

HYMNS AND EELS

'My mother made large quantities of food – hop picking made you hungry! We walked to East Farleigh hop fields from our home at Barming, running down the hill before the gates on the level crossing were closed for the 8 am train to Maidstone. We wore aprons of sacking to prevent the hops staining our dresses. The village shopkeeper boarded up his shop (there was trouble at times), but stalls abounded and the eel stall was popular.

The church was very good to the hoppers. There was a magic lantern show in a big tent every weekend down by the bridge, a first aid tent and a coffee stall. "Tea, coffee and buns," was the cry from the gentleman with his trolley in the hop fields. Hymns were sung with gusto, accompanied by an accordian outside the Bull pub. Fights between the locals and the hoppers were common but were dealt with efficiently by the local policeman.'

FRESH AND BRIGHT WITH DEW

'In 1920 my father was a constable attached to St Mary Cray police station. There was a holiday from school in late September for hop picking. The early mornings were fresh and bright with dew outlining the spiders' webs as we walked to May's hop gardens. The men pulled down the bines to enable the women and children to strip them of their hops to be measured in a bushel basket by Skinner, the overseer. My father brought us breakfast of bacon and mushrooms, cooked together, and eaten between thick slices of bread.

Work continued until late afternoon when the overseer called "No more bines". The men immediately pulled down as many as they could, the money earned being a good supplement to their meagre wages.'

AN AIR OF EXCITEMENT

'I suppose the biggest change in Collier Street is hop picking. When I was a girl in the 1940s, there was an air of excitement in the weeks before September. Everyone was preparing for an invasion of people from East London to pick the hops. The shopkeepers would put up wire netting around their counters because, when all the hoppers arrived, there would be a certain amount of stealing. Also plenty of scrumping in the orchards, so farmers were also on guard.

The week before the picking actually started, the lorries, cars and buses would arrive with all these people with their pots and pans and bedding. One of my early memories is sitting at the window of our butcher's shop watching all these strange people arriving. My father was a very popular man with the hoppers so when they went past they all shouted to us. Then it wasn't long before they would be queuing for their meat. On a Saturday morning, they would be outside from 6 am onwards and then make such a noise we would have to open the shop early to get rid of them so they could get back to picking the hops. We also had a sweet shop and we would have special sweets for hopping. The one I remember most is a slab of chocolate toffee, wonderful! This would keep them happy whilst they waited.

On a Saturday night they would all go to the local pubs. One of our treats was to creep up to the pub and listen to them singing and having the odd brawl. After they went home about six weeks later, everything seemed very quiet and we missed them. But as the same families came each year to the same farms, we knew we would see them next year. They became our friends.

We didn't have a car so our mode of transport was either by bus or train to get to the town. We were fortunate because having a farm, we had horses so I could ride around the village on my pony to visit people. Also my father had various carts but his pride and joy was his governor's cart. On Sunday afternoons we would go driving round the villages and how proud I felt when he said I could take over the reins.

When I look back now I realise that I was living at the end of an era.'

IN SERVICE

For many a young girl, going into service was the only employment available when she left school, particularly in country districts. It was not only the rich who employed the servants before the 1940s, many middle class families and farmers also found their services indispensable. The life could be hard, though, if you did not find yourself with the right family.

BELOW STAIRS

'I was born in Eynsford in old cottages in Church Walk, one of four children. My maternal grandfather and great-grandfather kept the butcher's shop until it was sold to Pococks. Another of my great-grandfathers was the village policeman. One of the ways he maintained law and order was to escort wrong-doers along to the stocks, where they were left long enough to mull over their misdeeds and for friends and neighbours to witness their disgrace.

I started work when I was 14 at Saddlers Hall, occupied by a widowed Mrs Crossely and her two unmarried daughters known to all as Miss May and Miss Queenie. At some point the family had lost money and to help out they took in paying guests. The Crossleys were good Christian ladies, considerate to the small girl who had come to work for them for they certainly did not burden me with the worst of the household chores.

153

The huge black kitchen stove had to be cleaned out and black-leaded daily, which was done by one of the Miss Crossleys and so was the cooking. I carried the food into the dining room to be served and did some of the housework. I slept in an attic bedroom but was allowed the use of a small sitting room which was full of books so I could indulge in my love of reading.

The only other help kept was a gardener/handyman and it was he who milked the cow kept for domestic use. There was a dairy round at the back of Saddlers Hall then, pulled down when the house was converted into flats.

When the First World War broke out I went along to Lullingstone Castle where a small munitions factory had been established to make shell caps. My job was to inspect the finished caps and I remember that Miss Sidney Hart Dyke and her sister, the Hon Mrs Bell, also worked there.

After the war I went back to the castle in a different capacity – as a kitchen-maid. I didn't much want to do that but my mother and someone on Lady Emily Hart Dyke's staff had fixed it up and there was no use me arguing about it, so to the kitchens of Lullingstone Castle I went. I was actually quite happy there and sometimes, between cooks, I did all the cooking myself and was praised by Sir William Hart Dyke for my efforts.

One of my most vivid memories of those days was when rats got into Cook's bedroom, knocked over her nightcap of hot milk and ate the cherries off her hat. This caused a hullabaloo at the castle and the maids had to be moved out of their bedrooms and the keeper was called in to get rid of the rats.

An unhappy love affair prompted me to seek a change and I went to London. In those days girls obtained domestic work by going to a Register Office. After turning my nose up at offers of jobs in several well known families, including the parents of the Queen Mother, I went as kitchenmaid to a Lady Muriel Liddell Grainger, whose London home was in Charles Street and country place Ayton Castle in Scotland. But the kitchen in that household was dominated by a really nasty, bad tempered cook. I remember an occasion when my parents came to tea in the servants' hall. I went to the kitchen to make tea and put the pot on the hob of the stove. The cook snatched it off and put it on my arm shouting "That will teach you not to put teapots on stoves." I had quite a bad burn but I went back to my parents and told them I had done it myself. On another occasion the cook threw a whole batch of pastry at me.

It was the custom for familes to take the complete kitchen staff, butler and footmen when they moved their establishments, leaving the household staff in one place. So I went to Ayton Castle in late summer but I was so lonely there and so unhappy with the unpleasant cook that I gave in my notice. My employer tried to make me change my mind but I refused and because of this I was made to pay my own fare back to London – £3 – a huge sum to find in those days.

Later I went to work as second kitchenmaid at Londonderry House in Park Lane, the home of the Marquess of Londonderry. This was a household where entertaining was done on a vast scale and the guest list often included George V and Queen Mary and many distinguished people of the day. Kitchen staff consisted of the cook, two kitchenmaids, two scullery maids, a vegetable maid and a daily woman. Even so, no cakes or tea or coffee were made in the kitchens – these were provided by the still room staff. The cook there, although firm, was a vast improvement on the last one. I used to do the cooking for the 30 members of staff.

It was at Londonderry House that I first met my husband, Walter. He was the under butler and I remember the first time I saw him was when he came downstairs to select silver for a very grand party, looking gorgeous in his uniform of smart coat, breeches, silk stockings and buckled shoes.

This was a happy time for me. When the staff travelled to Newtownards, the Londonderrys' Irish home, we would see each other in our free time in the lovely surrounding countryside. But such attachments between members of the staff were frowned upon, so I used to leave notes in the boot room, inside my shoes, to tell Walter when I was off duty, and found replies inside his boots. In 1925, we came to Eynsford to be married in St Martin's church. I remember giving in my notice to Lady Londonderry, who was quite put out because she had earmarked me to be cook to her daughter who was about to be married to a son of the Duke of Devonshire. Eventually we took a post together, working as butler and cook to Sir Herbert and Lady Cohen at Highfields, Shoreham where we stayed for 20 years.

I have been asked what I was like to my kitchenmaids and I reply, "Well, they stayed with me".'

FOOD SUPPLIED

'When I was 16, in 1926, I went into service. The house was at Godden Green, near Sevenoaks. I was a kitchenmaid and had to wait on the cook and do washing up. My wages were five shillings a week. Of course, I lived in and had all my food supplied. I was very well fed at this house. My uniform was supplied but I had to pay for it from my wages.

I worked from 6 am to 10 pm and had a half day off every week and every other Sunday off. I used to go shopping in Sevenoaks,

A parlourmaid in the Rochester area in the 1900s. Going into service was often the only work open to young girls.

with the under-housemaid, on the half days.

I left after two years because the cook was very unkind to me. She was only two years older than me. Then I received a letter from my employers asking me to go back, which I did and stayed another two years.

I then went to work for a solicitor and his wife at Oad Street as a general cook. I stayed there for five years. There was not as much food to eat there as the parlourmaid used to get there first and I was left with very little.'

TESTING MY HONESTY

'I applied for a job as parlourmaid at a large house in Sittingbourne Road, Maidstone. It was a lovely house with beautiful things. The gentleman had made his fortune in tea in India. When I was accepted, I hurried to visit my aunt, who was a seamstress, and she kindly made me the two necessary print dresses, complete with calico linings (which made them very hot), for morning wear and one plain black dress for afternoons, with little white caps and dainty aprons. I asked for £20 per year and got it! I was 18 years old. My mistress tested my honesty by leaving coins under the settee, under the bed or perhaps at the bottom of heavy curtains. It also ensured I cleaned properly. I would find the money as I worked and hand it to my mistress who would say, "Oh dear, the master must have a hole in his pocket."

One morning after I had cleared and relaid the fire, and swept the carpet on my hands and knees (having first scattered used tea leaves to lay the dust), I found a half crown under the large settee and, in a fit of pique, put it back in the same spot. The next time I cleaned the morning room I did the same. Of course, a few days later the mistress sent for me. She said, "Rose, you have not cleaned this room properly." I answered by pulling out the settee to reveal the half crown. "If you mean this, it has been sitting there since last Thursday. The floor is clean and so is the coin, but I am sick and tired of finding money in odd places. I am honest, my mother and father brought me up to be and I cannot bear to be mistrusted." The master crept out into the garden. I thought I should get the sack without a reference, but I was sent to the kitchen to calm myself and later told I could stay.

They turned out to be good, kind employers and later sent me to the ophthalmic hospital for eye tests and paid for my first glasses and, for the first time in my life, I could see the leaves on the trees and the face on the moon. So, at 18, I earned £20 a year (£1 10s 0d a month), and had a good position. Hoovers were just coming on to the market and my mistress bought one for me to use.'

COOK GENERAL

'I was born in 1916 in Sunderland, and arrived in Shoreham to work in service with the Rev Augustus and Mrs Payne when I was just 16½ years old.

Lady Hedlem in Durham knew how difficult it was for girls, particularly, to find work. It was "bad times" for the miners, who could not always work, but apart from the mills there was little work for young women. Organising work in domestic service with the gentry was Lady Hedlem's chosen task and many girls left the north of England and travelled to the more prosperous home counties. Sevenoaks, in Kent, was considered such a place and I heard that I had "a place" at the Shoreham vicarage at two shillings and sixpence a week all found.

Like many of my young contemporaries, I was a good cook and my title was cook general. My duties began at 6 am when the brass containers were filled with hot water and carried to the bedrooms. Some of the 21 bedrooms were frequently occupied and beds were made immediately after breakfast. I served meals in the large dining room. When the family left the room, the china had to be carefully washed in the large sink in the scullery, adjoining the kitchen. Ellen, the housemaid, was older and had been in service much longer. She was a great help to me and often laid the table at breakfast, lunch and dinner. I wore a dress with a large apron which crossed over the shoulders and at the back. At lunch I changed into a black dress with white apron, trimmed with broderie anglais, with a smart stand-up cap to match.

Breakfast consisted of oats, main course and toast, coffee or tea. Lunch would be meat and two vegetables with a dessert. Perhaps Sir Roger Gregory sometimes made a present of a pheasant from a shoot in Scotland and then there was a party, and a lot more work for us. Afternoon tea consisted of dainty sandwiches and cakes or, sometimes, toasted teacakes and muffins. Dinner comprised several courses and was the main meal, consisting of meat or fish and vegetables.

Sexton of the church was Percy Stevens and he came and made up the fire which serviced the boiler just outside the kitchen. The big range in the kitchen had to be cleaned and the floors scrubbed with stiff brushes. Without gloves and kneelers, the work was arduous. I endeavoured to keep my hands looking as good as possible, not least for waiting on at the table later. Another help, Olive, came to the house each Monday to do all the washing – at the large sink, with a rubbing board. If the weather was wet, the clothes would be dried on clothes horses round the range. The beds were changed each week.

I had to be in the house all week with just one half day off. I also had a half day on Sunday once a month. I attended church regularly back home and would be at one of the services in Shoreham, being careful to ensure that there was always someone at the vicarage for security purposes. Lord and Lady Gregory occupied the Buckland Chapel (now known as the Gregory Chapel) and Lord and Lady Mildmay sat in their private chapel, named the Mildmay. Only a member of the gentry was allowed to read the lessons.

When I attended the village "hop" (usually once a month) I still had to be back at the vicarage by 9.30 pm. The sixpenny hop in the village hall was great fun. There was a pianist and violinist to accompany the dancers.

I met my husband, who had been born in Shoreham, while walking through the village one day. We just began talking, became good friends and were married in 1935. After this I left service and concentrated on a nursing career.'

LIVING IN

'My father died in India at the age of 39 from an acute gastric ulcer. Although he had been in the army from a boy of 16, the authorities refused to grant my mother an army pension as his death was not attributed to army service. We came to Wouldham, which was his home. My sister was 14 so had to get a job. My mother received a government pension of £1 4s a week to keep herself and four other children. I stayed at school until I was 14½ as she received an allowance for me, then I left to work five mornings a week for a local farmer's wife. I did most of the housework and every Monday helped with the washing, which was done by hand, and had to scrub a huge scullery floor after. I received five shillings a week for this. One highlight was bottle feeding two orphan lambs who used to nearly knock me over in their hurry to get at the bottles when I opened the gate to the field.

I left the farm after six months, when I was offered a job with a friend who lived in. She was parlourmaid to a gentleman of 70. There was also a cook-housekeeper and chauffeur-valet. I was the between-maid who did the dirtiest jobs. We all lived in a huge house overlooking the Medway. I slept in an attic room at the top of the house and the chauffeur was in the other one. I received £1 10s a month and was up at seven o'clock to clean the kitchen range and kitchen, scrub the front steps and sweep the store rooms which had apples on the stone floor and vegetables in sacks. The housekeeper used to preserve eggs, in a bucket of waterglass, when they were at their cheapest. By the time spring came round again they used to taste awful. I had a half day off on Wednesday (when all the shops were shut, which perhaps was a good thing as I never had much to spend), and every other Sunday afternoon.

I was taught to answer the front door so that I could take over the parlourmaid's duties when she was not there. Tradesmen were shown into a little room, gentry were shown into the drawing room; they put their calling card on the silver salver which I held out. I would then take it to the study, where my employer spent most of his time, and he would decide whether he would receive the visitors or be "out".

159

I spent quite a happy two years there. We were well fed and warm. The first Christmas I was there, my friend and I were given an umbrella by our employer. The second year he gave us money to buy a new dress. We went to Chatham and I bought a brown crêpe dress for 12s 11d. My friend chose a dark green crêpe dress with full sleeves which were embroidered with white chain stitch which she didn't like. The assistant offered to unpick the stitching so we went over to Woolworth's opposite and had a cup of tea and a bun. When we got back, she still didn't like the sleeves as there were marks where the stitching was removed so she was allowed to choose another dress, all for 12s 11d. Then tragedy struck. I bent down to pick up the bag with my dress in it and it wasn't there. I had left it at the tea bar. We dashed back, the manageress was called. She said a child had claimed the bag saying her grandmother had left it. When asked what was in the bag, the child said she didn't know as it was a Christmas present so they gave it to her.

I was well and truly in the doghouse and received a long lecture from the boss and the housekeeper and cried myself to sleep. But it all came out right in the end. My grandmother and my friend's grandmother were rival shopkeepers in the village where we lived and my grandmother sent for me and gave me the money for another dress. She wasn't going to have her granddaughter laughed at. I got another lecture from the housekeeper, she said I should have been made to pay for my carelessness and learned a lesson from it.

I left there when I was 17 and went to work for a retired naval officer and his wife. They had a lovely, but smaller, house and gave me ten shillings a week. I did all the work and most of the cooking. They were not quite the gentry of my previous employer but I was happier.

We used to wear a blue dress with white mob cap and apron. After lunch, we changed into a black dress with lacy cap with black velvet ribbon and small apron. There were washing bowls, jugs and chamber pots in all the bedrooms. I had to wash in cold water when I got up. After breakfast, the housekeeper, parlourmaid and I went upstairs and they made the beds while I emptied the bowls and chamber pots, washed them and replenished the jugs with fresh water. After that I prepared all the vegetables for the day and swept and tidied the huge scullery. I washed the stone floor once a week and also the long stone passage which stretched from the back door to the scullery.

There was a store room, butler's pantry, parlourmaid's pantry (where all the upstairs washing up was done), the kitchen and scullery all along the right side of the passage. There was a room with marble surfaces where all the fresh food was kept, a meat safe and always a barrel of beer. My employer had a half pint with his dinner at night. I helped to wait table when he entertained, when it was the parlourmaid's time off.

I stayed with them until the Second World War, when he was recalled to the Navy and she moved to the West Country. I was invited to go with her but I wouldn't leave my mum.'

I RESENTED IT

'Most girls went into service when they left school at 14, I did myself. It was quite a nice job really, not too far from home at Ide Hill, but I resented the fact that my brother could live at home and go to work and still be free evenings and weekends. Girls were mostly allowed one afternoon off a week and every other Sunday afternoon, be in by ten o'clock and woe betide you if you were late. The head maids in large establishments could be real tartars.'

THE BUTCHER'S BOY

'I worked as a maid in a big house in Swanley and on my first day, while dusting the drawing room, I noticed a penny on the mantelshelf. I was sure the mistress was testing me to see if I was honest, so I gave it a good polish and put it back.

I did not last long in this position as I was rather taken with the butcher's boy and when he came I used to take off my uniform cap before I answered the door to him. One day the mistress saw me and sacked me on the spot.'

CHEVENING HOUSE

'At Chevening House between the wars there were employed a cook, two kitchenmaids, two scullery maids, two laundry maids and four housemaids. The butler set the tone for the whole staff. They all ate together in the servants' hall, with the three outdoor manservants, but the butler had his in the housekeeper's room with the lady's maid and the cook.

I came to be a housemaid at Chevening, earning £36 a year, meals provided. On Sundays, if it was not your "Sunday out" you went to church in the morning. The family was away from January to Easter in London, when the staff were on "board wages" and the springcleaning was done. I had a half day once a week free and every other Sunday. After the springcleaning was done I had a weekend off in March.

When there were parties I used to receive tips, and these were put into a pool for the housemaids. The money was shared out on a sliding scale. The kitchen staff got no tips but received higher wages. We were all very conscious of our position as staff at Chevening House, dressed neatly when we went out, and were not encouraged to be friendly with the villagers.'

OTHER WAYS WE MADE
A LIVING

There were of course dozens of other ways we made a living and these are just a few remembered from times past – from fishing to working in the local bakery.

INSHORE FISHERMEN

'My father was a fisherman on the river Medway. The history of inshore fishing in the Medway towns is not widely known. When the Dutch invaded the Medway in the reign of Queen Anne and reached Upnor Castle the local fishermen helped the navy to repel the intruders and drive them back to the sea. For their help the Queen gave the fishermen the Freedom of the River. This is carried on by the apprenticeship system, which is of seven years duration – five years to the "master" and two years to the Crown, which usually meant that in the event of war the fishermen were called to serve in the Royal Navy.

At the beginning of this century as many as 40 fishing smacks, also called "bawleys", were fishing from Strood, Chatham and Gillingham but unfortunately this way of earning a living has almost died out now. The catches were mostly of shrimps (pink and brown) and also Dover sole, flounders, lobsters etc. The shrimps were sold to local fishmongers although my grandmother also sold them to people who came to the house, using half pint and pint glasses for measuring them. As children we often had shrimps, Dover sole or lobster for tea. The shrimps and lobsters were cooked on the boats and the fish were cleaned (gutted) before going to the shops. The Freedom of the River was very jealously guarded and anyone not a freeman using a trawl net in the river could be arrested and their nets confiscated. When fishing the boats would hang a basket from

The Hilda Marjorie *under way, the Wadhams brothers on board. Once up to 40 'bawleys' fished from Strood, Chatham and Gillingham.*

the masthead and this meant that all other craft had to keep clear. All boats were originally under sail but when engines came along most were converted which meant greater efficiency in returning to their ports and selling their catches.

My grandfather, Roland York Wadhams, was born in 1900 and didn't retire until 1974. He came from a family of fishermen and seafarers and was number eleven of 13 children (only two of whom were girls). He was apprenticed to his father and later joined forces with his younger brother (my great-uncle Josh) with whom he owned a bawley called the *Hilda Marjorie*. Since the best time to leave port was with the ebb tide they would sometimes "go away" at 1 am but if, in the summer, the tide was a late one at 6 am he would take us with him. We'd arrive at Strood pier and he would ferry us out to the bawley in his rowing boat. He only ever used one oar at the stern of the boat which he worked in a figure of eight to propel us along. I don't know the technical term for this but he always called it "wiggling".

Once we had reached the fishing ground for that morning a small net called a tell-tale was let down on a rope. After a few minutes it was retrieved and its contents examined. If the haul was promising, the main nets were paid out, the engine was cut and the bawley was allowed to drift for a while. The engine was then restarted to drive the winch which was used to haul in the net. Before the bawleys were motorised, this was done with a hand-operated winch – very hard work! Even with a powered winch the last part of the operation was still done by hand. The cod-end of the net was then undone and the haul spread on the deck for sorting. If there were eels in the net you had to catch them very quickly before they slithered back to the water through the scuppers. The fish were then removed and those large enough for sale were put in boxes whilst the others were thrown back. As a child I liked to gather up the baby flat fish – some only two or three inches long – and slip them surreptitiously over the side of the boat. This was in the hope that they would sink back to the riverbed before they were caught by the flock of following seagulls. Lastly, the shrimps were passed through sieves to extract the smaller ones and these were washed back into the river with buckets of sea water.

The copper had already been lit and filled with water and a generous amount of salt. The shrimps were then cooked and were ladled from the copper with a net that looked like a long-handled tennis racket. A drier – an oblong net stretched between two poles – was fixed over the side of the boat and the shrimps were spread on this to cool. There's nothing like the taste of fresh cooked, warm shrimps straight off the drier. Whilst fishing we would have pint mugs of coffee to drink made with consdensed milk as the boats obviously did not have fridges to store fresh milk in.

After two or three hauls we'd make our way (reluctantly for us) back to the pier to land our catch. On the way back the fish would be gutted and the waste parts thrown to the seagulls who managed to catch them in mid-air. My great-uncle Josh actually got one bird to swoop in and take food from his hand. My grandfather made all his own nets and went out to work in all weathers – hard work – but it didn't harm him as he lived until he was 88. He was a wonderful father and grandad and he even took one of my tiny dolls fishing in his pocket for me when I was about three. We have many happy memories of my grandparents and their way of life "on the water".'

THE BAKERY

'There was a large bakery behind the shop at Betsham at the beginning of the century. On one side was a huge heap of coke, while on the other side was a big shed stacked with sacks of flour. In between was the door to the bakery which was kept shut when

164

baking was in progress. Inside the bakery was a long bench where the bread was kneaded and shaped. There were two huge coke ovens which had to be fed often.

George Strong was the baker and people came from miles around to buy his bread. He did everything himself – he made the fires up, baked the bread and drew the loaves out to cool them off. The shop was a gold mine – you could get practically anything there, except a suit of clothes. I believe you could even buy corduroy trousers, so beloved of the farm worker in those days. Certainly there were always hobnailed boots hanging from the ceiling and most of the local farm workers bought their boots there. The shop also sold the most excellent bacon.'

'My mother inherited the bakery business at Fordcombe from her parents. I was born in 1916 and have lived in Fordcombe all my life. I can remember my parents telling me that the bakehouse was part of the house until my brother was born in 1910. It was then that the bakehouse was built at the rear of the house as it was not considered hygienic to have a baby in the same house as the bread was made.

After I left school I worked in the business, serving in the shop and eventually doing the bookkeeping. In those days the dough was made in the evening in a wooden trough. It was then transferred to another trough where it proved overnight and was ready to knead in the morning and be put into tins and proved again. My father and brother started work at 4 am and also one other man, Mr Ted Dawson. Our first dough mixer was bought before the Second World War and this greatly helped with the work. Our flour came from the Medway Milling Co at Maidstone and A.H. Allen & Co at Croydon. Yeast was obtained from the DCL yeast company.

We worked most of Maundy Thursday night so that the hot cross buns went out fresh on Good Friday morning. I wasn't very old when I had to be out in the bakehouse with my parents and my brother and when I got older I was allowed to stamp crosses on the buns. This was done with a wooden cross and had to be pressed down very hard. My father bought his first car in 1915 and before that the bread was delivered by pony and trap.'

'My father worked for the village baker in Lamberhurst. Every other Sunday evening he had to go and make the dough ready for the bread on Monday morning. He would often take me with him when I was a child and I would sit on one of the empty troughs and watch. Sometimes I was allowed to dissolve the yeast in the warm water ready for him to add to the sacks of flour he had already tipped into the large wooden trough. He mixed it all by hand and the flour came up to his elbows. He kneaded the dough and when it was finished it took up about one third of the space. By morning it would nearly have filled the trough and could then be cut and put into tins and baked in the large ovens which were heated by a coke fire. The bread tins were greased after each baking but were never washed.

When I was a little older I would sometimes go out on the delivery round with him. I was given a little basket and took bread to some of the customers. There were cottage loaves, coburgs, bloomers, sandwich and tin, twopence farthing a small loaf and fourpence farthing for a large one. What a delicious smell came from all those freshly baked loaves, all neatly arranged on the shelves in the van.'

THE GROCER'S SHOP

'I remember hearing our grocer say to my mother: "Have what you want for the children and pay when you can." Little did I think that this benign, silvery haired old gentleman would one day be my employer.

It was a firm of family grocers in Gravesend. My grandmother was a customer and one of my older cousins worked at the desk. As she was shortly to be married it was hoped that I might be able to take her place. I duly presented myself – 14 years old, hair tied back with a black bow and wearing a green overall – at 8.30 on Monday morning feeling very nervous. Although in a rather poor quarter of the town, I soon found that we served a great number of professional people including river pilots and several hoteliers. These people lived in the big houses in the town. Apart from the owner the staff consisted of a manager, two counter hands, two shop boys and me – the only girl.

I had a few weeks' instruction, but after that I was on my own. I had to make out accounts, weekly and monthly, do a little simple bookkeeping, give change and work out cheese and bacon in pounds and ounces, for example 9½ ounces at 1s 8d a pound. It was good training which I have never lost. Our hours were 8.30 am to 7 pm, half day on Wednesday and till 9 pm on Saturdays. We all had three quarters of an hour for tea starting at 4 pm and all of us went home for tea.

Saturday afternoons and evenings were usually slack periods with no orders to make up. These were collected twice a week and delivered by the boys on bicycles. The huge carrier baskets were packed with paper dividing each order and with paper bags of eggs on top.

Prunes came in three sizes as did currants, raisins and sultanas. Cooking salt came in 28 pound bars and was sawn up and wrapped in newspaper. Soda came in sacks and was weighed up into brown bags. Currants and all dried fruit was cleaned by the boys down in the cellar where the cheese and bacon was also stored. The cheeses, which were huge, came in big drums and had to be skinned and were cut in the middle first and then in smaller pieces on a board with a wire. We also had a cheese taster which looked something like an apple corer. Customers often wished to taste before buying.

Tea came in chests and we had a mixer in which our tea was mixed to a special blend. It was kept, until packed, in huge cannisters on a shelf in the shop. Pepper and spices were kept in drawers and were weighed up to customers' requirements – two ounces of pepper was 2½d. Butter, margarine and lard came in 28 pound boxes and were turned out onto special dishes behind the provisions counter and weighed up at slack periods. Butter was shaped with patterned butter pats on a slate slab. Eggs came in long boxes and were unpacked into special baskets. On Mondays we did a roaring trade with the loose pickles. The basin was weighed first and twopennyworth of piccalilli or onions put in afterwards. Friday night, pay night, was when the Dad of the family was treated to a gammon rasher and we always had a nice cut ready. Saturday evening was the time to weigh and pack sugar and tea for which we had a special packet – orange pekoe and travancore already mixed to our own blend.

Christmas was a special time in the trade. Ladies and house-keepers came in personally to give their orders, sitting on the spindly high chairs at the counter. They would choose from currants, raisins and sultanas displayed on paper and look at the orange and lemon peel and citron with large pieces of sugar between it all. Special joints of bacon were ordered for the occasion. Figs and dates came to us in 14lb blocks and pounds and half pounds were cut off with a knife. We also sold long boxes of green angelica. Muscatels were packed flat in boxes in bunches and the larger Jordan almonds were the ones to eat with them. Valencia almonds were used in puddings. In spite of the fact that we had a butcher opposite we sold turkeys at Christmas and everyone prayed that it would not turn mild.

As time went on I used to come out from my little box and give a hand. The men taught me how to cut up a side of bacon into the proper cuts. I got quite good at cutting ham off the bone and slapping up a shapely pat of butter. Every night the shop was swept out and twice a day fresh sawdust put down. On bonfire night a bucket of water was put under the letter box inside and all the boxes brought in from the yard.

All our scales and weights were checked regularly and I remember a visit now and then by the Inspector of Weights and Measures. The scale pans and weights were all of brass from ¼oz up to 7lbs and were kept clean by the boys. The knife grinder called to sharpen the knives on his machine in the road.'

'Plaxtol boasted two grocers, two butchers, a shoe shop, a fried fish shop, a post office and a forge. In 1946 the latter became the garage, with a hand pump for petrol but nothing to indicate how much petrol it was pumping.

The grocers stocked a wide range of drapery, including some much coveted art silk stockings at 10d a pair. They were a repellent orange colour; they looked better worn inside out. The other grocer employed a young man called Foster Clark, who invented a custard powder in his mother's Plaxtol kitchen. In 1907 the old post office advertised itself on its billhead as a general drapery, grocery, furniture and earthenware stores.

There was a good selection of village inns. At the centre of the village was the Papermakers' Arms where the hop pickers would gather for singing and merriment. Special rabbit pies (poached or not) were made for them. Another popular pub was the Golding Hop, named after John Golding who propagated this famous Kent hop in the 18th century. This family owned property in Plaxtol for 200 years, employing many people, good landlords and friends to all. The pub was once owned by a woman who brewed her own cider outside to a secret recipe, using a 100 year old cider press and wrapping the apples in eight horsehair mats. The result was very strong and had to be diluted with lemonade.

Plaxtol also had its industrial side. At the hamlet of Dunks Green, in the south of the parish, is Roughway Paper Mill on the banks of the river Bourne. One who started in 1919 worked a twelve hour day. They took great pride in the fact that their mill made stamp and airmail paper, paper for postal orders and the white "fivers", and had to have an excise man on the premises. All spoke lovingly of the old steam engine which had a big fly wheel and five big ropes; a man came down yearly from Lancashire to service it. The other industry was Hyders ironworks housed in a splendid 15th century house. One worker said he was paid £1 7s 6d a week in 1929. He also spoke of the beauty and craftsmanship of the hand forged wrought ironwork.'

'The main employers in the village were the Horton Kirby Paper Mills and the Westminster Mill which made shoelaces. There are vivid memories of starting work at Westminster Mill in 1934, putting tin tags on the bootlaces and being paid three farthings a gross for the effort. Both factories provided generous outings for their employees with trips to Southampton, Hastings and even Windermere. Each year the Paper Mills organised a special train for their outing to Margate with a huge decorated shield attached to the front of the engine for the day.'

'At Hadlow village they were still hand-picking the hops in the 1950s. Horneden was the largest farm, having Londoners as well as locals, and Dumbreck's had only local pickers, also Honey's hop field which was adjoining the Bourne river. Many men and women had work on the farms, also gardening and housework in the estate manor houses such as Oxenhoath, the Grange, Hadlow Castle and farm.

Kenward and Courts were the local brewers in the High Street, providing men with work, the wages being around £2 10s to £3 10s a week. There were several grocers in the village, a post office, a corn chandler, a bank, a baker and eight pubs. Soft fruit was grown in Court Lane fields.

Sir William Geary, who owned the big house at Oxenhoath, had Berkhampstead boys and girls for holidays (Butler Pomfret's wife and daughter looked after them in a cottage). Later he employed these children as parlourmaids etc and the boys on the farmland, giving them a cottage on the estate. He also employed many local men as gardeners, and the local builder Smithers for repairs.'

'Chart Sutton was, in the old days, a hop growing parish, but in the slump years for hops, the 1920s, the farmers grubbed them out and planted fruit. This was firmly established by the time the Hop Marketing Scheme stabilised the industry in July 1932, and so the farmers remained fruit growers.

Spile making was a very old craft in the village in 1926. Spiles and hurdles were made of chestnut which grew plentifully in the district, is very durable under and above the ground and splits easily. The wood is cut into suitable lengths, peeled of bark and split. The butt end is pointed and soaked in hot tar for 24 hours. Spile fences are the most common kind in the village. Rolls of spile fencing are erected in strategic places at the beginning of winter to prevent snow drifting across exposed sections of roads. Ladder making was the other old craft practised by Mr Peen, who also made furniture and was a wheelwright.

There were also two brickfields in the parish where the bricks were made by hand. The blacksmith was a jack of all trades. He shod horses, made tools and repaired anything that came his way. He would charge three shillings a shoe and three shillings and sixpence for the old shires of Kleinworts.'

'Pre-war life in Marden was slow and peaceful. Most of the population was engaged in agriculture and money was very short. Only the farmers and tradesmen had cars or vans; a few dashing lads had motor bikes. There were many shops – five butchers, four shops providing food and household requirements, three coal merchants, and two blacksmiths. The Southern Railway station was a hive of activity, with coal wagons and fruit containers transporting apples and other fruit to Covent Garden, Manchester and Newcastle. Mr Back with three clerks, three signalmen and four porters manned the station from 6 am to 11 pm.'

NURSERIES EVERYWHERE

'Hextable began to emerge as a village at the beginning of the century. As it was a very fertile area, it was destined for horticulture and this developed by the end of the First World War. Nurseries began to open everywhere and the produce was taken to the London markets by horse and cart. The produce would be gathered and packed during the day and it was ready to be loaded on to the carts by about 6 pm and they would set off to London by about 7 pm. The horses had been well fed and the road was literally covered with horse droppings. All the householders were keen gardeners with allotments and they would go out and gather it all up to put on their gardens.

The nurserymen began to specialise in tomatoes and cucumbers which grew well here and with the growth of nurseries it soon became a necessity to have better transport than the horse and cart. Hextable Haulage Company was founded which had Foden steam engines and trailers and a few Model T Ford vans which could get to the markets more quickly.

With the horse and cart, the horses knew the way so the driver would drop off to sleep. It was an offence to be found asleep in charge of a horse, but it was difficult for the police to catch them asleep because, as soon as they stopped the horse, the driver woke up.'

DIVERSE PRODUCTS

'The Crystalate Works (now a housing estate) was for many years one of the largest employers in the area of Golden Green. They made such diverse products as 78 rpm gramophone records, electrical and radio parts, toys and dominoes. My mother was a deft "domino spotter" – this was a sought after job amongst the employees. The shrill "time hooter" was missed long after the factory closed its doors.'

'We lived at Little Mill, a hamlet of East Peckham. My father worked at the tanyard (now Brymores) in the old barn where the bark was kept and sorted to use for dyeing the hides. These were made into leather for seats etc in cars and railway carriages. At the age of 13

I joined my father in this work. I earned a penny an hour, totalling five shillings a week working from 6 am to 6 pm Monday to Friday and 6 am to 1 pm on Saturday, with an hour off for lunch and half an hour for breakfast.

When I was 15 I changed my job and went to work for Crystalate in Golden Green. There we made billiard balls which were exported all over the world. I joined the army in 1916 when I was 18. At the end of the war I returned to Crystalate until 1939 when I moved to the chemical plant in Yalding where we produced chemicals for plant protection. Here I started at £3 a week from which sixpence was deducted for pension. When I retired after 24 years this gave me a pension of £3 a week.'

WASHING AND COFFINS

'My mother took in washing during the 1930s when we lived at Hadlow. One day while she was ironing an embroidered sheet of Fay Compton's (the actress) my muddy ball sailed through the window right on to the centre. She was cross and I can understand why as it had to be washed again – it was king-sized and its return was delayed.

My father was a carpenter and sometimes stayed late making a coffin. He had been known to snatch a few hours' sleep in it if he was particularly late.'

THE HOSPITAL LAUNDRY

'St Bartholomew's Hospital laundry was at Swanley Junction set in woodlands. I started work there in 1923. I was very lucky to get this job as it was the only other alternative to agriculture or domestic service and was better paid; I earned more than my father. Because of this, people worked there all their lives. You could only get the job by knowing somebody who worked there. There were 21 people working in the receiving room, 42 in the sorting room, 33 in the washhouse, 27 in the drying room, 80 people in the ironing room and 54 in the packing room. The laundry was brought down from the hospital by horse and cart and the horses were stabled overnight.

It was very hard work. I stood and ironed all day. No creases were allowed otherwise Matron would return them. The hours were Monday to Friday 8 am to 6 pm, Saturday 8 am to 11 am. The door was shut promptly at 8 am; if you were late you had to ring the bell to be let in. Our only holidays were Bank Holidays and women were not re-employed until four weeks after childbirth. I worked there for 32 years, leaving in 1955.'

'In the mid 1930s, the German barque *Peking* arrived in the Medway to replace the old *Arethusa*, which had been in service as a Naval Training Ship since the 1860s. The new arrival was fitted out in the dockyard to be adapted as a residential training ship for boys. The beautiful *Peking* became an object of admiration as soon as, under her new name, as the Training Ship *Arethusa*, she took up her station at Upnor. There was also much speculation as to her reason for being in the Medway. The letters "TS Arethusa" worn on the cap band of the boys' naval uniform caused some people to say that the ship was some sort of approved school for naughty boys, and drove home their argument by saying that the TS stood for Truant Ship. Even after the letters were removed, this belief persisted. Another suggestion was that the ship was a floating orphanage. Neither theory was correct.

In the first place, the boys were destined to enter the Royal Navy. Under no circumstances was anyone with a criminal record (including probation) ever accepted by the RN. Any boy coming under this category could not, therefore, be accepted by the *Arethusa*. Practically every boy in the ship's company came from a broken home, or from a children's home and the fees for tuition and upkeep were supplied by donations from well wishers or children's departments.

There was a form of entrance exam, roughly equivalent to the old eleven plus. When a boy had been accepted and had joined the ship's company, he was given a medical and was then allocated to one of the ship's six divisions, thus following naval practice. There was a staff of qualified schoolmasters and Naval or Royal Marine instructors. Boys attended school in the normal way with normal school subjects – English, maths, science etc. The instructors, a dedicated body of men, gave instruction in naval subjects – knots, splicing, signalling, sailing etc. Much of this was continued after school hours, not only to keep the boys occupied, but also because the instructors were so enthusiastic they wanted to continue after school was over.

There was one very important point to consider. Each boy had to become a proficient swimmer by the end of his first term. It was essential that this should be so, they did not want to lose boys overboard. Any boy unable to swim by the end of his first term was sent to another of the Shaftesbury Homes. Boys were forbidden to swim in the river, but it was remarkable to note how many managed, by sheer accident of course, to slip overboard and into the water. The cure lay in the hands of the SRN, who was ever present. She worked on the theory, firmly pointed out to her victim, that the river was dirty and carried diseases, for which the only cure was a very unpleasant tasting nostrum to clear out the internal organs of microbes, followed by a period of 24 hours without food. Very few boys "fell" into the river twice.

Each morning the boys were awakened and the day's duties began. There was a task for every boy in the ship. This could at times lead to awkward moments. On one occasion a boy was required to explain why the Sister had complained on being awakened at a very early hour. With some indignation, the boy remarked that his duty each morning was to bring a mug of hot water for the officers to shave. In his eyes, the Sister was a ship's officer, and to bring hot shaving water to her was only in compliance with his normal duty.

After breakfast the day's schooling began. These continued until midday, when the midday meal was served, usually of very good quality and quantity. The afternoon saw more activity, on the field, in the swimming bath, at the rifle range or in the classrooms. At about 4.30 pm tea was served and the boys had time to follow their own pursuits, under the guidance of the Instructor Officers. These sessions were voluntary but were always well attended. When time came for the boys to turn in, they fetched and slung their hammocks. Then, towel in hand, they went to the shower room for their nightly bath. This procedure went by Divisons. Each boy handed his towel to his Divisional Officer, went into the shower and then out at the other end of the shower room, collected his towel and gave his number to the DO before drying himself. This ensured that no boy missed his daily bath. On one occasion the system caused some merriment. When a child is transferred from one school to another, his/her medical and scholastic record goes to his/her new school. One day, the Sister remarked to her assistant that we must be receiving girls as well as boys. One lad, who was attending Sick Bay for some minor ailment, said that it was impossible for girls to be aboard, his tone of voice indicating that was a jolly good thing too. Sister showed a medical record card which had arrived with the records of new recruits to the ship, and, sure enough, one was for a girl. The boy obviously could not accept that the tone of the ship was being lowered by the presence of girls. The next day he came to Sister and said, in tones of triumph, that there were no girls aboard. He proved this, he said, because he had taken six showers that night and his eyes proved to him, beyond any doubt, that no girl had gone through the showers.

Discipline was strict, but never severe. In line with Naval regulations in effect in those days, a boy could be caned for smoking. This, in a ship, could be a very dangerous practice. In the Royal Navy, a boy under the age of 16 was also caned if caught smoking. The staff were firm, but fair, and all had a great attachment to the

173

pupils, many of whom had experienced much trouble in their young lives. The staff aimed to bring the boys back onto an even keel and fit them out for a successful life. I remember one boy saying when he came to bid me farewell, that he had been in children's homes all his life, and this *Arethusa* period had given him the only real home he had ever had. Many boys went on to great success. A boy who gained a commission in the Royal Navy was presented with a sword, a beautiful piece of craftsmanship. A boy who reached the position of ship's captain in the Merchant Navy was presented with a magnificent pair of binoculars.

The departure of the ship for America, in 1974, was a sad day for us all. The local population still miss the sight of a truly beautiful ship lying offshore in the Medway. On our part, we miss the pleasure and satisfaction of knowing that we played an important part in helping boys whose young lives had been shattered and caused them to lose their way. We are glad to know that we were able to help in setting their feet in the right direction.'

CHATHAM DOCKYARD

There are many memories of the years when the dockyard at Chatham was a bustling and thriving place, the very heart of the area. As one man looks back on his working life there, he can only ask, 'Where have all those skilled trades gone?'

THE FOCAL POINT OF EVERYTHING

'The dockyard was the focal point of everything really. Nearly every family had at least one of their household working in the yard. Apprenticeships were numerous, and you could almost guarantee a job there. All the barracks were situated in and around the dockyard – Brompton, Pembroke, Kitchener and Southill.

The Brook was commonly known as "cut throat alley", with eight public houses in it, and knife fights and brawls were commonplace. Children were warned not to go anywhere near there!

The town was full – full of people, servicemen, employment, and most of all, full of life. Sadly it will never be the same again.'

'The ropery at the dockyard was always my favourite place. It fascinated me. It has a 1,128 foot long ropewalk and you could see the strands being twisted to make ropes using traditional methods and machines dating back to 1811. There was also wire splicing by hand, rigging, knots and canvas work. Sails and flags were made in the sail and colour lofts, and there was mastmaking as well as ship repairing and restoring.'

THE DINNER GIRLS

'My mother was born in Chatham in 1908 and lived in a little house at Luton Arches. She was a dinner girl – not to help with school dinners, there were no such luxuries in those days. Before the other children went home for dinner, the dinner girls were allowed out of class to run home and collect the plated dinner for fathers and uncles who worked at the dockyard. The meals were tied in white cloths, with the hot gravy separate. They then caught the bus to the dockyard to await the hooter sounding. The gates opened and they hurried to where father worked, handing over the meal and hoping they had not spilled any. She can't remember if she had any dinner, it was probably a piece of bread and dripping before returning to school. Living at Luton Arches, it was quite a way to go to the dockyard.'

WHERE ARE ALL THE SKILLED TRADES GONE?

'The year was 1936, and after three years at Chatham Technical School and some extra cramming during the Easter holidays, finally came the news of success in the Dockyard Apprentices Entrance Examination. Instructions arrived to report to the Dockyard Central Office Block for selection of trades on such and such a date. The big day arrived – what trade to choose – electrical fitter, shipwright, engine fitter, pattern maker, boiler maker? At the time, 15 years old, I was always interested in pulling things to pieces to find out how they worked and was absolutely fanatical about motor bikes. All right, I will be an engine fitter; at least it will have something to do with engines. And so the future pattern of one's life, career, friendships, relationships are all determined by a simple decision at a tender age.

At last came the great first day of my working life – report at 0700 hours 24 September 1936 to the engineering factory. I was living in Sittingbourne at the time, which required that I got up at 5 am, rushed to Sittingbourne railway station to catch a train to Chatham at 6 am, rush from Chatham station to the dockyard, and be in one's place of work by 7 am and not one minute later. I had no idea where

175

the engineering factory would be and did not appreciate that it was about one mile from the main dockyard gate. The main gate, a large Georgian arched entry complete with a coat of arms was quite intimidating and the only thing missing seemed to be the motto "Abandon hope all ye who enter here". The policeman at the gate said, "Straight down that road, lad, and you can't miss it. It's a very large building on the left." For some reason a bell was tolling intermittently. I wondered who had died, for I had yet to learn that at five minutes before starting time the dockyard bell would be rung slowly and that one minute before time it was rung continuously, and explained why all the workmen were running in all directions and disappearing into various building and cubby holes.

At last I found the factory and went in and the small door set in a pair of huge sliding doors. Inside was a gentleman (a recorder) who said, "What's your name, son? Quick! Take this card and put it in the slit in that machine and bang down the brass handle." The machine had a clock in the top of it and was my first sight of a time recording clock. When I took my card out of the slot it read 07.01; this would normally mean that I would have been docked a quarter of an hour's pay. The recorder was a kindly man and said, "Don't worry, lad, I will put a note on your card that the clock was running fast, but only because it is your first day. You'll have to be on time in future." He consulted his list. "Take this lad down to the submarine section" he said to another chap. Off we went to the far end of the factory and I was dumbfounded by the noise and activity. Overhead travelling cranes rumbling along carried all sorts of oddly shaped chunks of metal, lathes of all shapes and sizes, short and big fat ones used for machining gun mounting rings, long and skinny ones used for turning ships' propeller shafts, milling machines, slotting machines, drilling machines, huge cast iron slabs at waist height where large chunks of cast and fabricated pieces were set up on jacks and marked out with scribing blocks for subsequent machining.

At the far corner away from the machine tool section a submarine diesel engine was being built, and around this were benches and vices where the fitters were working on bits and pieces for the engine. I was left with the chargeman of the section who took me to a short sandy haired gentleman in glasses. "This is Mr Crawford and he will be your instructor for the next two years. So behave yourself, or he will be after you." It is hard to be sure whether grown-ups are pulling your leg or not at that age: anyhow, Charlie turned out to be a second father to me and looked after my welfare. I worked at the next vice to him and he instructed me in the gentle art of filing, hacksawing, chipping etc, how things were put together and what was their purpose.

After three years in the factory one was then sent "afloat". This did not mean going to sea, apart from the occasional sea trial at the end of a ship's refit, but meant working on ships in various stages of refit or being newly constructed on the building slips at the top end of the yard in the present Historic Centre. There were three huge refitting basins and nine dry docks. There is always a fascination in seeing a ship being brought into the dock, the caisson being put back into place and the water being pumped out by huge pumps way under the ground until the ship gently settles on blocks on the dock bottom and side shores are wedged into place to prevent the ship toppling over onto its side. This docking process has to be a carefully controlled operation, to ensure that the ship is exactly in the right position over the dock blocks that must be clear of all underwater inlets and outlets and protuberances such as sonar domes, and that the side shores go in exactly the right place to avoid damage to the ship and at the right time as the ship loses stability. This operation comes under the control of the foreman of the yard and his shipwrights and riggers. It carries an enormous responsiblity; one could imagine with a few million pounds worth of warship lying on its side in a dry dock that a few heads would roll.

For the war years I stayed with the "afloat" party, sometimes working on cruisers, sometimes destroyers or frigates, corvettes and occasional periods on submarines. Submarines – what congestion, everybody working in each other's pockets, there was scarcely room to change your mind. It became fairly routine, with the occasional air raid to liven things up or something a bit out of the ordinary, like refitting a Polish destroyer with instruction plates on machinery in a funny language. During the time of the American Air Force daylight raids on Germany, a Flying Fortress crew had to bail out over the dockyard and one of them landed next to us in No 9 Dock, and was taken into the wardroom by the ship's officers for a stiff gin, and was later seen walking nonchalantly in flying boots and his crumpled parachute tucked under his arm, escorted by a dockyard policeman to the gate.

By the end of May 1944 we seemed to be running out of work – no ships except those in dock; in fact, anything that would float was out of the yard. There was obviously something afoot. Sure enough, a few days later – D-Day, so that is where they all were. In subsequent days some ships came limping back with holes in them or bits missing, then it was all work again.

In 1947 the Reconstruction Examinations began to enable people to qualify for permanent promotion into the Inspector of Trades or drawing office fields. By then I was a little tired of being up to my ears in hyraulic oil or frozen to death in winter, sweeping snow aside to get at the nuts and bolts. I decided it was the drawing office for me, as machine drawing was one of my pet subjects and one which I enjoyed. It was a case of back to all those academic studies.

The hard work paid off and into the dockyard drawing office I went. I was now a Dockyard Officer, although I did not feel any different and began a period that was the happiest time of my career. This was designing equipment for launching aircraft from scratch and it is the only time I can remember lying in the bath at home thinking up new ideas and hardly being able to wait for the Monday morning to get back to the office and try it out on the drawing board. This went on for some five years until promotion again, and off I went complete with family to Bath, Admiralty Headquarters. In 1953 my close connections with Chatham Dockyard ended and my nomadic career with the Admiralty began.

I cannot leave my thoughts of Chatham Yard without reminiscing on the characters I met along the way. There was Big Fred, the slinger in the factory, whose job it was to assess the weight of load, decide where the centre of gravity was, arrange his lifting slings and strops accordingly and control the movements of the overhead travelling crane and its driver by mysterious flicks of his hands like an inebriated traffic policeman. Fred's lunch consisted of a loaf of bread cut in two and inside an order of fish and chips from the local shop and down went the lot, including the bones. I remember Bill the driller whose job it was to drill tiny delicate holes in a semi-spherical fuel injector nozzle, and during the morning was surrounded by a blue cloud of profanity as broken drills zinged off in all directions but who, after having four or five pints of best ale in the dockyard canteen at lunch time, could drill holes contentedly all afternoon without breaking one drill. There was Bluey, the odd-ball who had an ancient fabric-covered Austin 7 motor car that he would tar and grit every spring, like a country road: and Tiny, of our afloat party, a giant of a man with enormous strength but as gentle as a lamb, who, under cover of a gun shield would stick paper strips to his eyelids and prance around fluttering them to the sound of the Marine Band on the deck below performing their ceremonials. Characters all who would help each other and pitch in and get down to it when the chips were down and jobs were urgently required.

Of course, there must have been a few loafers and scroungers, which often made the dockyards disparaged at times by the Navy, but in my experience the yard saw that the Navy had the top brick of the chimney if it was in their power, and the standard of workmanship was amazingly high. Where are all these skills and a myriad of trades now? Defunct? Overtaken by modern technology? Ended by the removal of the Russian threat? Probably gone to the same place that the Grand Fleet has gone – down to their last 30 serviceable ships.'

WAR & PEACE

THE GREAT WAR 1914-1918

As the men took the King's Shilling and marched off to the war, we could never have imagined that very soon the skies over Kent would see the first air raids, bringing the war home to us. Families left behind often found it hard to struggle on without the breadwinner, but we managed when we had to and greeted the end of the war with relief, and with sadness.

FROM BALLOONS TO AIR RAIDS

'In the years before the First World War it was a common sight on fine summer afternoons to see perhaps 20 or 30 balloons drifting across the sky at varying heights. Some were quite low, and, as youngsters, we eagerly followed for them to land. The occupants in the basket often called on us to hold on to the trail rope to prevent it landing in some awkward place. For this we were rewarded with a penny which, in those days, represented a fortune, as it was possible to get four ounces of sweets for that amount. These balloons used to take off from the Crystal Palace and carried three or four passengers. There was no likelihood of interfering with aeroplanes as they were almost non-existent. At the start of the war this sport had to stop and small aeroplanes began to make their appearance but it was a long time before they were seen in any numbers.

Air raids that took place in the early part of the war were made by Zeppelins, huge airships that looked like sausages. The raids were mostly made on moonlit nights and it was fairly easy for the searchlights to light them up. Although they were big, the bomb loads were small compared to what we were to have three years later. Two smallish bombs dropped in the village, both near the Old Mill; one fell into the river and the other behind the cottages opposite the mill. The latter one caused Bexley's one and only air raid victim in the war.

These Zeppelins were to become fairly easy prey to defence units and were eventually superseded by aeroplanes. The first daylight raid by aeroplanes was on a Saturday morning and caused quite a sensation. I was on Dartford Heath when the warnings were sounded and found it hard to realise what was happening, seeing these, by far the largest ever, aeroplanes flying towards London and aircraft guns banging away.'

TIMES WERE HARD

'A small house in Crayford High Street was the place of my birth in 1914. My home was situated between the Crayford Arms public house and the local "milk shop". My grandparents owned a fish shop, also in the High Street.

The standard of living in 1914 was very basic and work was scarce. My father, who was a carpenter, was out of work more than he was in. There was no guaranteed time or unemployment money so we eventually had to leave our home to go and live with my grandparents in the fish shop. Life was very busy and how hard my mother and grandparents worked – my father joined the Army and was sent to France. My grandmother would get up very early to go to Billingsgate fish market to buy the fish. She would return by train with the fish in wooden boxes, ready to be sold when the shop opened. As we also sold fried fish and chips, opening hours were long. Closing time was often as late as eleven o'clock, even later when the fair was in town.

As the war went on, Vickers factory began employing men and women from all over the country and Crayford began to grow. Houses were built all around and new roads began to appear.'

TELEGRAM GIRLS

'At Barming during the war, when most able-bodied men were in the forces, young women were employed to deliver telegrams etc. They could be seen in their navy blue uniform, cycling along the roads to deliver their sometimes sad messages to families who waited at home.'

THE KING'S SHILLING

'When the First World War was imminent, I was four years old. I had a six year old brother and my mother was expecting her third baby. Men were being persuaded to join the army. To this end, a band would march down the High Street, carrying placards, playing well known catchy tunes. Men joined the marchers to the Town Hall where they received the King's Shilling and signed on.

My dad never could resist a challenge of this nature. Imagine my mother's shock when he announced that he had joined the army, leaving her with a six year old, a four year old and a new baby. We were every proud of our soldier dad who returned home from time to time in his Royal Fusiliers uniform. He was posted to Leiston, near Sizewell in Suffolk. We stayed in a little cottage on the seafront just down the hill from the barracks when he was in training.

The cottage had a trap door in the scullery, which led into an underground passage and went two miles to Leiston station. When my mother was told that we could use the passage in an air raid, her retort was, "I'd sooner face the Germans than go down there and face the rats." However, for us children it was a prolonged holiday. We virtually lived on the beach which came up to our front gate.'

TAKE COVER

'I was born in London in 1911 and in the autumn of 1914 I caught diphtheria and was very ill. On recovery I should have gone to a convalescent home but these were needed for wounded soldiers, so I was sent to stay with an aunt and uncle in Rainham in Kent.

My uncle kept a jewellery shop in the High Street. He also sold gramophones, records and mouth organs, which were very popular with the soldiers as they were small enough to put in their pockets and take back to the trenches. The parish church of St Margaret's was on the opposite side of the road and had a lovely peal of bells. There was a row of horse chestnut trees in front of the church. On Sundays in spring, people from Chatham and Gillingham came on the open top tram to admire the blossom and get a breath of fresh air.

My uncle's shop was between the bank and the post office. Next to the post office was the vicarage. Once a year there was a garden fete in the vicarage grounds. My aunt helped with the strawberry teas and uncle ran the bowling games. I loved the donkey rides. In the evening there was a concert in the vicarage drawing room. It was a very jolly affair.

A very large sign at the entrance to Rainham read "Motorists must not exceed 8 miles an hour through the village". Of course, a great part of the traffic was horse-drawn vans and carts and bicycles during the war years. One Saturday morning I was playing in the garden when I saw some planes coming over. The black crosses on them were plain to see as they were flying low. I rushed in to tell my aunt that German planes were coming over. She did not believe me until she came to check as the air raids had always been at night. The planes were on their way for the first daylight raids on London. We had numerous raids and heard heavy gun fire, sometimes a plane was shot down. My uncle was medically unfit for the army but, when a raid was coming, he had to cycle round the outlying villages crying "Take cover" and when it was all over return and shout "All clear". He had a connecting bell from his bedroom to the post office next door which received the first warning.

The streets had gas lamps and a man went round with a long pole to turn them on at dusk and off again at about 10 pm.'

Unveiling the First World War memorial at Loose. The war touched every town and village in West Kent.

PEACE

'I was five years old when the Peace Celebrations took place in the village of Brasted after the First World War. There was a wonderful fancy dress procession, amongst the many other events, and I think that every man, woman and child in the village was involved. Of special interest and excitement to me were the costumes of my two older sisters. One was made up with the flags of all the participating nations who fought so bravely against our enemies, the other was a wonderful creation depicting the Angel of Peace.

I must have been considered too young to take part and I wept bitterly until Mamma trimmed my little dress with fresh flowers from the garden. A basket of flowers for me to carry completed "The Flower Girl" – and peace, the operative word, was restored.'

THE SECOND WORLD WAR
1939-1945

Just 20 years later, bombs were falling again over Kent. Night after night, we rushed into the air raid shelters and many are the tales of near misses and of tragedy averted.

PRIME TARGETS

'The wartime years in the Medway towns were very traumatic. Not only were there all sections of the forces stationed here – Navy, Army and Marines – but the dockyard at Chatham and Shorts Brothers aircraft factory were prime targets for the German bombers. They were also on the flight path to London.

I was a child living in Strood during the war and we were bombed out four times. The first time, early in the war, an oil bomb dropped on our house burning all the upper part of the house.

It was the custom at that time to change the furniture around, making the lounge upstairs and bedroom downstairs, to enable an easier dash to the Anderson shelter in the garden when the sirens went as they did every night. I had just passed the scholarship for the grammar school and my mother had sat all evening sewing Cash's new name tapes on my new uniform, only for it to be burnt where it sat in a neat pile on the sofa. Next to it were two dolls, a white one and a black one. When searching through the debris afterwards we came across the dolls which had changed colour. The oil in the bomb had blackened the white doll while the heat had stripped the paint off the black doll.

Later on, nearer the end of the war, when we had moved house, there was a very bad raid killing many people, of whom I might have been one if my father hadn't shrieked to me to dive under the table. The ceilings, windows and French doors crashed in burying me. I remember lying there in total blackness wondering if I was dead.

One day, when I was about eleven, a German plane came down in the allotments near our house in Broom Hill, Strood. The pilot was unharmed and was apprehended by the police as he stepped out of the plane. They had to march him through the allotments and all the local women turned out with brooms and sticks ready to assist in case he escaped.'

SURVIVING THE BOMBING

'While we were picking hops in Dumbreck's hopfield at Hadlow, the Battle of Britain went on overhead. Sometimes a few Spitfires broke up waves of bombers and some retreated while a few went on to bomb London. A few women went on picking hops through it all. One very stout picker would bend over the bin, putting her head into the hops – her rear end was a hilarious sight.'

'When the war started I was nine years old and we lived at Waterworks House in Higham. When my mother was at work my sister and I went to stay with a neighbour, Auntie Pearce, who had a son called Gordon. One day we were there while she was cooking lunch for her husband who worked on the farm. The air raid siren went off and my sister went to hide in the cupboard under the stairs. Gordon hid under the table and I was standing in front of the fire. Auntie went up the garden to put the peelings on the compost heap. She heard the bomb coming and threw herself onto the ground. The bomb landed at the front door, pushing in the wall which in turn pushed the table towards me, trapping me between the table and the fireguard. We all came out alive. If we had gone upstairs to play like we normally did we would have been killed.

When my mother came home the police told her she could not go down the road because the water pipes had been damaged and the road was flooded. She asked where the bombs had dropped. When she was told she replied that her children were in that house and Hitler himself could not stop her from going home. She later took a photograph of my sister and me on the rubble, but when she went to get them developed they were confiscated until after the war.'

'In 1939 I was seven years old. We lived in Chislehurst, which was considered a safe area even though it was less than 15 miles from London and very close to Biggin Hill aerodrome. Many bombs intended for London fell on Chislehurst. We had no shelter or cellar so my brother and I slept on a mattress in the cupboard under the stairs, which was the strongest part of the house.

The other thing we lacked in our house was a bathroom. We had a long metal bath which hung on the wall outside the back door and once or twice a week this was placed in front of the fire in the living room and filled with hot water so that the whole family could have a bath.

Late one afternoon, a bomb dropped onto a rather stony piece of land about 200 yards from our house. When the raid finished we found the paved area in our back garden resembled a beach and our bath had been peppered with stones, although there were no actual holes in it. It would probably have been better for us if it had been punctured, as it was impossible to buy a new one, but had ours been useless the emergency services would have supplied us with one. As it was we had to sit on innumerable bumps for about the next eight years! It was bliss when our bathroom was built and we had a nice smooth bath installed in about 1948.'

'There were soldiers billeted in nearly every large house, hotel and school in Hawkhurst, so the village was the target for German planes. A bomb dropped onto a house near ours and did not explode so we were all evacuated. Another time things got a bit scary was at Gills Green, when a German plane machine gunned everything on and around the railway station. I worked near the station and had been to the little post office at Gills Green. I was walking back through the station yard when all this noise started. A voice down by my feet said, "Get under here quick." Very frightened, I got under the lorry. There were about four people under there and we stayed there until it was all quiet again.

In 1944 a doodlebug dropped on to the Moor church, doing a lot of damage to the church and surrounding area. All weddings, funerals and other services had to take place at Highgate church.'

'I can remember the bombs dropping on Frindsbury – a landmine dropped on Frindsbury Hall. My mother's neighbour shouted that the bombs were coming, so my mother threw the three of us down the shelter. When we came up we had no front door and the ceiling had fallen into the custard that my mother was cooking – she was more upset about the custard than anything else.'

'When the war started I was living at Dartford Heath and had two children. It was a very frightening time. We had an incendiary bomb through the bedroom window which burnt a few bedclothes. We were able to replace the blankets with special coupons but we had to have blue ones. The first winter we spent nights in the Anderson shelter buried halfway up the garden.

We had some near misses. A string of fire bombs narrowly missed the shelter where the children were sleeping one evening. Another bomb was discovered deep in the ground just outside our french window and we all had to stay in the front of the house while bomb disposal engineers dug it out. This took all day and late into the night.

On D-Day 1944 I remember the radio announcement and being so relieved, thinking the war would be over soon. How wrong I was. A few days later the flying bombs started. The first night the siren went I bundled my young family down the shelter; I had three children by then. The night dragged on without a sound. I thought we were the only ones left alive and was almost afraid to come up. We were not told the reason for the alarm for some hours.'

'Just before the war Air Raid Precaution (ARP) exercises took place at West Malling and one necessitated the rescue of a casualty from a bedroom in Churchfields. While we were waiting for the stretcher party to secure their volunteer casualty to the stretcher the crowd were entertained by the warden at the foot of the ladder who could waggle his helmet on his head without touching it, and a boy demonstrated his double-jointed fingers, and we kids thought it splendid entertainment which concluded with the stretcher coming down the ladder.

During the war an anti-aircraft gun was sited somewhere on the outskirts of East Malling. One day in 1941 the neighbourhood's boys and girls were playing "parachutes" in Offham Road. The "parachute" was a handkerchief tied at the four corners with string, and a small stone used as the weight, and this was thrown up as high as possible and then floated down – we hoped it would not get caught on any gutters or shrubs and be lost to us. Suddenly a tight formation of twelve aircraft flew over, and we fled to our homes, just as the East Malling gun opened fire and hit one of the German bombers. From nowhere it seemed Hurricanes and Spitfires came to force the crippled plane down onto the aerodrome where, we learned afterwards, every gun was trained on it, but it landed just off the runway and the crew was captured.

Another day a parachutist was seen coming down and people flocked out of the town, along Norman Road, to see him land, but as I was only nine I was not allowed to go and join in the fun.

When the doodlebugs or V1s started the flightpath from one launching site in France seemed to be straight up our garden path. Fortunately they did not come very often. Also from our house we could see the barrage balloons being floated up at nearby Wrotham Heath. Another wartime memory is that of standing in the backyard and seeing a doodlebug flying towards London when a Spitfire flew alongside it and, at great risk, the pilot put his aircraft's wing under the doodlebug's and tipped it off course and it plunged earthwards.

One night we heard a doodlebug's engine stop and had no idea where it was going to land. Shortly afterwards there was an explosion and it landed on a walnut tree in Fartherwell Park and caused a lot of damage to the Hall and its greenhouses, as well as to property in Offham Road.'

'We had a lot of Canadian and New Zealand soldiers camping in the woods at Kingswood. I remember how tasty the chocolate and army biscuits were. Walking home from school one day we heard the German planes overhead, though the sirens had not sounded, and then we heard bombs exploding on Detling aerodrome. Mum said that even the hen gathered her chicks under the hedge when she heard the roar of the engines. We could always tell by the sound if it was a German or an English plane. We saw many overhead battles and one Spitfire was shot down and landed about a quarter of a mile away. This was recently recovered from the field.'

'Holidays were out of the question in 1944. A few days off work meant getting out into the countryside and relaxing. So, on a warm and sunny August morning, a friend and I took a walk out from Rochester to Halling and then branched off up the hill to find a spot to sit and read. I would have gone to the top of the hill but my friend was not so energetic and suggested we sat a bit lower down. I agreed and we had just settled comfortably when we heard the sound of a doodlebug coming over. We looked up and saw it flying much lower than usual. It appeared to be coming straight for us. There was no time to seek shelter so we just laid flat, face down on the grass, and the bomb went right over us and crashed into the hill, where we would have been sitting had I had my way. Fortunately we were not hurt, just covered with leaves, and naturally, badly shaken.'

INTO THE CAVES

'People from St Mary and St Paul's Cray went into Chislehurst Caves to escape the bombing. One night there were said to be 10,000 people in the caves. At first it was very disorganised with people bringing beds, bedding and even small stoves to cook supper. Eventually all these were turned out. Bunk beds and electric lights were installed, wardens appointed and one cave set aside as a first aid post. There was also a cave for mothers with babies and milk was distributed by the health visitor. One night bombs fell demolishing houses above the cave. Nobody below felt even a tremor.'

'The caves under Rock House in Chipstead High Street were used as a wartime shelter. They resulted from the old whiting works where the chalk was dug out, dried on the huge wooden drying frame which was a landmark until recent times, and sold to housewives to whiten their doorsteps in the cities. Some was ground up for use as fine powder or French chalk. John Pudney, known for his war-time poems, stored a lot of film there after the war. Many theatrical people used to come and stay here in his time.

One villager who had refused to shelter in the caves as she was not allowed to take her dog, remembers a landmine coming down in the field where Chipstead Lake now extends, and having the windows and doors blown in upon her. These mines came down attached to parachutes and one villager panicked thinking parachutists were coming. The stones of the old house never stirred! Relatives from London had far less damage and were glad to return to London. There were lots of dog-fights overhead, and a string of incendiary bombs fell across the village. A member going up to shelter in the caves with her sister recalls pausing to admire a chandelier in a house in Stone Row, opposite the cottages at the end of Chevening Road, near The Crown, when they heard the noise of the descending bombs. Her sister dragged her little boy up the steps into the pub while she crouched in the gutter.

Another villager recalls pulling back the blackout after some unusual noises to find incendiary bombs in the fields outside. The men went out with forks and put manure on them, which put them out! Another bomb fell on the footpath nearby, the blast hurling her husband, who was looking out of the window, across the bedroom. It looked just as if the wall came in and went out again. They thought it must be out on the main road but did not go out to look. Some time afterwards an ARP man came to the door and asked, "Do you know where the people next door are?" They answered, "No, but they will be in there, under the stairs" He said, "Well, they ain't in there now! I can see the stairs and there's no one there!", and when they went to have a look the side of the house had been blown out. The German pilots used to jettison unused bombs over this part of Kent. The Home Guard were on duty as well as the ARP. One large bomb blew windows and doors out of a great many houses.

Recalling how as children we used to be taken out of the classrooms when there was an alert to shelters underground, we remembered the Anderson shelters in people's gardens which were cut down into the ground, lined with concrete, and had turves and soil put over the curved corrugated iron roof. There were some of these in Chipstead despite having the caves in use. The Morrison shelters were like steel tables with heavy mesh screens at the sides which were put up inside people's homes. There was a barrage balloon on Chipstead Common, and another on Bessels Green. If they caught a "doodlebug" (pilotless plane) they used to put a cross on the balloons. They got a couple at Bessels Green which landed up Polhill way. There was a searchlight in Deans Field, and an AA gun where Quarry House now is, in Chipstead Lane. One of the first V2s exploded over Chevening House, and the warhead went into the wood, doing very little damage.'

WRITTEN AFTER THE AIR RAID

'This letter was written by Joan Mortlock following the air raid on Bromley on the night of Wednesday 16th April 1941. Joan lived with her mother and sister-in-law, "Ginge", over the shop, Mortlock and Son, at 25 East Street, Bromley. The shop sold antiques and second-hand furniture.

"It really has been like living through hell here this last week; plenty of people besides me have lost their nerve.

The report goes now that we had 16 landmines as well as dozens and dozens of HEs [high explosives] on that ghastly Wednesday night. I have never been so terrified in my life before and thought the house was sure to fall in on us, with the blast of the bombs all round. When it got a little bit quiet about 4 am Ginge and I (hand-in-hand) went upstairs to inspect damage. I was never more surprised than when I found we still had a roof over our heads and that the only damage upstairs was a few windows gone at the back of the house. Two doors were damaged and the little wall on our showroom roof was knocked about a bit by the incendiary that landed there. I found it on the next morning laying there, a beautiful silver, and I unscrewed the end and shook all the black powder out of it; so that it couldn't suddenly explode when I got it indoors. We took it to the police station, plus the part of the frame that the incendiaries came down on, that fell through the roof of a shed in the yard; the incendiary was dated 1936.

I was up the road fire-watching when the first bombs fell and also when a landmine fell on our beautiful parish church. There is not any of the church left, except for a piece of the tower which will probably fall down at any moment, it is cracked in two. I went to church Easter morning and it was decorated. That was the last time I went into the church and now it is just a heap of rubble. The vicar is very upset; but when Ginge and I went to the service held in the little hall last Sunday morning he was very brave and got through the ordeal well. There were four churches damaged in the raid and three of them were completely demolished.

Lots of shops were burnt out. Dunns the furniture place in the Market Square is completely gone; not one piece of furniture was saved. Also, Isards warehouse behind the post office and whole rows of private houses as the water supply went.

I thought nothing of laying there in the doorway in all the dirt as the bombs swished down; before I have always laughed at the thought of it. Then the bread-baskets came down and there was one mad rush; I got a stirrup pump and bucket of water and then dashed and got the axe for the Home Guard (who were fortunately at the drill hall) to break into a shop whose roof was on fire. There was a continual cry of "water" coming from a darkness that was gradually getting more and more into a nasty red light as fires started.

The AFS had 58 fires to deal with in Bromley on that night. We took buckets of water out into the road at every cry and bombs were coming down then in a steady flow. It took me nearly ten minutes at one time to get a bucket of water through our shop as at every few inches I had to lay down owing to a bomb screaming down too close for my fancy.

Mum, Ginge and I spent from between 10 pm till about 4 am sitting on our basement stairs clinging to each other. I kept dashing up between the bombs to see if any more incendiaries had come our way but we were there nearly six hours. It was freezing cold; the back door had been blown in and the scullery window out; the back windows of the shop had also gone and the wind and blast of bombs just whistled through the place.

The casualties here were very bad and the ambulances were up and down the road all the time. You remember Aunt Ave's house; just a little further down the road there is an awful lot of damage and they did not finish getting the people out of there till Sunday; about ten people were killed there, three that I knew. Our doctor says that Bromley had it worse than anywhere in London on that night.

I expect you've heard that Wallis's is gone? There is nothing left at all and the men are pulling down the outside walls now. I think they are starting up again somewhere but don't know where yet.

The City Temple and the church next door and also Buchanan's were burnt out in Holborn.

I had to fire-watch again last night and was very worried in case the warning went; but we had a lovely quiet night and I even got some sleep.

Well so much for the ****** war. I do so hope and pray that it will soon end and that we shall all be able to live happy, normal lives again."'

THE LAST V2

'Towards the end of March 1945, in fact the 27th, found me one afternoon standing in the playground of Charterhouse school in Orpington, and I can remember with great clarity what happened in the next few minutes. Although it was late in the afternoon the sun was shining and it was windless and, therefore, a very calm and tranquil spring afternoon. Charterhouse school was situated high above Orpington and I can remember noticing how peaceful the town looked. The visibility was very good that afternoon.

Whilst staring down towards the end of Orpington High Street, my eyes saw what appeared at first to be a daytime shooting star flash down from the sky to the ground. It was very fast, rather like a lightning strike but both fainter and faster and above all was the impression of the flash moving downwards. There then came a big flash at ground level, clearly a bomb-type flash, followed by an almighty bang and the end of the High Street and surrounding area disappeared from view. A huge black-grey plume rose with stunning speed to the height of more than 200 feet. At the same time, I heard a long rumble in the sky, not unlike thunder. It all happened so quickly, it was only afterwards that I realised I had been staring at the exact position of a V2 rocket strike. I never mentioned this to anyone mainly, I suppose, because I thought nobody would believe me, now I no longer mind, what I do know is that what I saw was the last V2 rocket to fall on England.'

LIFE GOES ON

[   ]

The war changed all our lives, whether we stayed in home villages faced with an influx of soldiers and prisoners or set off on travels round the country. We learned to take it all in our stride, from rationing to 'make do and mend'.

THE WAR CHANGED EVERYTHING

'About 1937-38 the aerodrome at Detling was reopened and that made quite a difference to the village. Some of the airmen brought their wives to the village and by that time houses had been built in Hockers Lane, Pilgrims Way and Harple Lane. They were unable to rent cottages or houses and then, of course, the war came and changed everything.

We only had an hourly bus service and no relief buses because of petrol rationing. We could hardly ever get on a bus because they filled up with airmen over the hill. Mr Rogers, at the garage, had a large taxi. He could carry six and we used to band together and get him to take us into town. It cost us sixpence each, almost the same as the bus which was fivepence each way. Later, quite a few of us bought bicycles. It was all right going in, but what a pull coming home with a basket full of shopping on the front and more on the carrier on the back.

An open air service held at Bearsted in 1945 during a local Red Cross event.

I worked at East Court, the doctor's house, during the war for four years until I had to get permission to go home to help Mother at The Cock as my father was ill. I was only a young teenager and was considered to be in a reserved occupation at the doctor's house.

I started work at 7 am (living at home most of the time), and often did not get home until after 9 pm and then sometimes had to help in the bar. I was able, some days, to go home in the afternnon or to the village shop but only if there was someone to answer the phone as the doctor was always on call.

I had one half day off a week, leaving at 3 pm, and every other Sunday afternoon and evening. I was allowed to go to church most Sunday mornings as I often had to play the organ. Our organist had to do his Home Guard duties on Sundays as he worked long hours in a grocer's shop in the town and could not be spared any other time.

We had about every sort of bomb dropped around us and quite a lot of damage at times, especially when a landmine fell on the hill. East Court was badly damaged by the landmine and a string of incendiaries was dropped in Harple Lane; one penetrated the roof and went into the bath and they turned the tap on it. A doodlebug fell at Harple Farm and killed two horses and slightly damaged the house.

There were great jubiliations when the war ended; we danced in the school playground. We raised quite a lot of money for various charities during the war. Mother used to run small musical evenings or games of whist. We had a weekly raffle at The Cock with, quite often, a loaf of home-made bread among the small prizes.

When the aerodrome was badly bombed in 1940, for several days they had no kitchen and we were kept very busy serving bread and cheese to the boys. A lot of them were sleeping in the woods above the village. When Dr Bernard heard about this, he bought mattresses and allowed them to use the surgery waiting room. We also slept a lot of the officers at the Cock Inn.

One morning, a route march of about 250 soldiers came through the village and an officer came in and asked my father if we could serve them in ten minutes. There were only the three of us, but by giving them the bottles and glasses to pour out themselves and working quickly, they all got a drink of something. While we did that, their medical officer was attending to some of their blistered feet with bowls of hot water and towels, also supplied by us. So, in a small way we were sometimes called on to help the war effort.'

SOLDIERS AND POWs

'During the war, soldiers from the Royal Engineers were stationed in the oasthouses which were part of the old farm buildings at Mill Hall, Aylesford. They used to practise building Bailey bridges across the river.

There were big petrol tanks on the river bank near our house, owned by Power and Regent. The barges came up the river to deliver the petrol. German prisoners of war, stationed at East Malling in a Nissen hut, were brought down to work at the Regent petrol tanks. During their break time they used to go to the coal yard, where my father worked, and make all sorts of things from string, like slippers. One man asked my father if he wanted to buy something and my father sent him round to see my mother. We had quite a few things made by the POWs. When I had mumps, food was rationed and fruit was difficult to get. The prisoners brought grapefruit, sugar etc to the house from their camp. One of the prisoners was a doctor at the camp. He had been training before he had to go into the forces. His name was Ludwig.

During the war, my uncle was a night watchman at Snodland Mill. A landmine was dropped on the mill and he was buried under the rubble. He was sent for treatment to Preston Hall hospital, which was also used in the First World War for soldiers gassed in the trenches. The patients were allowed to walk out of the grounds. Eric Winstone, the band leader and Bryn Jones, who played for Arsenal, were patients there. My uncle brought Bryn Jones to our house for a visit, which was something special. I remember my brother was putting his football boots on ready to go out and play. Bryn Jones offered to tie them for him, which he did, and off went my brother, really excited.'

'I attended St Peter's Church of England school at Southborough throughout the war years. I can recall sheltering by the church wall with shrapnel falling all around us. When the air raid siren sounded, we all went to the brick built shelter in the playground. I suppose it was safer than staying in the classrooms as it had no windows to shatter. But I hated going into dark, poorly lit rooms. When the war was over we were all given a card with a message from the King.

Towards the end of the war my father, who had been in the Fire Service, was sent to work at the prisoner of war camp at Tonbridge. His job was to take the POWs out to work on the local farms – hedge laying, ditching, haymaking etc, doing the work that machinery does today. During their dinner break, the prisoners would occupy themselves with basket making, carving ashtrays and other such crafts. They knew my father had a young family and one German prisoner made a ring for me. He fashioned it from the end of a spoon with pieces of coloured toothbrush for the "jewels".'

RATIONING CAME IN

'In June 1939 my family moved over the border from Sussex to Kent to the village of Cowden. My parents were taking over the village stores. We had not been in the village long when war was declared and with it came rationing. Dad had to go away on war work and Mum was left with three children, her grandfather and a shop to look after.

One of the things I remember is the bacon being delivered. A man would carry a whole side of bacon on his back and hang it on a hook in the larder, as of course there was no fridge. The cheeses were round and weighed about half a hundredweight; they had a type of muslin skin on them that had to be peeled off before it could be cut with a wire. My mother had to cut the side of bacon up into joints with a carving knife and then cut them into rashers. We had no bacon slicer, and she got complaints if she cut it too thick, as the ration was about two ounces a week. Cheese was also two ounces a week but if you were a farm worker you had three quarters of a pound.

We didn't need to leave the village very often as we could get most things we needed. Miss Miles at the draper's shop sold shoes, clothes, wool and most of the necessary things. There was not a lot of choice in clothes and most of the children ended up looking alike, with all the boys in brown cord shorts and lumber jackets. We were lucky, our Mum used to make most of our clothes from hand-me-downs.'

'I was born in Kemsing, near Biggin Hill, a quiet village until 1940 when an influx of troops arrived. A team of barrage balloon men took up camp in the garden of my parents' home, Dynes Farm. My mother, amongst other duties, was an ARP warden. The Army took over a large house, Box House, for their own use. We spent most nights in a Morrison shelter under the table for safety from bombs.

On the farm we had chickens and fresh eggs. These were preserved in "Ottegg" for later use. Butter was made from the cow's milk. Fruit trees provided for jam and bottled fruit and vegetables were also grown. It was a time of rationing and "make do and mend" for clothes and household items. Everyone was issued with a ration book with very meagre amounts of food each week.'

'My grandparents lived at Tug O'Mutton Green in Farnborough. My grandmother had always kept hens, so war-time saw a large part of her suburban garden converted into a chicken run. As a child, I delighted in collecting new laid eggs from the laying boxes. The hens were fed on household scraps and meal. To supplement their diet, my grandmother took me gleaning to find grain in a field close to Tug O'Mutton Green.

There was always a smell of baking in the house. My grandmother had been cook to Miss Matilda Talbot at Lacock Abbey and delighted in feeding her seven children and their families when they visited her. Roast chicken or baked rabbit were her speciality, with vegetables from my grandfather's allotment. Pies were made using windfall apples and blackberries from the hedgerows. War-time shortages were not allowed to affect her family's visits and nobody ever went home empty handed. A piece of chicken, new laid eggs or a few slices of brawn made from a pig's head, went with any visitors to supplement the meagre war-time rations.'

'Lectures and films from Government and company sources were provided to aid the work of food production. The Dig for Victory campaign was heeded. Extra allotments were bought by Wateringbury Parish Council and heartily cultivated by the local people. Wateringbury school had a garden, too, on the site of the village car park. The Cottage Gardens competition was still held. Specially packed seeds by Sutton & Sons were available to Women's Institute members and in 1942 the WI were granted six packets of tomato seeds which were raised by Mrs Norton (Wateringbury station). Many pounds of tomatoes were grown aided by an allocation of artificial manure from America. Chickens were kept in many gardens, the egg ration being substituted by a corn ration. Rabbits were also kept for meat.

Hopping continued as usual, with the arrival of hundreds of Londoners. During the Battle of Britain, when the airfield was often under attack, Mr Frank Blest (Broomscroft) could not persuade anyone to pick his hops growing close by. He arranged for the hop bines to be carted to the forecourt of the Queen's Head pub for the ladies living nearby to pick the hops. When the raids came they were able to run to their homes for shelter. Many other families picked hops brought to their gardens.

Clothing was strictly rationed and often, when the correct number of coupons had been saved, the desired goods were unavailable. "Make do and mend" was the order of the day.

The WI instigated many courses which were well attended. Glovemaking and slipper classes taught ladies how to cure rabbit skins; some even progressed to lamb skins. It took one rabbit skin for one glove or mitten. Great skill was needed, and a bit of luck, to get two similar skins for a matched pair. Wool was also rationed, but WI members were given a special allowance of a pound and a half of wool each year to knit garments for family and friends.'

'We returned to Kent in October 1944, before the end of the war, so were there for the V1s and V2s. I travelled to my school in New Cross by train and never quite knew if I was going to make it. New Cross Road along which I walked had sometimes had a rocket or buzz-bomb overnight and looked different. Woolworth's disappeared this way one weekend, the mother of one of my friend's being killed there.

Lessons were interrupted by sirens for the buzz-bombs and by the bangs of rockets. Rockets banged twice, once in the air and once on the ground. We were taught to slide under our desks at the first bang to protect ourselves from flying glass in the case of a near miss. This became automatic and many times Mum found herself sitting at the dining table alone as we three slid under it at the first bang. There were no alerts for rockets but buzz-bombs could be seen and so the sirens went and we trooped to the shelters. The lower classrooms were strengthened and sandbagged and that is where we went during raids. My class had a large cupboard under some stairs.

At home at night we would grab a blanket from our bed and go to our shelter or latterly under the dining room table. Mum kept a Mars bar and a knife handy and would slice it for us. In this way a raid was a treat as sweets were rationed.

We had rationing during and for some years after the war but, in fact, bread was only rationed after, not during, the war. During rationing we had to be registered at the grocer and butcher we used and we could get our weekly ration only from those shops. Sweet coupons could be spent everywhere. If we went away for more than a few days our ration books went also and we had to register on a temporary basis with the local shops. Being a family of five we never went out to tea without taking some tea, butter and sugar.

In spite of, or perhaps because of, rationing we had a very healthy diet. My father had a large allotment and we had lots of vegetables and never went hungry. Eggs came dried in packets, there were very few fresh ones and children got priority. At Christmas we got extra rations and in the summer one could have extra sugar to make jam.

Clothing and furnishings were also rationed although blackout material for windows was not. My grandmother had a cousin in America who was very large and who had a lot of very large friends. She would collect clothes from them and send them to us. My mother was a good dressmaker and would take them apart and make clothes for us. One coat we received was so large that it made coats, leggings and balaclava type hats for both of my two year old brothers. Aunt Tillie also sent food parcels of tea, sugar, candies, cookies and sometimes bacon. On one occasion she included a box of face powder for my mother but it split and we had scented tea and sugar.'

WARTIME JAM

'It was compulsory under the Ministry of Food's directions for two "lay" members to serve on a bona fide Women's Institute committee applying for a sugar ration to make jam in bulk from surplus garden fruit. I was one co-opted and I have vivid memories of that period.

The sugar ration per person was not sufficient to spare any for jam, so the Ministry of Food allocated rations to groups such as WIs. The fruit was brought to a centre (in our case the dining room of the primary school at Harrietsham) by members of the public, being the produce of their gardens. The sorting, cleaning and cooking was done on a shift system.

The MOF had very strict rules about the standard required. Only jam jars could be used which had MF stamped on the bottom as these were the official containers for one pound of jam. The personal ration was a pound a month and people were very fussy that they got their full weight. The jam jars were filled to the brim and after cooling would sink about one eighth of an inch. They were covered with a wax disc and finally parchment covers (the official issue) and tied with string (also issued) with a special knot which did not waste an inch of string. Then they were labelled with the WI labels.

The fruits used were all the varieties grown in gardens as well as rhubarb. In those days people's gardens were well kept up and productive. There were also certain rules about the stoned fruit – no more than two stones were allowed in each pound of plum jam and only four in damson. To make sure we kept to this precise ruling, our cooks removed all the stones in the boiling and when it came to filling the jars popped the required number back in!

The jam then had to be sold to shops and schools against their allotted quota. At the end of the season it was essential that all the jam was sold and so the MOF made a deal with the Co-operative Society to take the surplus at what was called first-hand price, a much lower price than wholesale which the shops were paying. We did not care for this arrangement especially as we discovered all our carefully labelled home-made jams had their labels removed and Co-op labels substituted.

Between 2nd June and 9th July 1941 the following jams were made: rhubarb 670 lbs, gooseberry 297 lbs, strawberry 381 lbs. In September 1941 the production for the year was 7,196 lbs of jam, 108 lbs chutney and 30 pots of mint jelly; 4,713 lbs of sugar was used. A sales day was held for chutney and scum at the end of the season, the price to be charged to workers being ninepence a jar for scum and a shilling a jar for chutney. The head cook was rewarded with three pounds of scum for all her noble work during the season and the driver who conveyed all the jam to Maidstone was presented with four pounds of scum. The cleaners were given one jar of scum free.

Letters were received from Lady Denman and Lord Woolton thanking members for their magnificent work at the Preservation Centre.'

SEEING THE FUNNY SIDE

'She wasn't so bad as cooks go, but as cooks go she went! – leaving me with a task which no doubt helped to send her away post haste. About to descend on Chevening Gardens were two big parties, on one week in high summer. The first was to be a party for the local rather large Women's Institute, followed on the very next day by a school treat for something over 100 children and evacuees from the local school. With little warning I found myself having to make cakes and bread for over 200 women and children, on top of my war work looking after a contingent of land girls, German and Italian prisoners of war, farm labourers, plus the Estate Office and complicated records which had to be kept for various Ministries.

The cakes managed to get cooked, mostly in the night hours, and were duly set out in the vast kitchen quarters in Chevening House, carefully separated for the two parties.

Alas, the WI ladies descended upon me to help. They certainly did help, and they also helped themselves to the cakes intended for the children. They brought out their paper bags and, before I could stop them, with exclamations of "Oh, how my husband will enjoy having cakes for tea for a change" away went all my supplies, and I had then to set to work on yet another "midnight feast" making more bread and cakes for the children.

How we lived through those war years was a miracle for these undertakings were achieved in the midst of bombings and alerts, and yet we managed to see the funny side, and laughter kept us going.

You may ask where all the food came from. The answer in this instance was from a Merchant Navy brother of a member of staff who was nothing if not generous, ingenious and obliging!'

GIFT FLOUR

'I was born in Cowden. During the war I can remember walking with two friends up to the bakery at Horseshoe Green owned by Mr Hawkett. We were going to collect "Gift Flour" as it was called, allocated annually to families from a charity at Cowden church. We each took a pillow case to get the flour in. On our way back home passing Cowden station, a German plane flew over the railway line and fired its machine guns. We sheltered under the railway bridge and then picked up some of the bullets and took them home with us. We were more excited than scared.'

'My aunt ran a baker's shop during the war. My mother used the flour sacks to make pillow slips.'

DOING OUR BIT

From making meat pies to be sold locally, to joining the Women's Land Army, we all did our bit during the war.

WE ALL DID OUR BIT

'With the coming of the war, Bearsted village bonded together, people joining the ARP, Red Cross, Home Guard, Observer Corps, Wardens etc. Mr Stanley Johnson of Bearsted House gave over most of his home for the ARP and Red Cross. He bought an ambulance for us and equipped his billiard room as a casualty receiving station. He also equipped one of his cottages as a gas cleansing station. The Women's Institute hall was used as a canteen and rest room for the forces. We worked in shifts providing hot meals and drinks and the troops really appreciated somewhere to relax.'

'During the war I was in the Red Cross. When the siren sounded, and it was my turn to report for duty, I had to put on my uniform and my tin hat and walk all the way from where I lived in Chevening to Sundridge, about two miles.'

'I was a trained dressmaker before the war, and when war came I was busy making blackout curtains for the big houses around Downe. We went fruit picking, bottled fruit and preserved beans. We also collected jam jars, making sure they were the correct type, and sterilized them for jam making.

We made thousands of meat pies for the village, with a grant from the government for the ingredients. A team of women made the pies. They had only meat in them and were three and a half inches in diameter. We made them on Mondays and Fridays and each household was allowed one pie on both days. The gravy was distributed for soup. Although the pies were only threepence each, we were able to make a donation to the Nursing Association and pay the helpers a small amount out of the profits.'

'My mother belonged to Maidstone Centre WI and remembered when France fell and troops were evacuated from Dunkirk and taken to Headcorn railway station. The WI were asked to make tea and jam sandwiches for the starving men.

We lived on a hill in Maidstone and fire-watchers used our flat roof during air raids to look for incendiary bombs. One night they saw a light flashing from somewhere near the bridge. It proved to be an enemy agent signalling. My father was very excited to think the spy had been caught.'

'During the 1930s and 1940s my father "Buster" Simmons was a member of a famous Kent dance band – Albert Card and his Band. They played in ballrooms all over Kent and at Rochester Casino, their signature tune being *In the mood*. They were featured on

Albert Card and his Band were popular entertainers during the war, often playing at the Rochester casino. Albert Card is on the right, 'Buster' Simmons on the left.

Workers' Playtime, a programme on the wireless that was very popular during the war years. My father played in the band all through the war and apparently travelled home in many an air raid. He was an air raid warden and when he was playing in the band, my mother would don his tin hat and do all the necessary duties.'

'When I left school I got a job as a machinist in Lloyds Bank, Threadneedle Street. Due to the bombing of the railways during the war I had to travel from Bromley to London Bridge. In the evening after finishing work, twice a week I helped at London Bridge YMCA, and I will never forget going home on the unlit train after ten o'clock at night. When I got to Bromley the last bus to Keston had gone, so I had to walk from Bromley bus garage with shrapnel falling around me. I also helped at the canteen in Holwood Park, which was under canvas and run by the Canadian YMCA for the army. Once a week a dance was held at Keston village hall and I'm afraid hardly any of them could dance, so yours truly had her toes stepped on many times.'

'Maud worked at Shorts factory at Rochester, as a fitter on Sunderland Flying Boats. After being picked up by the workers' bus at 6 am at Sandling, they would start work at 6.30 and work until 6 pm. She did this for two years from 1939, then moved to airport works at Rochester, for another year, doing the same work (lots of hacksawing). The pay was £2 8s a week. Maud's husband worked in a factory and was also in the Home Guard, so usually when she came home from work he was going out again. During this time Maud had three miscarriages, probably due to the long hours and hard work. Although she did not like the work, Maud made a lot of good friends and had some happy times.'

'It was in May 1952 that I was introduced to the beautiful Kent countryside. In a rather decrepit hospital transport bus, I travelled with four other pupil midwives, about ten ladies whose babies were due to be born in the very near future, and an assortment of equipment from a maternity hospital in war scarred south-east London to Moatlands near Paddock Wood.

Bomb damage had reduced the number of beds available at the hospital in Woolwich, so Moatlands had been acquired and the mothers were brought down to the country where their labour was induced and they had their babies. In spite of the peace, fresh air, greenery and lovely apple blossom, they loathed it. They longed to get back to the smoke and the 5.30 am train coming through the tunnel.

As pupil midwives, we were to spend eight weeks of our training at Moatlands. We loved it and I still remember the beauty and scent of the early mornings when on night duty, chasing round our dormitory attempting to expel a maybug, sitting in the sun and studying, playing tennis and the luscious bread pudding the cook produced. The one real problem we had was keeping the Aga alight when on night duty. One was in great disgrace if there was no hot water or heat to cook the breakfast in the morning.

The first baby I delivered was born at Moatlands at midnight one moonlit night. He was duly dispatched to the oak panelled nursery and the mother returned to her bed in a rather ornate room which served as a ward.

The mothers travelled back to London after 14 days with more colour in their cheeks than on their arrival and the babies looking bonny.

I have heard that Moatlands is reputed to be haunted. I never saw a ghost, but I wonder if any of the little people in their oak panelled nursery ever saw the lady in white bending over their cot.'

HOME FROM HOME

'The Glorious Twelfth, 1939! On that day my husband and I were married and set off on our honeymoon in Wales in an Austin 7 car, knowing like most other Britons that the days of peace were numbered.

We returned home to the cottage in Kilndown, near Goudhurst. We had cleaned and scrubbed it clean and furnished it with love and care. Imagine then my surprise when a friend, who had become the Billeting Officer, approached me and said, "You've got three bedrooms, I've put you down for some evacuee children." Truth to tell I was a little afraid of her and felt that there was little I could do to object.

On 3rd September, the blow fell and we were at war. Immediately the plans made by the government of the day to evacuate children from the big cities went into action. We in Kent of course were to look after children from London.

So it was that I, a bride of only a few weeks, who had hardly got used to looking after myself and husband, went to the village hall to meet my guests. There were three! A brother and sister, Reggie aged eight and Patty aged seven. Then there was Marie, aged six. There she was, certainly far from clean, with long gingery coloured hair – also far from clean!

The children settled down quite quickly really, as children do. My lovely new home lost a little of its sparkle. I cooked for us all on the kitchen range. Gradually everything became in short supply and we were rationed with coal. I read in the newspaper of a good way to keep the fire going. I kept a galvanised bucket into which I put coal dust (there always seemed a lot of that). Whenever I made tea, the leaves were carefully dried and put into the bucket. Then after mixing, I made little parcels wrapped in newspaper. They were a bit smelly when they burned, but did the job and we all felt that we were helping the war effort.

Because there was such an influx of children into the village, the school had to institute a system of shifts. Some went to school in the morning and others in the afternoon. Reggie and Patty weren't too difficult to look after, but Marie was a little pickle. She fell in the lake, she had accidents with her clothes, and one day when we were out walking I noticed that her feet and legs were not moving normally and she kept falling over. I looked at her feet when we got home and found that the poor little scrap had grown out of her shoes which were by then several sizes too small. I wrote to her mother and eventually a new pair of shoes arrived. She stayed with me for some time, but Patty and Reggie's mother went to live at Yalding with a relative, and so of course they went too.

By late 1940 the Battle of Britain was at its height and most of the children left to go home. Then I was sent two Land Army Girls who worked in the Timber Corps at Bedgebury. This was very hard work, but very important because the wood which they were cutting was for pit props. Of course all our factories were powered by coal, and so the mining was of first class importance. One of the girls came from Northumberland and the other from Brighton. The girl from Brighton used to go home on leave sometimes, and when she came back there was always a little something for the larder because her father was a butcher. What luxury, a few extra sausages, perhaps a marrow bone, all to supplement the one shilling and twopence worth of meat which we got per person per week.'

A VERY ORDINARY LOCATION

'For many years right in the middle of the strawberry fields of Sutton Valence there was an Air Ministry Communications Station. My father was stationed there from 1937 until it closed in 1957. It was a very ordinary location, its high radio masts being its only obvious feature, in which a very interesting job was being carried out 24 hours a day – listening to and transmitting messages to and from all parts of the world. The entrance was a large farm gate with a hut just inside which was the "gatehouse". Further up the track, in the middle of a field, was another hut they called the "cabin". This had wireless sets along the sides. All information was exchanged in morse code which was just like a second language to them all.

There were about 35 airmen working there and at one time during the war 24 WAAFS came to release some of the men for duties elsewhere. They all worked shifts, midnight to 6 am, 6 am to 4 pm, 4 pm to midnight. Many of the WAAFS lodged with the airmen's families. My father would come home in the early hours to find our floor full of sleeping people and lucky to find himself a space. When he came off duty in the early morning he would sometimes have a rabbit, caught in the field, to supplement the meat ration. After the war the same job was done with the airmen changing into civvies but basically carrying on as before until 1957 when the station was closed and everyone went to larger establishments which had better facilities, but not the special character of Sutton Valence.'

THE HOME GUARD

'The Home Guard at Tonbridge used to hold exercises against the Army on Sundays. One day, I was coming back from church and saw a Home Guard man going into a public house. A man asked him what he thought he was doing. He replied he was dead so it didn't matter!'

'As my husband was blind in one eye he could not serve in the forces. He was a builder on bomb damage work in Maidstone. At first there was no first aid in East Peckham where we lived, and he joined a group of volunteers. Later he transferred to the Home Guard. Four of five of them guarded the Bainbridges every night, and on Sunday mornings they had to dig trenches along the river – all felt hard done by as "the powers that be" said they were in the wrong place and more had to be dug, a good way, it was felt, of getting all that were needed.

Local pubs ran pig clubs. The men took turns feeding and keeping the animals clean and all swill and kitchen waste was saved for food. When the pig was large enough it was butchered and the members of the club shared the meat.'

I JOINED THE LAND ARMY

'My memories are as a Londoner who came to Kent as a land girl. My first job was on a milk round in Beckenham in February 1941, delivering quarts of milk with a tricycle like the one the Wall's ice cream man used! Finding the work too heavy on the snow and icy roads, I was transferred to a farm in the Weald to learn milking by hand and the care of a herd of cows. Then it was on to another milk round, this time with a horse and float. First catch your horse, groom it, feed it and harness it, then load up with milk for a daily trot round the Bat and Ball gas works in Sevenoaks. It was not my idea of helping the war effort and eventually I came to Tenterden to a small mixed farm, to look after a dozen cows and work on the land between times.

Work was long and hard, starting at 6 am and finishing at 5 pm, with a half day on Wednesdays and a weekend off every three weeks. I had to get a special pass if I wanted to go home to London as Tenterden was in a restricted area. All for £2 10s a week plus a pint of free milk – £1 for my landlady, £1 for spending and ten shillings for saving. To supplement my wages I went primrosing in the spring, bunching them up in the evenings and putting them on the rail for the London markets. If I was lucky, sixpence a dozen bunches was a good return.

Nearly all the work on the farm was done by hand, with three men, an old horse and a secondhand tractor. Besides corn there was the hop garden, soft fruits, potatoes, kale and mangolds for the cattle. During haymaking and harvesting we worked till dark when the weather was fine, hand loading on the horse-drawn carts. I was spared hop picking owing to looking after the cows, so enjoyed apple picking in the orchard with the help of some very jolly workers from London.

Nancy Arthur and the threshing gang. Land Army girls kept food production high during the war.

My recreation was the cinema and sixpenny hops, dances arranged in the town hall on Saturday nights for all members of the forces. Tenterden during the war was a quiet town. All the shops were privately owned, the baker baking his own bread and cakes, the butcher slaughtering his own meat, a fish shop, two family grocers with tins of biscuits on display, cereals and sugar measured into blue packets, and cheese, bacon and ham sliced to order. At the end of the town was a good old fashioned general store selling men's and women's clothing, footwear, millinery, haberdashery, furniture, china and glassware and groceries. Overhead was the pulley cash dispenser that whizzed to and fro to the closed-in cash desk.

Sheep and cattle were driven on foot through the High Street to the market on fair days, when all the pubs did a good trade. One of note was The Cellars, which was a typical farmer's pub in a basement cellar with barrels and stools to sit on, beer being drawn from barrels in the corner. The low ceiling was thick with dusty billetdoux, notes, cards and foreign money from visiting servicemen and holidaymakers.

My most impressive memory of those years is of the glittering formation of Flying Fortresses going out to the Continent early in the morning and straggling back in twos and threes later in the day. Also the dogfights overhead as we loaded the corn, and later the terror of the flying bombs being intercepted by the valiant Spitfires. All in all a very memorable time!'

'I left school in 1939 and went to help my father on my grandfather's farm. At 17½, in 1942, I joined the Land Army as I enjoyed being in the open air. I was sent to a fruit and arable farm, initially as a tractor driver. Altogether there were eleven land girls, German and Italian prisoners of war and conscientious objectors working together.

In 1944, for working a 52 hour week, we were paid £2 8s 11½d with many hours overtime for little extra money. We had to pay £1 a week for our lodgings. Our jobs included spraying, picking and carrying fruit, cultivating, ploughing, spreading manure, threshing, planting cabbages and numerous other things.

It wasn't very pleasant driving a tractor in 1944 when doodlebugs were coming over, you couldn't hear them so you had to try and watch the sky and be ready to dive under the tractor, making sure you had your gas mask and tin helmet with you.

Long working hours and nights in the air raid shelter did not leave much time for socialising. We did have occasional get-togethers with land girls from other farms. It was the comradeship during the war years that helped you through. One highlight was a "day out" at Allington near Maidstone, with competitions for everyone doing farm work. I remember taking part in the ploughing (I won a certificate) and cabbage planting – what a back aching job that was!'

'When war broke out I lived in Hayes. My parents had a shop and I remember standing outside when the siren sounded to see when the planes were coming! I joined the Land Army in 1941 and I had my month's training on a farm on the Weald. I was up at five o'clock to fetch the cows in. It is hard trying to find cows in the dark, and I learned quickly that Jersey cows are very difficult to milk, so I opted out and decided to work in the dairy. The water was heated by steam and all the milk bottles were washed by hand. We did have a machine to fill the bottles, but the cardboard tops were put on by hand. One day while I was washing the milk bottles, the foreman came in and said: "What will you say when people ask you what you did during the war?" Little did I think then that I would be writing it down now.

After my training I worked on a milk round in Sevenoaks. I had a horse and float – she was a lovely horse and knew every stop on the round. I felt like Boadicea when I was standing on the float! When the manpower got shorter the land girls were taken off the milk rounds and then I went threshing. That is very heavy, dirty work but I enjoyed it. The first day I was halfway up the straw stack pitching to the top and there was a man below pitching to me, as fast as he could go. I didn't realise that he was trying me out so I kept up the same pace. I had blisters on my hands and I soon learned that the way to slow him down was simply to let the bale of straw fall back on him!

After three years I had an accident and lost my leg in the threshing machine, so I was discharged in September 1944. I really enjoyed those years moving from farm to farm and meeting different people.'

A CHILD'S WAR

Children soon came to accept war and its restrictions as part of life, even taking the bombing and destruction in their stride. Some children endured the trauma of evacuation away from family and friends, but often found compensations in a new way of life.

JUST IN CASE

'After a rather tranquil existence there seemed to be a lot of unusual things happening in Dartford.

One day the teacher said we were to have lessons in our own homes and a few days later my mother said I was to sit ready at the dining table and wait for the teacher to arrive. When she came there were three little girls with her and she directed them to the chairs that Mother had put ready for them. I cannot recall what lessons we had, only that it seemed very strange but fun. A few days later we were told to report back to the school on the following day ready for lessons there once again. We were not told why we had had lessons at home. I found out years later that it was so blackout could be installed.

Then another day there was a knock at the door of our home and there was a man standing there who lived further down the road. He had come with our gas masks and was to make sure that they fitted correctly. I was only seven at the time and when I saw my mask, I was rather frightened as I had never seen one before; they did not look very nice. However, after my mother had tried her one on and had a good laugh which made the eyepiece steam up and made me laugh too, I put mine on as the man had told us to. I thought I looked very funny in it and was glad when the man said we could take them off. He said that we must carry the masks with us wherever we went "just in case". Mother made some covers for the cardboard boxes in which the masks were placed as she thought the cardboard was not very watertight and she also put a shoulder strap on the covers so that we could carry them more easily. When I asked why we had to have the masks she said "just in case" too.

One day Father did a strange thing. He dug a big hole in the garden and put three pieces of corrugated iron sheeting in it, then he prepared and poured liquid cement into the bottom of the hole. When I asked what it was going to be, he said a shelter. I wondered why we needed a shelter, if it rained we could go indoors – he said it was not that sort of shelter; this one was "just in case". There was that phrase again but no one enlightened me. Whatever it was never seemed to come about.

Then father did another strange thing, he dug up the lawn he had so carefully sown earlier that year – he was going to dig for victory he said. I did not know what victory was and wondered was it treasure or a person. When we were staying in London one time my mother had shown me a statue of Queen Victoria and I think I had visions of the Queen being who he was digging for.

Mother gave me a card one day and said I was to carry it everywhere I went. "Like the gas masks?" I said. "Yes, and do not let anyone else have it, it has details of your name and address on it", and then she said, "just in case you get lost" and then I knew what that phrase meant at long last (or thought I did). I thought it was a good idea as I had once or twice got lost but I always knew the way home. It was a blue coloured card called an Identity Card. Now we had the blackout I thought I might not be able to find my way home if I got lost in the dark.

Then one Sunday when I was lying about in the garden feeling rather bored I asked Mother if I could get my bike out and go over to the field to play. She said I might go but not for long as it was nearing our dinner time. I had just been cycling round some partially completed houses in the field when a lot of hooters started up, then a man rushed into the field waving his arms about and shouting, "The war has started and bombs will be dropping. Go home, go home." We did not know what a war was but we were so alarmed by the man that we dropped our bikes and ran to our homes. I ran all the way, it was not very far – just up the road and round the corner – but being an asthmatic I was not supposed to run and I arrived at the back door quite out of breath. When I nearly fell into the living room I was hushed quiet, although I could not have spoken anyway being too breathless. The wireless was on and someone was talking about the war having started – so my parents knew too, but then they had already lived through one war and knew what might come in the near future.

In May 1940 I was told to get ready as we were going to see one of my aunts. We usually went for the day on the train so I did not ask any questions until we got to the station and saw a lot of little children with labels attached to their coats and bundles in their hands. One or two grown-ups seemed to be with them and a lot of the children were crying. When asked, my mother said they were going on a sort of holiday but they would have lessons too. I found that I too was on that sort of holiday when my mother left me with my aunt at the end of the evening and I had to understand that

Mother was going home to be with Father while I stayed there for a while.

My mother had been a book-keeper when she was single but upon marrying had had to give up her job because it was considered that married women should be at home to look after their husbands and families. After the war started and I had been evacuated Mother was "called up" to do a job as a civil servant. She worked as a clerk in the local women's employment bureau and then in the evening she fire-watched (to see if any bombs fell on the town, which started fires).

My father was deferred call up as by the time the war started he had become chief cashier at the factory where he was employed. In the evenings he spent his time in the Home Guard on manoeuvres in the Dartford marshes, or learning first aid, morse code, signals and such. He had a uniform and tin hat as well as his gas mask. If he had a weekend off and Mother could get the time off too they would come to see me at Windsor where I was staying with my father's sister "for the duration". Father would cycle all the way after work on a Friday evening while Mother came by train.

In 1943 I returned home because there were rumours of the war ending and my mother had got fed up with me being away during my formative years. It seemed no time at all before the doodlebugs started flying overhead and one evening when the air raid siren had sounded and we had gone into the shelter Mother and I were really afraid when one of them stopped over our garden but then it started up again and came down on a house near the junction of Shepherds Lane and Princes Road. One person was killed. When we got indoors again after the all clear went we found that the explosion had caused some ceiling plaster to fall down on the pillows of my parents' bed just where their heads would have been if they had stayed in bed. Discussing the day afterwards, we found that we had both prayed hard that evening, particularly as my father would persist in standing outside the shelter watching the night sky.

Of course, by this time I had realised why we had to carry our gas masks and identity cards about with us, "just in case" we were killed in the bombing so we could be identified easily or if there was a gas attack. Fortunately in the latter case there never was in this locality so I did not have to wear my mask. One day I did see a man with blood on his face when a house had been demolished by a doodlebug. I had been attending a friend's birthday party when the air raid siren went off and her aunt, with whom she was staying, sent all the guests home as she did not want to be responsible for them. Fortunately I had gone by bike so was able to get home fairly quickly.

Sometimes at the Dartford West County Modern School (as it was then called) if an air raid commenced while we were having our last lesson before dinner time, we would have our dinner in the air raid shelter, which was a long underground room with forms in it on which the pupils sat. The catering staff brought in cutlery and huge pans of minced meat, potatoes and boiled cabbage which was followed by stewed fruit and custard, and ladled it out into large soup dishes which the teachers handed to us. I think we had to eat with the dish balanced on our laps as I don't think there were any tables. After the meal we would sit and sing the popular wartime songs; if the raid went on a long time then we would go through the whole range of songs again.'

NO CHOICE

'My arrival in this world on the 31st December 1937 must make me one of the last claimants for a Coronation mug, which I received and still treasure! Of course the memory of this is a folk one and it can honestly be said that all my earliest memories are of "the war". I knew no life before and until I was seven or eight I knew no other. Silence from children during the six o'clock news was absolute, although this meant nothing to me at first.

Our lives had very small parameters indeed. In fact we hardly went anywhere. My father, through a childhood injury, stayed at home, but this did not prevent him working long hours as a carpenter/joiner (building pontoon bridges I understand), and in the evenings joining a band of ageing schoolmasters as a member of the Home Guard in and around Coxheath and Tovil. Actually he was wounded whilst on this service by a man who stabbed him in the behind with a bayonet whilst going through a hedge. "Sorry, mate" he said, "I didn't know it was so sharp!"

On reflection the theme of our lives in those days was No Choice. My grandmother queued up in Maidstone for fish, I'm almost certain it was either cod or herrings. Fruit and vegetables were only those grown in the garden. We traded scraps for eggs, which were stored in waterglass in a big metal crock in the larder. We had no choice of travel. I went nowhere at all except to visit my grandmothers who both lived in central Maidstone, although I have no memory of getting there, but I suspect we walked. Once I did make a bus journey to Gillingham Strand. However, even though the only sweets we had were the occasional lump of boiling misshapes from Sharp's factory I still grew up with poor teeth.

Choice did enter my life when it came for me to start school. My mother refused to send me to the damp Victorian infants department of Loose School and instead I went to a brand new infants school in Park Way. It was then called Plains Avenue and everything was

213

delightful. My mother walked me there and back every day, pushing my sister in her pram, and my dinner was carried in a little wicker basket. The teacher boiled an egg for us at lunch time and her housekeeper brought her lunch in a wonderful plate with a hot water compartment underneath. This school was in vast contrast to the old Victorian school at Thurnham, with outside toilets and temporary classrooms, in which I spent most of my teaching career. Some children came across the "plains" where soft fruit grew all the way from the wilds of Willington Street! We collected ship halfpennies, sang songs in the shelters and at the end of the war were allowed to scratch the tape from the windows.

Perhaps there was some excitement – evacuees from Plumstead in London and soldiers billeted on us from what was whispered to to be the intelligence service. Sad to say we slept through the incendiary bomb's arrival in a neighbour's bungalow but I did visit the scene and admired the scorched sofa. Hiding under a hedge in the Loose Road whilst a doodlebug landed in Lancet Lane was quite exciting, and in the evening we went round to my sister's godmother's residence to admire her windowless house. There even exists a rare photograph of me winning a prize dressed as a landgirl – photographs were so small in those days!

In 1942 I developed pneumonia and spent about five weeks in the West Kent Hospital. This was traumatic for a four to five year old. The regime was harsh and so were the lights! Ward sisters crackled in starched uniforms – Sister Jackson refused me the ritual sweet and I hated her. We sang very rude songs indeed! I fell in love with the boy in the next bed who had broken a leg falling out of a Kentish cobnut tree, somewhere in the Weald. Being treated by M and B tablets, an early form of antibiotics, is about the only thing I have in common with Winston Churchill. On being released from hospital I had to be pushed in a Suncar, a heavy form of pushchair, vastly different from my grandson's buggy!

After the war my horizons began to broaden. Our first holiday was to a boarding house in Broadstairs. We sent a truck, via Carter Paterson, to await our arrival. Portions of food were very small and on the way to the beach we bought buns to fortify us. Those were the golden years; trolley buses crackling in frosty weather, making camps in the woods, little traffic on the roads, riding bikes around Sutton Valence and going no-handed down the middle of the road, playing complicated skipping games and bouncing balls against the wall of the house. The only thing that I envy about the modern child's life is their easy access to wonderfully written and illustrated books and even so in 1948 I thought the Dimsie books were wonderful!'

HAPPY DAYS

'For the first ten years of my life I lived in Middlesex but in 1941 with my mother, sister and brother returned to the cottage where I was born at Biddenden, moving in to live with my grandparents, a cousin, and later an aunt joined us. So there were eight of us living in a three bedroom cottage (one of the bedrooms being on the second floor), with a "front" room in which we lived, a kitchen, pantry and porch. Electricity had been installed but no running water. For drinking, cooking and cleaning teeth the water was collected by Grandad from the farmhouse, it having been in the pantry. Water for washing oneself was rainwater collected in a big butt, one having to break the ice on it in winter. Water for washing clothes was collected from a pond across the road from the cottage. The pond had a "dipping board" on which one walked out a few feet over the water to make it easier to fill the pails.

Not having running water there was no indoor toilet, this being in a little building halfway down the back garden. Being war-time one was not able to have a decent light to find one's way along the Bethersden marble path in the winter. If it was dark I never shut the door because I wanted to be able to see if there was anyone about in the garden. I did not want to get a shock opening the door and finding someone, maybe a German, there.

Coupons were needed when buying clothes and children over a certain size were given additional clothing coupons. The headmaster measured our height and feet with what must have been a magic rule as I qualified for extra clothing coupons even though I only took size three shoes when my feet were fully grown.

Soldiers were stationed on the farm for a short time, and one day gave us some of their tinned peaches, delicious. Coming home from school one afternoon we were startled by armed soldiers on manoeuvres lying in the long grass along the roadside.

We schoolchildren contributed to the war effort by knitting socks for servicemen, picking rose hips for syrup, and collecting books. According to the number of books collected one was made a corporal, sergeant, etc. We also picked blackberries and other fruit for the school canteen. We took part in the village concerts held to raise money for Navy Week etc, the school choir opening the proceedings. On these occasions we would walk home from school, have tea, put on our Sunday best and walk back to the village hall for the concert.

It was whilst walking home from one of these concerts that we saw one of the first doodlebugs. During the doodlebug era some of the children were evacuated, and my grandmother and cousin went to live with a relative out of the danger zone. One evening I saw a doodlebug heading for our cottage so placed a pillow over the heads of my sleeping brother and sister to protect them , but the doodlebug turned and landed near to where I now live, killing the boy next door. While the doodlebugs were terrorising the country children took turns in being on duty in the playground listening out for their drone and on hearing one coming rang a bell, when the school took to the shelters. If we heard one coming when walking to or from school we used to get in a ditch.

On Sundays we attended the Strict Baptist chapel in the morning, went to Sunday school in Frittenden in the afternoons, and sometimes in the summer went to chapel at Worsenden in the evening. Grandad was a lay preacher but he did not have to walk, having a bicycle with a smelly carbide lamp. A lot of cottages had stands on the grass verge on which to lean bicycles. These were simple affairs made with three pieces of wood.

The main social event of the year for us children was the church garden fête. This took place in the garden of the rectory on a Wednesday afternoon, and we were allowed out of school early so we could join in the fun. Because of the war there were no Sunday school outings to the seaside, but instead we had games in a field followed by tea and a small gift. At Christmas we had a party and also entertained parents with recitations.

On Easter Monday we would collect bread and cocoa from the Old Workhouse. The Biddenden Maids, Siamese twins joined at the hips and shoulders who died aged 34 years in 1100, had left lands to the parish the proceeds from which were to be spent providing bread and cheese to the poor at Easter. During the war cocoa was substituted for the cheese which was rationed. The loaves were twice the size of a normal loaf.

On an excursion to Ashford we were stopped by a policeman at the station and asked for our identity cards. I was very worried because I did not have mine. During the war the distance one could travel was restricted. To get to Ashford we would catch a train on the Kent and East Sussex line at Frittenden Road to Headcorn where we would catch a train on the South Eastern line. One could also get to Tenterden on the K&ES line or go by bus.

We used the K&ES train as a clock. Out playing in the fields we knew it was time to go home for dinner when we heard the train go by. We were very fortunate in that we were allowed the run of the farm, riding on the running board of the farmer's old car, or sitting on its roof with our legs dangling through the sun roof, and at harvesting and haymaking being allowed to drive the tractor in the fields. A horse was still being used on the farm which my grandad looked after. Though there was a war on they were, in the main, happy days.'

MEMORIES

'My sixth birthday, about a dozen children attending the party, the siren goes – Mother drops the tea caddy and herds us into the centre of the house and takes our minds off the war by producing some cream biscuits. Where she had them hidden and for how long I know not and at the time never gave it a thought! There is a crash and the house shakes – we play games until the all clear sounds when we file back to the dining room for tea, some broken windows and daylight between the flat roof and the walls but my candles are still upright on the cake!

Sugar coated butter balls for a sore throat but it's war-time and rationing is in force! Father kept bees which produced honey; he was a chemist and in those days they made their own cough syrups for which they received extra sugar so Father used the sugar for feeding the bees (and for the butter balls!) and the honey for the cough syrup. The butter? Well, the grocer next door was a bachelor and he loved steamed puddings so Mother used to put a large portion of pudding on the wall and from time to time it was exchanged for half a pound of butter.

Standing at the spare bedroom window fascinated as a V2 bomb went past on fire, totally unaware of the danger. It came down at the end of the village, fortunately in a field.

Sitting at Sunday lunch as a German plane flew straight down our drive (or so it appeared), low enough to see the pilot's face, and headed for the gasworks two miles away.

The extra "uncles" that came from the nearby barrage balloon site for weekly baths and some home cooking.'

BABY'S GAS MASK

'When I was nine years old a baby sister arrived at home. But there was a problem. We had all been given horrible black rubber gas masks and I worried how such a tiny thing could wear such a contraption. I came home from school one day to find the answer. A huge box had been delivered which contained a peculiar globe thing which we were to put the baby in.

Happily, we never had to use it. When we went on the bus to town, we could never have taken it with us. When my little sister was toddling, it was swapped for a mask with a Mickey Mouse face. I thought I should like a Walt Disney mask too, but I was much too old!'

217

PLENTY TO DO

'There seemed to be plenty of things of do in Strood, going to the pictures about three times a week, sometimes four. As a cadet with the St John Ambulance I was involved in voluntary work which included helping at a day nursery, washing up at St Bart's Hospital and the YWCA. At that time the St John's meetings were sometimes held in Rochester Museum and to get to the meeting room we had to go through the stuffed birds section; this was of course in the dark. On one occasion we were inspected by Lady Mountbatten and another time by Princess Marina of Kent.

There were large numbers of the armed forces in the area. The sight of hundreds of sailors with their little brown weekend cases streaming up Military Road towards the Chatham railway station on Friday afternoons had to be seen to be believed. The daily exodus of the dockyard workers who all seemed to ride bicycles was also a sight we took for granted. From time to time foreign vessels were in the dockyard and a stroll through the Victoria Gardens on a Sunday would reveal which nations were actually in port. Of course language was a problem but could be overcome. Station Road school was occupied by Italian POWs and they were allowed a certain amount of freedom. They spent a lot of time sitting on the school wall and they would greet passers by with a "Good morning" or "Good evening" either in English or Italian. At the end of the war the German POWs replaced the Italians until they were repatriated.

In spite of the rationing I have no recollection of actually being hungry though some of our food involved ingenuity. One thing I remember especially is mashing parships and adding banana flavouring and putting this in sandwiches. Actually it didn't taste too bad! One day a week I was despatched complete with basins to the British Canteen in the old Union building to collect our dinner. It always seemed to be some kind of stew and had loads of pearl barley.

My father was considered too old for active service and he worked for the Pool Petroleum. He worked very long hours and he was on the fire-watching rota, but it seemed to be my mother that handed over to the next person, sometimes in the middle of the night.

In spite of being very close to a railway junction and the dockyard being just across the river, it wasn't until 1944 that we became a victim of a bombing raid. Our house was badly damaged, but we were able to live downstairs, although I had to go and stay with my sister. My grandfather who was in his nineties had to go into hospital, but he had only had a few cuts in spite of being covered in plaster as he lay in bed. As soon as it got daylight I walked to Rochester to tell my sister, but it wasn't until I reached her that I realised that I had walked the two miles looking absolutely filthy with plaster in my hair. I didn't have to tell her what had happened!'

WE DIDN'T FEEL DEPRIVED

'Back in 1944 there was just as much obsession with the past as there is today. The older generation then would get very nostalgic over, of all things, food. Endless lip-smacking, eloquent debates went on about the texture, flavour, taste, smell of such mysterious objects as a "nice piece of ham", or "steak and chips". These ramblings meant absolutely nothing to us children who had known only basic ration book food. Not that we felt in any way deprived, just the contrary, we considered ourselves superior to those who found it so difficult to adjust to the austerity of war time rationing.

So what of war torn Swanley of the 1940s? The highlights were the convoys of Belgian troops to be supplied with water, but even better the convoys of American troops who would shower us with sweets. As children we quickly learnt the art of begging: "Got any gum, chum?"

Of course there were air raids, preceded by the siren's wail and concluded by the "all clear". Excitement is all that can be remembered, not fear. We must had have our share of terror, but nothing of it remains. There was the memory of the direct hit by an incendiary bomb on the wooden barn that stabled the milkman's horse. That upset us because of the effect it had on my sisters. Us boys could not wait for the following morning to go out and gather up all the chunks of shrapnel we could find and deliver for recycling. The war did not go on forever and at the celebration street party I think for the first and last time in my life I ate junket, then another, then another, then another, until I was violently sick.

Another memory connected with eating was that the girl across the road refused to take her cod liver oil, so as it was good for you, I was given a double dose! You can hold a grudge for 50 years!'

IT MEANT LITTLE TO ME

'I lived with my parents, grandmother, brother and sister both older than me on a 13 acre smallholding, near to ʌne North Pole Pub, between East Malling and Wateringbury. At the back of our land was the Barming Woods and to the front was the West Malling aerodrome which played quite an important part in the Battle of Britain.

I was five years old when war was declared so the actual meaning of war and all its implications meant little to me at that age.

I can remember my family excavating a dug-out near to our house

219

Wherever we went, our gas masks went too – four of them stowed in Mother's basket on a family visit to Coxheath in 1940.

that we would all run to when the air raid siren sounded. Indoors in our front room we had a Morrison shelter. This was like a large metal table to which wire mesh sides could be attached. My mother made up two beds in this shelter for my sister and I. If we were restless at night and turned over too near to the metal frame we got a very rude awakening. The top of the shelter made a lovely surface for our games of table tennis!

Sometimes my brother, sister and I were in the dug-out on our own and I suppose got rather bored and wanted to see the action going on above, so we would leave the dug-out and watch the "dog fights" and puffs of smoke left by the exploded shells in the sky. During some raids we became quite daring and unbeknown to our parents (I cannot think how!) we would climb up one of the oak trees at the back of our land as high as we could, to get the best view and watch the aeroplanes take off and land at the airfield. My brother lowered us down from the branches by holding our hands until our feet touched the branch below. My mother never knew about this until many years after. We often picked up empty shell cases and shrapnel after the raids.'

OUR LIVES WERE UNFETTERED

'During the early war years, life as a child in Tonbridge was curiously unfettered provided one obeyed the general edict of coming home "immediately you hear the siren".

220

We played topical war games in the woods and hop fields which surrounded the Cage Green area. Being the only girl in the group usually meant that I was invariably the forgotten hostage when the siren sounded. When they eventually came back for me there were certain bribes to stop me "telling Mum" such as promising I could bat when they played cricket. (Girls were usually only allowed to field in those days except on the rarest occasions.)

In summer, we used to fish in an area called the Winklebarge, which sounds more like a pub than a pond. To reach it, we had to cross a field containing a fearsome solitary Hereford bull who used to chase us regularly. One day, I was particularly reluctant until my older brother said reassuringly, "It's quite safe, they've taken the bulls in for milking." Naïvely, I marched with great confidence across the field which was strangely deserted. I fear the Hereford had an appointment with the butcher!

One afternoon during the war, a pilotless Flying Fortress made a cushioned crash landing on trees in the Trench Wood area. As the plane was left unguarded later, the local boys decided to help themselves to souvenirs. To my mother's horror, my brother arrived home in the evening complete with a dozen live shells in a cake box. Announcing that they must be taken to the police immediately, my mother walked with grim determination to the local hostelry The Greyhound to deliver my brother's booty in its flimsy container to the local special constable. I vividly remember whispering fearfully as I ran to keep up with her, "Don't drop them Mummy, will you?"'

BULLETS IN THE HOPS

'We always went hop picking to Enfield's, Goddards Green. When an air raid started there were trenches at the side of the hop garden for us to get into, but most times, if the planes were not near we would go on picking. One day a German fighter took us by surprise. My dad was with us this day and I remember him throwing me to the ground, shielding me as the bullets flew in all directions.'

'It was difficult to get pickers from London during the Battle of Britain. We even had a circus artist who entertained us by walking on the high wire above the hop field. The ditches around the fields had to be dug deeper so we could dive into them when the siren went. When the air raid was over it was back to the picking. Mum used to pack food for us to take to the hop garden – I had four brothers so a lot of food had to be packed, and every day Mum had to make a Kilner jar full of custard just for Dad!

At Marden, where my grandmother lived in the middle of the village, they were able to pick hops without going to the hop garden, because the farmer took the hops to the pickers in the village.'

TOYS WERE SCARCE

'The war made a considerable impact on my childhood and my first term at school coincided with the commencement of the war in September 1939. First priority was safety – of keeping together, if possible, to face whatever was to happen to us all. My father had to go away and Mother was left to cope alone with the full responsibility of home, small daughter and supporting ageing parents several miles away. Just the thought of coping with "dad's duties" in the home must have been very daunting to my gentle mother, as women still led a very protected role – worrying for my father's safety and no doubt longing that the war could soon be over and life return to normal with Dad at the helm as decision maker and protector. Cope she did, though, and very well, as much of the awareness of the war went over my head and I can still recall a happy childhood with sunny days and simple pleasures such as a picnic, playing with my dolls etc.

Toys must have been scarce because factories went over to making armaments. I remember one very sad occasion when several of my best toys, including a much loved teddy and a rubber baby doll, were stolen. I had left them in the back garden under the shelter of a verandah and had gone on an errand to post a letter for Mother. They were taken by a tramp with a sack. I cried myself to sleep that night and for many days after as they could not be replaced.

I can remember "doing my bit" in making a big hole in the garden. This was for the air raid shelter. When the hole was deep enough and the shelter was up, we covered it with some of the earth and planted marrow seeds on top. Going down into the shelter was not very pleasant. It smelt musty and the bedding felt damp and cold. We had a candle for light and just stayed there waiting and listening until the all clear sounded. My mother used to sing to me as we tried to get some rest.

One day the siren sounded just as we were starting our tea – a special treat that day of shrimps and bread and butter. We took it all with us and sat in the half light taking off the shells. Another day the siren sounded just as Mother was washing my hair, which was long, thick and curly. The shampoo was still in it but we had to run and it dried sticky and full of tangles.

We all had gas masks, which we were expected to carry at all times. They doubled as a lunch box for school and the "tuck" used to taste slightly of rubber I seem to recall.'

'Many of our lessons at Maidstone Girls' Grammar School were taken sitting on benches in the underground shelters which had been dug into the playground and surrounding grassy banks. All were numbered and each form knew exactly where to go when the air raid sirens wailed. We all had our free third of a pint of milk, sucked through a straw. Halfpenny and penny currant buns and penny pink-iced ones were available on long wooden trays. At the beginning of each week we bought as many dinner tickets as we required. They were sixpence each.

School games consisted of netball and hockey in winter and tennis, stoolball or rounders in the summer. Only those who showed good potential as tennis players were allowed to play due to the shortage of tennis balls.

As a family we didn't have an air raid shelter. My parents appeared not to be too afraid and my sister and I resorted to lying in the cupboard under the stairs during bad raids. When there was a prolonged spell of raids my sister and I occasionally went down our neighbour's Anderson shelter which they shared with their other neighbours. It was quite snug down there with two tier bunk beds, an oil stove and primus stove on which to heat water for cups of tea and soup. It smelt a bit earthy but then we were four or five steps down and the roof was piled high with soil.

The enemy planes would sometimes follow the line of the London Road to London and being so close to West Malling and Detling aerodromes we had an exciting time watching the "dog fights" and identifying the planes. There were always plenty of barrage balloons in evidence on Wrotham Hill and we would watch the enemy get through or get caught by fighters or ack-ack fire. At night when the clouds were low the roar of enemy bombers overhead would be amplified and we'd watch the searchlights trying to spot them.

We kept 20 to 30 rabbits as pets and for pocket money, selling them at six weeks in Maidstone market for ninepence to two shillings each. Many was the time we put the sack of rabbits' food (weed collected from neighbours' gardens) over our head as protection from the shrapnel, which often showered down around us. After any raid we would hunt for shrapnel souvenirs.

Once a German fighter was brought down in the field above Allington Way and we rushed over hoping to find someone in the cockpit but the pilot had bailed out. One night an enemy bomber crashed in Barming Woods, fortunately causing no damage. A stick of bombs fell harmlessly in the fields 300 yards from our house, shaking us all and the house, dislodging a few bricks and bringing down some plaster from the kitchen ceiling. A window or two cracked but didn't break, thanks perhaps to all the sticky tape which we had criss-crossed over them for just such an occasion.

My friend wasn't so fortunate on her fifteenth birthday on 18th June 1944. A birthday party had been arranged and food was ready in the dining room, which had casement windows leading to a glass verandah outside. Just before her friends were due to arrive a doodlebug fell nearby, shattering many windows and the verandah. Quickly the food was transferred to another room and the party proceeded.

Army manoeuvres were fun days, with masses of troops in camouflage and with blackened faces, some "friend" and others "foe". We fraternised with all and were sworn to secrecy not to give away strategic positions. We never had any trouble with the army. They were always polite, asked for permission if they had to intrude upon your land and we were as safe as being with our friends.

We travelled everywhere on our bicycles; up to the hills for picnics and down through the Weald. Not a signpost in sight to guide us on our way. We often rode six abreast and blushed at the whistles received when passed by convoys of trucks or tanks.

Father was an air raid warden (ARP) and had his "W" helmet, waterproof cape, gas mask in a hessian bag and whistle. This he blew when the sirens sounded. He shared the duty with a friend about once a week and when not patrolling the streets looking for chinks of light through the blackout, or fire bombs, they were able to sleep on lilos on the kitchen floor of their chief warden's house.

Every week my parents would call on local houses and the Sir Thomas Wyatt Inn and sell stamps for National Savings. Another lady had a similar weekly routine but collected pennies for the Red Cross.

Entertainment was provided by the Sheila Wilcox School of Dancing. They would put on an excellent pantomime-like musical show at Christmas time. On the first or second Christmas after the start of the war, the ARP wardens arranged a fancy dress party for all the local children.

We used to attend the London Road area Social Association, which organised old time dancing, whist and beetle drives, all of which were held in St Nicholas's church, the sanctuary being closed off by large sliding doors.

When peace was announced I remember dancing with lots of happy people in Maidstone and outside the Carlton Cafe watching a large lady dance "Knees Up Mother Brown" with a soldier. At a later Victory Parade, dressed in my Guides uniform, our war hero, handsome fighter pilot Guy Gibson, was on a float just ahead of us. What a thrill!

With rationing post-war, eating out wasn't easy but one could obtain an excellent meal for two shillings at the British Restaurant which was on the site of the Hazlitt Theatre.'

READY FOR EVACUATION

'As war was about to be declared in 1939 the schools in Gravesend were ready for evacuation. My sister was 13 years old and I was ten. Arrangements had been made so that by 3rd September we had already left home.

We were taken to Suffolk on the MV *Royal Daffodil*, each with a small number of belongings and a ration of Ryvita and Fry's Sandwich Chocolate. Our first port of call was Lowestoft where we were accommodated in the cinema for the night. The older children watched a film, the younger ones were settled down in the foyer on bales of straw. From there we were taken by bus to Diss in Norfolk. On arrival at the village school we were greeted by a large group of prospective foster mothers (called "hostesses"). It was a bewildering experience, having never been away from home before and feeling very tired. It had all the excitement of the doors opening at a rummage sale. My sister and I were chosen very quickly (probably because we were small and didn't look as if we would eat very much) but many children and teachers felt rejected. The earth closet at our new home was the greatest shock to us, and my sister spent most of her pocket money using a toilet near the Co-op hairdresser's. After a few weeks we were moved to another house in Diss where the sanitary arrangements were more to our liking but homesickness soon took over and we returned to Gravesend.

We lived on the outskirts of Gravesend with fields at the back of our house and open country extending for about three miles. On the horizon was a small aerodrome, where before the war Amy Johnson had landed. We saw a great deal of activity as the Battle of Britain took place overhead. When the air raids were at their worst my sister and I slept in the cupboard under the stairs, my parents under the oak dining table.'

EVACUATED TO BIDDENDEN

'My memories of Kent start on 1st September 1939 and the declaration of war. I was 14 when war was declared and living at Grove Park. My parents had agreed for my brother and I to be evacuated with my school, Downham Central School for Girls. There was three years difference in our ages but he was to come with me. We had the message at school on Friday 1st September that we were to go but we must have had some indication before that as our cases were there. I was given permission to run home to collect towels and so was able to say goodbye to our mother. We then walked up to Grove Park station in a crocodile. We boarded a train which took us to Headcorn station and then on buses to Biddenden.

It was dark by this time and we were led into the village school where we were given lemonade and biscuits. The village billeting officer gradually sorted out children to hosts. My brother was billeted with six other boys with a lady in the High Street. I was billeted with another girl in my class further up the village through the churchyard. She didn't stay all that long because she became homesick and was also a Roman Catholic and had to go into Tenterden to go to church. I then had another girl join me.

The boys where my brother stayed never looked clean, it was too much for her and they had to wear their shirts several days. My headmistress took me aside to point out that my brother was coming to school in a very dirty condition which was very embarrassing because I knew that he had the clothes but she made them keep them for church and so they grew out of them and they hadn't had much wear. They all had to do jobs before school such as cleaning the school boiler fire and getting the coal in, and so their hands were dirty.

My billet was later changed to a beautiful country house owned by the head of the Red Cross in the village whose husband was a retired country farmer. They had one son and daughter in the air force and one daughter who had her own chickens and sold free range eggs. We had to call her Miss Betty. We were very lucky living there, we had our own sitting room, and we had our meals over the coachhouse which we had to carry up a ladder! Quite a lot of our meals were served in silver tureens. I must admit we were a bit of a handful at that age as the country boys were cheeky. One day during the holidays my friend Christine and I decided we would cycle to Dymchurch. We did ask if we could go for a long cycle ride but didn't say where we intended to go. When we got back that evening we were in great trouble as we had been across the Romney Marshes and it was considered dangerous. We were reported to our headmistress and very nearly expelled!'

THE UNDERRIVER TAPESTRY

'A remarkable reminder of the coming of the first evacuees to Underriver is now in the Sevenoaks Museum: the tapestry illustrating the journey of the evacuees from Camberwell to Underriver. It was the brainchild of Lady Freda Wilson of Catts Cottage (one of the founders of the Bach Choir), designed by Sylvia Ball ("Œuf", the wild life artist) who lived at the Old Forge, and executed by the evacuee girls and the village girls with their help. It was taken and shown to the little princesses Elizabeth and Margaret Rose and Queen Mary, who expressed herself as "very delighted".

One of the girls who worked on the Evacuee Tapestry, Mrs Josephine Moir (nèe Bagley) sent her memories to the Underriver Newssheet in 1989. She was a pupil at St George's School, Camberwell.

"On the 31st August 1939 we had a message from the school to say the evacuation of the children from the school was to be the next day, 1st September. We had to be at the school at nine o'clock. It was quite exciting for me, as that year I didn't go away with the school and it would be like some sort of holiday. I was twelve years old at the time. My parents had a shop which sold cats' and dogs' meat so, as they were busy, my eldest sister took me to the school. I was carrying my small case and gasmask with a label tied to my coat lapel with my name on it. The coaches were there waiting to take us to the station. We arrived at Denmark Hill station and boarded the train. Nobody knew where we were going, but we arrived at Tubs Hill station, Sevenoaks. From there we were taken to the cattle market which was just across the road from the station, we were then put into cattle pens, ten children to a pen. The teachers had tears in their eyes as they looked at some of the little five and six year olds in those pens where the cattle should be, it didn't seem too bad for us older ones. From there we were taken by coach to Underriver, the boys went to Seal nearby.

We were taken into the village hall and each given a small white carrier bag containing a large bar of Cadbury's chocolate, a tin of corned beef, a tin of evaporated milk and a packet of biscuits. People came in and started to take their pick of the children. A lady came in and looked at my friend and I, my friend's name was Olive Sales, she was just three months older than me. We were good friends at school so we did hope that we would be billeted together. This lady asked if she could have us, so we went with her. She told us that she had chosen us as she couldn't afford servants and we would be able to help do the housework. Our bedroom was a very untidy boxroom with a single bed for the two of us to sleep in, she explained that we could help her tidy it up the next day. When we went to bed Olive and I felt near to tears but we did not cry.

Next morning for breakfast, just us two in the kitchen, we had cornflakes with evaporated milk (from the carrier bag) which was awful. After breakfast she put a piece of newspaper on the kitchen table and every bit of silver, brass and copper that she could find. We seemed ages cleaning all this, then we had loads of washing up to do, there were pots and pans and dishes from the meal the night before, then we had to do the hand washbasins, to clean all the bedrooms, then the bath which at that time was something we had never done before. During this time all the other children were going round the village rounding everyone up. We did manage to get out in the afternoon. War was declared on the Sunday morning while we were in church, but during that weekend word had got round about us, although Olive and I never complained.

In the house opposite the church there lived an elderly couple named Mr and Mrs Ascot. They had taken in one of the lady helpers, Mrs Smith, and she asked if we could live there with them, and she gave up her nice comfortable double bed to us and slept on a camp bed in the same room. We were made very welcome, we had very good food and they were very kind to us.

In the village lived a lovely lady named Lady Wilson. She invited us into her house to do some tapestry. It was a long piece of material something like calico, and a picture was drawn on it of us evacuees leaving London and arriving at Underriver. We all embroidered our initials at both ends. We went there sometimes once or twice a week, we would sit in her window seat with it across our laps.

Time went by and we moved twice more, then one day we were both sitting on a fence opposite Underriver House when we heard machine gun fire. When we looked up we saw fighter planes having a dog fight in the sky. We ran to the lodge belonging to Underriver

It's over at last! The Victory party held at Plains Avenue, Maidstone was typical of events all over the county.

House and the man and lady took us in. They were also frightened, they pushed the settee against the wall, tilted it back and the four of us sat underneath.

We both wrote home telling our parents all about it, it all seemed rather exciting to us but our parents were horrified as up to that time London had been very quiet and nothing had happened at all like that. Next we knew my brother-in-law arrived at the house, he had hired a car and had come to fetch us home. That was in the middle of August 1940. We were home just a couple of weeks when the Battle of Britain started."'

IT'S OVER!

At last the war was over, and we celebrated with enthusiasm.

'VE Day had come at last, so the idea of a street party in our corner of Maidstone was greeted with enthusiasm. A committee was formed, the landlord of the Kent Arms, on the corner of Wyatt and Tufton Streets was voted chairman, Mr Brunger, the grocer on the opposite corner of the two streets was the treasurer. The children of Wyatt, Tufton and Astley Streets would attend the party and money had to be found in a hurry.

Mr Brown, a jobbing builder, made a rough coffin, over which was thrown a very large Nazi flag, bright red with a big swastika. This flag had been given to my husband by a friend in the Airborne Division, who had brought it back from Stavanger in Norway. Coffin and flag were placed on the builder's handcart, about half a dozen men and women, dressed in black, with top hats draped in crêpe, widows weeds etc, made up the cortege, and they processed around the streets inviting folks to pay to see the last of Hitler! When the flag was lifted, a chamber pot, with a pint of beer and a cooked sausage met their gaze. Much hilarity ensued and people gave freely. Enough money was collected in one day to pay for all the things needed for the party, and people from the three streets donated ration points, which enabled our grocer-treasurer to get a very good deal with the wholesalers.

Old sheets were dyed red and blue and I cut them into triangles and sewed yards of bunting to criss-cross Tufton Street where the party would be held with permission from the police.

The great day at the end of May was fine and trestle tables, borrowed from Trinity church hall were set up. A large roll of white paper from one of the mills made excellent tablecloths, everyone lent a few chairs each. The ladies had made little cakes, sandwiches of paste, spam and cress, jellies and even hoarded tins of fruit appeared. Paper hats, balloons, flags and whistles had also been found. Please remember younger readers, all the above were in very short supply and the people had worked wonders. Tea was made in one house and passed out of the window, that was my job, and not many cups were broken.

When the party was in full swing, Mrs Taylor arrived with Bill her husband, who had been a prisoner of war in Poland for over four years and with one of the "Gibbons boys" had just arrived home.

An old piano was dragged into the street junction of Astley and Tufton and we all sat around singing and dancing till the small hours.'

'One day at the beginning of May 1945 I was upstairs in my room doing my homework when the rest of the family started making a terrible din. I was told that the war in Europe was over and the next two days were holidays. We knew this was coming and had been saving wood for a bonfire and food for a party. The road at the bottom of ours at Barnehurst was flat and everyone piled their wood in a heap and it was lit. Someone brought out a piano, sandwiches were made and stored beer etc was also produced. We had a railwayman living nearby and he had got hold of some of the "flash bangs" they had used on the railways to warn trains that they were approaching a blacked out station. The searchlights were all turned on and weaved patterns in the sky. We had a wonderful party, even the children were up until after midnight.

The victory in Japan in August 1945 was celebrated with a daytime children's party for which we had much more time to prepare properly. However, it did not have the atmosphere of the VE party which, for those of us in the southeast of England, was a tremendous release of tension.'

HIGHDAYS &
HOLIDAYS

WE MADE OUR OWN ENTERTAINMENT

In the days before television, and even before the wireless, we had to make our own entertainment, whether that meant joining in the local drama group or joining a cycling club, so popular in the 1930s.

NEVER A DULL MOMENT

'Looking back there never really seemed to be a dull moment in our lives. Classes were held regularly at Ryarsh for the ladies and Mother never missed one. She was taught tailoring from schooldays and made gym slips and kilts for us three girls. Now from the classes she took up in turn crochet, smocking, drawn thread work, tapestry and embroidery. The classes were always held at the rectory. I hated having to go as the dainty cakes I was offered at tea always broke and I was inclined to try to put them back and take another. This did not go down well with Mother.

Both our parents belonged to the Stansted Seven, a small group who felt they should be "walking the boards". They used to get up hilarious concerts and social events. My uncle and aunt also belonged and were very gifted musically which must have been a saving grace. Another thing I remember is other villages joining in. We always heard all about the pageants at Wrotham. Mother was in demand to sew all sorts of costumes and finally agreed to take part, then I was roped in as a page. I suppose I was about eight by now, then a rumour went round it would be Lady Godiva this year. I was scared it might be Mother, but it wasn't. By now a group of grown ups had joined the English Folk Dance and Song Society and were invited to dance at various events. By the time I was twelve I was allowed to join. I was very tall and really enjoyed the dancing. I've a feeling we were affiliated to the League of Health and Beauty because three years later in 1937 we were given the marvellous chance to dance at Wembley before King George VI and the Queen and the then two young Princesses to celebrate the Coronation. The day dawned fair and sunny and at the finale we danced in our thousands, a scarf dance. No, I believe it was handkerchiefs, then a grand march past the Royal Family. It really gave our village plenty to talk about for several days.

Cricket too played a part in our lives, sport and social wise. The club dances were always fun on summer evenings and the games were well supported by our own and other villages. The church too was very active, the festivals being celebrated spiritually and socially; Christmas carol parties with hot toddies and cocoa, and the Harvest – a real Service of Thanksgiving on a Friday night to which all the farm workers and families came to join in praise that all was gathered in and then afterwards a glorious Harvest Supper at which one small child piped up one year, "All the men are drinking beer".'

'We had in our village a Brownie pack, Guide company, and later a Scout troop. There was a Chelsfield Glee Club to which my father belonged and village football and cricket teams. Apart from this, most activities were centred around the parish church and the – then Wesleyan – Methodist church, with which my parents, and later I, were greatly involved.

Then in 1920 Chelsfield village life took on a new dimension. The first Women's Institute was formed and my mother was a founder member. She was an enthusiastic member, and once a month my father and I could look forward to an entertaining tea-time as she regaled us with stories of the afternoon meeting. The "Pudding Lady" had given a talk on "eating for health" and we were persuaded to boil our cabbage for a few minutes only, then pour off the water, reboil and drink the second water as a cocktail! There was a monthly competition – the "largest number of things in a matchbox", "the funniest thing that happened to me", etc and there was always a social half hour. Soon a drama group was formed, followed by a WI choir, both of which, together with a later Toc H concert party, made a welcome contribution to the social life of our village.

It was also in the 1920s that domestic life began to be enlivened with the coming of "the wireless". Some of the more adventurous of our community were to be found crouched over a box in their parlour as they pressed earphones to their heads and tried with varied success to listen to the early broadcasts from "2LO". A tiny wire that made contact with a piece of quartz was their method used, shortly afterwards to be superseded by valves, but the proud owners became the envy of their neighbours and I remember one evening when we were invited by our more prosperous friends to "listen in" for the first time.

The summer brought forth signs of great activity. The village fête was the event of the year. Side shows in abundance surrounded the recreation ground, and tension ran high as local teams heaved their way through the tug of war competition, while other opponents armed with hay bags fought each other sitting astride a greasy pole.

Running the basket race at Chelsfield fête in the 1920s.

My father, having donned an old cap, hurried down the field to victory with a tier of bushel baskets on his head, in the basket race.

My mother was, meanwhile, busy in the large Women's Institute marquee, for they organised the flower and produce show. She would set off after breakfast for a mile walk to the village in time to receive and record the entries to the various classes. Having welcomed the judges, and then left them to their deliberations, she would walk home for a quick lunch, and soon after returned for further duties.

Early in 1924 came the news that the West Kent Federation of WIs was to stage a pageant at Lullingstone Castle, early in July. "A pageant of Kentish History performed by Kentish Women – the first pageant ever produced in which only women were taking part" it was said. Scenes were to be allotted to various institutes in the county. Naturally we envisaged ourselves in beautiful Elizabethan gowns or the like. In the event we were chosen for Episode I involving Ancient Britons, Druids and Roman Soldiers. As children we were allowed to join our mothers and were dressed in animal skins and tattered tunics. My mother, with ivy entwined round her head and hair hanging over her shoulders, carrying a pitcher on her shoulder, was the first woman to appear in the pageant as she walked "wearily" (as directed) through the gates of Lullingstone Castle.

We were very much in awe of Miss Gwen Lally, a remarkable lady with a stentorian voice which rang out through a megaphone as she directed us in our inexperienced efforts. We rehearsed at local level in a large house in the village and when the day arrived travelled in my father's lorry, with all our props to Lullingstone. The castle and environs made a wonderful setting for this journey through history. With seat staging high around we were left with an arena complete with a growing oak for King Charles I to hide in!

Living at Well Hill we overlooked London. We had an almost panoramic view and the lights at night were quite a feature of interest. In the foreground stood the Crystal Palace, where, on Thursday nights one could see a distant grand firework display. Alas, one night in 1936, it was not fireworks that met our eyes but a huge conflagration, and the Crystal Palace was with us no longer. No more fireworks on Thursday evenings but still the lights of London remained, as we took our quiet summer evening stroll along the ridge of the hill.'

'Entertainment at Brasted in the 1920s was largely self-made, with the exception of a touring group called the Mummers. They called at the houses and as a reward for their kitchen antics and dramas sometimes received a glass of beer.

During particularly hot summer days the village children would brave the cold waters of the recreation ground swimming pool. It had been built by local residents and many were put through their first strokes, paddling from side to side. It was freezing cold even at the warmest time of year. It was fed by a spring that came out at the bottom and could only be used on hot days. It opened in 1914 just before the war started and the first gala there involved wounded soldiers from Dunsdale. It had changing rooms on the bank, diving boards and a chute.

One of the most popular yearly events was the joint village fair with Sundridge at which Petisgroves would hold a flower show. The event had stalls, a roundabout, coconut shies and a hoop-la.'

NO WIRELESS OR TELEVISION

'We had no wireless or television in those days so we made our own amusements. We had three cinemas in Dartford then – the Scala, the Gem and the Rialto – and, looking at my schoolgirl's diary for 1924, religiously kept, I am amazed to see how many times I went to the cinema. Some years later I came to know a lady who played the piano at the Gem cinema in those silent picture days, when serials always ended with some terrible catastrophe so we just had to go the next week to discover what happened next. We paid sixpence and crept up to the better seats under cover of darkness.'

'We were often to be found on a Saturday morning lined up outside the back entrance of the Kosmos cinema in Calverley Road, Tunbridge Wells. Sixpence would get us in for a full morning of Roy Rogers and cartoon films. "Chums Club" was very popular with hundreds of children over the years.

As teenagers we would dress in our best clothes on Sunday and walk to the Calverley Grounds or the Pantiles to listen to the many military bands that visited the town.'

'Every year in the 1930s we looked forward to the theatre that visited Lenham. Town Meadow was the venue. It was produced and acted by amateurs and Mr Bert Weight was the owner and leading man. *Murder in the Red Barn*, *Sweeney Todd the barber* and *Danny Boy* were just a few of their many plays and in the glow of an ember fire we would sit there enthralled by their performance.

We also had an annual flower show and fair. This was held in the cricket field. Children's and adults' races were run, and a local foreman at the basket factory would organise a race for the men which involved balancing as many baskets as possible on their heads.'

Love From a Stranger *was being performed at Chatham's Theatre Royal in March 1947.*

A POPULAR PASTIME

'Cycling was a popular pastime in the 1930s, with many clubs exploring the countryside. Large parties would tackle the lanes and hills, bringing their own sandwiches and flasks of tea. But if the signs of the National Cycling Union and Cyclists Touring Club were seen, they would know that teas and light refreshments would be to the standard of these organisations. Behind the scenes, teas would be produced on an oil stove, in a brick-floored kitchen, with only a cold tap over its shallow stone sink. Nonetheless, meals were provided efficiently – a plain tea was three slices of bread and butter, with jam and a pot of tea for a shilling, with one cake an extra threepence and two cakes sixpence. Poached egg on toast with tea and cake cost one shilling and threepence, salads took more preparation and could be one shilling and sixpence.

In the spring it was a regular sight to see a string of cyclists going home with large bunches of bluebells strapped on to their saddlebags.'

ROYAL OCCASIONS

Royal jubilees and coronations were celebrated with enthusiasm all over West Kent, and there are more personal memories of royalty too, especially for those who lived by the Thames.

CORONATION FESTIVITIES IN 1902

'A local press cutting described the occasion.

"Probably few of the Coronation festivities in Kent have passed off more successfully or proved more enjoyable to all concerned than the one held at Swanley Village on Wednesday last for Hextable and Swanley.

The Hextable children assembled about eleven o'clock and marched to Mr Hooper's meadow, Swanley, where they were joined by the Swanley children. Here they formed up four deep and, headed by the Farningham Boys Military Band, marched through the village and down the church walk to Mr J Alexander's meadow where the sports were held. It was a pretty procession with the girls in their bright summer garments and wearing appropriate favours and carrying flags, whilst the boys were turned out smartly and waving their flags and cheering as only British boys can do in these circumstances.

The children were cordially received by the Vicar and leading residents of the district. The National Anthem was sung by the children and all present. The children's dinner followed and later the old folks were entertained to a substantial meal at the Swanley school. Later the old folks were photographed on the Rectory lawn and the children were amused with a Punch and Judy show. The sports which followed proved unusually interesting and varied. The Sutton-at-Hone Fire Brigade gave a very fine display of manual drill and Mr Tom Moody, the famous Kent pedestrian, walked one mile against time.

The funny events of the programme, such as "Tilting the Bucket", "Ringing the Turkey" (with competitors blindfolded) etc etc excited roars of laughter. Of the ladies, Mrs Pomeroy had the honour of winning the Coronation Pig, presented by Mr Hooper.

Each of the children received special mementoes of the occasion in the shape of a book – *King Edward's Realm* – and a specially designed Coronation Mug. The prizes for the sports were numerous and well chosen and these were presented by Mrs J Alexander and Mr WC Jackson (the well known coaching whip). It was quite eight o'clock before the happy children, laden with their treasures, toddled homeward.

Later, dancing commenced and all the fun of the fair with roundabouts, swings, sideshows etc were liberally patronised.

Altogether it was a right royal day, thoroughly enjoyed by one and all. A word of praise is due to the Farningham Boys Military Band and the Dartford Volunteer Band for their excellent performances, and to all the officials who worked hard to make the festival one of the best that has been held in the district.'

FAMILY MEMORIES

'In 1863, Princess Alexandra of Denmark arrived at Gravesend by sea, on her way to marry Edward, Prince of Wales, later Edward VII. Two small girls, Pattie and Pollie, our family great aunts, were there with other young girls, strewing flowers over the royal pier when the princess arrived. Today some of those flowers, now very dry, are among our family keepsakes. That same Prince Edward came often to Rosherville which is between Gravesend and Northfleet, to the yacht club beside the river, a popular place in the 19th century. The Rosherville Hotel was converted to a hospital in the First World War. An aunt was a VAD there. Forty years later, colleagues and I used this venue overlooking the Thames to see the young Elizabeth II sail past in *Britannia* on her way to the Pool of London after one of her visits abroad. We had a wonderful sighting as the river there is quite narrow.'

'As with most people who live in the Medway towns, I had relations who worked in Chatham dockyard, some as far back as the 1800s.

On 18th July 1959, I went to the launching ceremony of HMS *Oberon*, by Her Royal Highness the Princess Marina, Duchess of Kent. She arrived with full ceremony but there it ended. Princess Marina was never one to stand on ceremony and put back the launch by a few minutes. She went under the bow of the submarine to ask the workmen questions. My dad said that she had done her homework and everyone was surprised by her knowledge.

When the *Oberon* was finally launched, after the choir singing and the obligatory bottle of champagne being broken, it slid sedately down the slipway amidst cheering and waving. The whole ceremony was very moving and all I could think of was that my dad had been a part of that and I had a great feeling of pride.'

ROYAL CONNECTIONS

'Jubilees were always celebrated in style in the villages. In 1902 the Horton Kirby Parish Council decided not to provide intoxicating liquor to celebrate the Coronation of Edward VII, but 177 gallons of ginger beer were provided at a cost of £3 10s 2d. The Silver Jubilee of George V and Queen Mary was celebrated in the local recreation field with separate races for single ladies (60 yards), married ladies (50 yards) and married couples.

Connections with royalty in the local villages came through the Farningham Homes for Little Boys. Set on the hill above South Darenth, this refuge had always attracted attention as it was the first time an attempt had been made to give destitute boys some sort of real home with a house-father and house-mother. The Duke of York, later George VI, was President for 16 years and the Homes were regularly visited by members of the Royal Family. In 1920 George V said: "These homes are not only a great charity, they are also a national and imperial asset." In 1926, the Duke of York was accompanied by Prince Chichibu of Japan and on this occasion the royal car was pulled up the drive by the Homes' Scout troop.

A special railway platform was built alongside the Homes to save visitors the journey from Farningham Road station and on open days as many as 1,000 to 2,000 visitors would take the special train from London. The Homes provided training in a large number of trades and examples of the boys' carpentry can be seen in the local church.

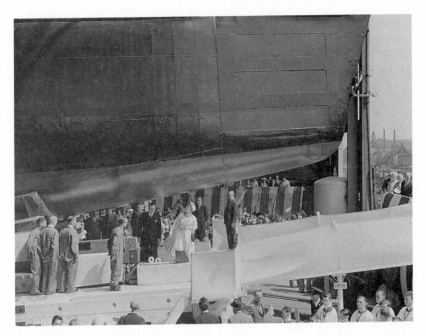

The Duchess of Kent launches HMS Oberon *in July 1959 at Chatham dockyard.*

On Sundays they could be seen walking crocodile fashion to local gardens, churchyards and woods.'

'I was eight years old in 1935 when the Silver Jubilee was celebrated. I can recall attending Barnsole Road Junior Girls School at Gillingham at that time. It was a beautiful sunny summer day in May and we children were marched out onto the school playground where we were addressed by some local dignitary. To my delight, we were then presented with a china mug and a book full of photographs of royal occasions. Sadly, neither of these items are in my possession now as my home was bombed while we were evacuated in Cornwall.

I was a civil servant in the Torpedo Depot offices in the dockyard from 1947 to 1952. The office was situated beside No 1 basin and consequently afforded the staff a grandstand view of ships' arrivals and departures.

Two such arrivals stand out in my mind, the first being of a Royal Navy ship returning from the Far East after three long years. There was a newsreel camera on top of a van filming the reuniting of families which was very emotional to watch. I can recall clearly an officer running down the gangplank to embrace his wife. In her arms were ginger-haired twin boys and it was obvious that it was his first sight of his young sons.

The second exciting visit was of King Haaken VI of Norway in his beautiful yacht. He was on a courtesy visit. He resided in Britain during the Second World War when armed resistance aginst Germany was no longer possible in Norway.

Whilst employed at the dockyard I remember well a visit of the Duke of Edinburgh, then Prince Philip. He came to unveil the names of the Second World War victims on the cenotaph situated on the Great Lines field, a hill overlooking the town. At that time there were just three of us young clerks in the Torpedo Depot. We got word that the prince was lunching at Admiralty House nearby. We hurried along during our lunch hour and were rewarded with a smile and a wave from the tanned and handsome young prince who was still in his twenties at that time. As we were the only people at the gateway to Admiralty House to greet him, it not being on the official itinerary, we considered ourselves very privileged indeed.'

JUBILEES AND CORONATIONS

'The Jubilee of 1935 was celebrated with much enthusiasm at Lenham. The highlight of the day was a torchlight procession, with Mr Tommy Gilbert leading all the village children with their torches, up the Faversham Road, along the Pilgrims Way to the Cross then back to the village. We were all singing and laughing and it was a wonderful end to a perfect day.'

'There was a firework display on Chislehurst Common in 1935 to celebrate the Silver Jubilee of George V and Queen Mary. We all received commemorative mugs at school and the firework display ended with a crown and the King and Queen portrayed on either side.

The coronation of Queen Elizabeth II, in 1953, was celebrated in Pratts Bottom with a tea party at the school for all the village children and a sports day for all ages including grandparents.'

'The coronation of the Queen in 1953 was a great excitement. At Barnehurst we had two days holiday from school. My parents let me join a party of people they knew who were going up to London to watch the procession. We left at about 6 pm the night before, well armed with rugs, mackintoshes, sandwiches and flasks of tea. We obtained good places in the Mall with a large party of Australians to one side of us and we had a very happy time, singing and just watching the other people. By 1.30 am we were getting cold and damp but then Hillary's conquest of Everest was announced and that cheered us all up. Soon things started to happen and the various army bands got into place and entertained us but we were allowed to stay where we were, spread out sitting on the pavement until about 7 am when we had to move into position as further crowds were arriving. After that we didn't dare move, not even to visit the mobile toilets that had been installed in Green Park, as we would have lost our prime positions.

Everything that passed got a cheer, which startled one or two officials but it was a very long wait. Finally the procession started. Apart from the Queen, Churchill and Queen Salote of Tonga got the loudest cheers but there was total silence for the Prime Minister of South Africa. This was very noticeable as his carriage stopped for some time in front of us. The service was relayed to us and now whenever I hear "Zadok the Priest" the day returns to me. After the return procession we made for Charing Cross and home. I went to bed having had no sleep but the phone rang and it was my boyfriend to say "Let's go to London and see the fireworks" and I did.'

'In June 1953 my father bought us a black and white television so that we could watch the Coronation. My granny, aunt and uncle came up for a day from Newhaven, to watch the Coronation with us, which took all day. Some weeks later we went to the cinema to see the film of the ceremony in colour.'

'I was nine years old in 1953. My mother and Nan had spent the past week busily preparing my fancy dress costume for the Coronation Day procession. It was all made from crêpe paper with silver painted cardboard accessories.

When the day came at last there was so much excitement but when we looked out of the window it was overcast and miserable. Never mind, we were going to have a good day no matter what.

We all assembled in the village (Hadlow), there were hundreds of us or so it seemed. There we were my cousin and I in our costumes. We thought I would be so original as Britannia but there were at least ten more – never mind. My cousin was more originally dressed as an Indian Maid.

As the procession started so did the rain, and boy did it rain. Can you imagine Britannia dressed in red, white and blue crêpe paper in the rain!

After the procession I had to go to my cousin's for a bath as we had no bathroom at home, no hot water either, only by boiling a kettle. In those days we were gas powered!

We had our lovely day, it was truly a day to remember.'

AWAY FROM HOME

Any kind of holiday was a real treat, whether it was just a day out or a whole week by the sea.

THROW OUT YOUR MOULDY COPPERS

'In 1922 I moved with my family to Farnborough police station. The White Lion, an old coaching inn on the London to Hastings road, stood next to the police station. On Bank Holidays it was a favourite stopping place for horse-drawn brakes carrying Londoners from Shoreditch to Farnborough to enjoy the countryside. On their arrival, local children would run round them shouting out,"Throw out your mouldy coppers!" The cart stood in the pond on the other side of the road to cool the wheels, while the horses were watered and the travellers refreshed themselves.'

COACH OUTINGS

'One of the highlights of our year was our family's annual holiday in a caravan at Seasalter, where we went cockling on the mud flats, having great fun and then back to the caravan for fish and chips.

We also had good fun going on coach outings with the public houses where we lived at Gravesend. Having loaded the back of the coach with beer, we would stop on the way to Margate or Ramsgate at the side of the road, where the beer would be unloaded and the merrymaking would start. It took about four hours to get to the coast, what with the beer and the traffic. We would walk beside the coach through the Medway towns as they were so congested. All in a day's fun though, life was not so rushed then.'

ONE WEEK A YEAR

'Father had two weeks' holiday a year. One was spent at home, the other generally in a private boarding house in Cliftonville. A lovely quiet place, we didn't wander far, just played cricket and ball on the sands, scrambled amongst the rock pools and watched the big tractors hauling in piles of seaweed. Sometimes we ventured into the sea and I remember my great embarrassment when my mother would make me wear a vest under my swimsuit to prevent me getting sunburnt. There wasn't another child on the beach dressed like me! The biggest attraction for me was the donkey rides. We were allowed a sixpenny donkey ride one day and a sixpenny ice cream the next and on our last day both a donkey ride and an ice cream.'

ALL THROUGH THE YEAR

There were high days to be enjoyed throughout the year, that came around regularly and were part of all our lives, from May Day to Christmas, and 'special' days that have stayed in our memories.

MAY DAY

'In 1937 I remember my mother taking me to meet Mrs Everest. She was the lady organiser of the "May Queen" in Chislehurst and her front room was cram full of furniture and clothes in various stages of being altered. She was very kind and said she would see if there was a place for me. When you are only six the choice was: if dainty, a Fairy; if a bit solid, as I was, a Herald. Mother then had to go to our nearest town Eltham, to buy buckram, gold paper, and other bits to make up a pill-box hat and a small banner. The gold paper was used for edging the banner and the numbers of the year. I do not remember a dress being made at home, it must have been made by one of Mrs Everest's many helpers.

Came the great day, it was a cold start so on went the liberty bodice, and the woollies, all under a silk dress. We arrived at Edward Road and found many children dressed in a variety of costumes, we did not know there were so many in the procession. The Boys' Brigade band led the way, into Albany Road up the High Street and then on to the common where we stood in a big circle while the May Queen was crowned. As I was very new I don't remember a lot more that year.

In 1938, after the Chislehurst crowning of the May Queen, we all went to Hayes Common. There all the village May Queens met, processed to the village church where all the Queens received a blessing – we had to stand outside whilst that was going on – then back to the common. There the May Queen of Merry England was crowned; she had been chosen from the previous year's queens. I think 1938 was Chislehurst's year. There was also a London May

May Day at St Mary Cray in 1931, the May Queen enthroned overlooking the maypole.

Queen. Then we were chosen to dance round the maypole and that was great fun. I continued being part of the group until I was Prince to the May Queen and that was during the war – we did not let the war stop us. In fact Mrs Everest used to hold concerts and the May Queen group took part, past members coming back when on leave.'

'The National school at St Mary Cray celebrated May Day in the 1920s and 1930s. A maypole was put up in the school hall for practice sessions and moved out to the boys' playground for May Day itself. Girls danced around holding coloured ribbons. The girl chosen as May Queen sat on a decorated platform, was crowned with may, and attended by two pages and two maids of honour dressed all in white. Each class performed a play or did a country dance to complete the celebrations.'

EMPIRE DAY

'I was born in Langton Green in 1908 and started school there at the age of four. Creative activities were rare – singing for special occasions and sometimes a concert was performed, when the audience had to bring a chair. Empire Day, 24th May, was celebrated with marching past the flag on the green. A local Indian Army colonel and a sergeant major had drilled the pupils. As they marched they would sing a verse something like:

Unfurl the Empire standard
Sing aloud today
One glad great song of triumph
That echoes far away
For God, for King, for Country
Thy Empire shall be set.'

'On 24th May, at school at Rainham, we celebrated Empire Day. The Union Jack would be flying from the flagpole and all the children would be in the playground ready to salute the flag and sing the Empire songs we had been learning. Sometimes we stood still and sometimes marched round the playground. After this the head-master would tell us about the Empire and we would sing "God save the King" and the rest of the day would be a holiday. The sun was always shining on that day so Mother and Father would take us for a picnic. Charlie would be harnessed to the waggonette. Mother and Father sat in the front and my sisters, brother and I sat in the seats at the back, facing one another. We usually went to the cherry orchards all around, because Father used to buy cherries on the trees later on and he wanted to see where the most cherries were growing. After eating our sandwiches and playing games in the orchard, we would ride home. Charlie knew he was homeward bound and would trot all the way. If it turned a bit cold we had a rug to cover our knees and if it rained there was a shiny mackintosh cover to keep us dry.

There were other regular pleasures we looked forward to. Sometimes the "Hurdy Gurdy Man" came down our road. He was Italian and wore very bright red and green clothes and a yellow handkerchief tied round his head. He wore big gold earrings which dangled when he turned the handle of the hurdy gurdy. He would have a monkey or a bear with him. The man would start up the music and the monkey would dance and turn somersaults. Then when he was tired he would hold out his hat for pennies. The brown, shaggy bear was very big. He had a collar round his neck which had a long chain and was fastened to the hurdy gurdy. He did not do tricks, but he would dance when the music started. He would hold out a hat for pennies, too. Mother would usually give us a penny to give them because it was such fun to see them and they only came about three times a year.

Another man who used to come down our road was the "Balloon and Windmill Man". He was a little man with a big wheelbarrow and all coloured balloons or windmills would be tied to his barrow, blowing in the wind. To get one, we had to go home and ask our mothers for a nice clean jam jar. Back we would go to the balloon man and he would let us choose a balloon or windmill and we would play with them until teatime. The little man would put all his jars

Everyone joined in the fun and fancy dress at Bearsted Fair in the 1920s.

into a sack and take them to the jam factory where he would be given money to buy more balloons and windmills for the children in the next village.

Every year the circus travelled through our village. We used to get up at five o'clock and take with us a paper bag filled with apples and buns for the elephants. We had to go to the top of the road and cross over the High Street to the church path and stand behind the railings. First would come the big horse-drawn waggons filled with everything to make the Big Top. Then would come the performing animals and the circus people in their brightly coloured caravans drawn by horses. At the rear came the elephants. There would be seven or eight of them and we would drop the apples and buns in front of them and they would pick them up and put them in their mouths. We were sorry to see the last of the circus go through and hoped we would be able to go to Chatham or Sittingbourne to see the animals perform in the ring.'

NAVY DAYS

'Chatham dockyard had Navy Days prior to the Second World War, when members of the public were admitted every Bank Holiday. It was a day out for the family, who were allowed aboard various boats and submarines and were shown round by sailors who explained how they lived and occupied their time. The sailors and Royal

248

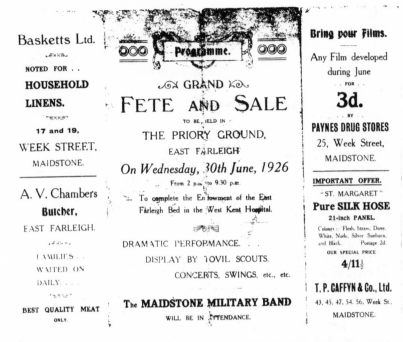

Programme.

∽ GRAND ∽

FETE AND SALE

TO BE HELD IN

THE PRIORY GROUND,

EAST FARLEIGH

On Wednesday, 30th June, 1926

From 2 p.m. to 9.30 p.m.

To complete the Endowment of the East
Farleigh Bed in the West Kent Hospital.

DRAMATIC PERFORMANCE. .

DISPLAY BY TOVIL SCOUTS.

CONCERTS, SWINGS, etc., etc.

The **MAIDSTONE MILITARY BAND**

WILL BE IN ATTENDANCE.

*Programme for a 'Grand Fête and Sale' at East Farleigh in 1926. Before the NHS,
hospital fundraising events were common.*

Marines put on various displays, drills, climbing the mast to the
music of the Royal Marines band, gymnastics and finishing with
Beating the Retreat. Aircraft did flying displays during the day and
visitors were allowed to go on the river in small launches.'

THE DICKENS FESTIVAL 1951

'In April 1951 I sang in the Co-op choir at Rochester and one evening
we were all invited to take part in the Dickens Festival being held in
June that year. Of course, the most attractive aspect of this was a
whole week off school. The school duly gave its permission and my
mother set about making me into a sweet "Victorian Miss" which
was a bit difficult as I was happier climbing trees and playing cricket.
My dress was pale pink with puffed sleeves with a frill round the
bottom. I looked as if I had long pantaloons but they only started
from below the knee and were held up by elastic. A straw bonnet
tied with a pink ribbon completed the outfit.

The festival was to be held in the Castle Gardens and based on the
Pickwick Papers. My part was a girl-with-a-hoop, only I didn't have

a hoop. I felt quite deprived for a while but when one of the girls dropped hers and went to pick it up she nearly got run down by a horse so I didn't feel so bad. We all had to follow the coach in, containing Mr Pickwick, plus all the horsemen, which was a problem. I wasn't sure I liked horses and I had to stand next to them before we ran on, but it all worked out very well, and for weeks afterwards I would only draw horses.

We had to wait in the Vines until it was time to move on to the Castle so my friend and I went round collecting autographs from the actors and the riders who all wrote the name of their horse as well. Dame Sybil Thorndyke was at one of the performances and I really would have liked to have got her autograph as my nan was her maid when her father was vicar of St Margaret's parish many years ago.

There is a regular Dickens Festival now but it is very commercialised and not half as much fun.'

BONFIRE NIGHT

'At The Moor at Hawkhurst there is a patch of green where I can remember each year a huge bonfire was stacked up and on 5th November would be lit. There was a good display of fireworks, watched by a large crowd. The First World War ended that.'

'In the 1950s a group of local men formed the Headcorn Bonfire Boys Society. They arranged a procession and giant bonfire every November. Having gone round the village, the floats went onto the large field where the bonfire was lit. Money collected was used to help local people, such as a girl who was given text books to enable her to go to medical school. Unfortunately the field was taken for building houses so the end came and the Bonfire Boys are just a happy memory.'

CHRISTMAS MEMORIES

'Christmas in the 1920s was a time of treats, puddings and fresh fruit. Presents consisted of one toy, fruit and nuts in the Christmas stocking. One year my brother who worked in a butcher's shop in Chatham brought home a turkey for dinner and when it was cooked it was so tough that even the dog wouldn't eat it, the grandfather of all turkeys!'

'Christmas began when Mother started to make the mincemeat. We all "helped" to stone raisins, chop peel and pick over the currants. The same again for the puddings, this time grating breadcrumbs and suet. Stirring was a proper ritual, everyone having a secret wish.

For paper chains, Mother made a basin of flour paste and we seemed to make miles of them all linked together. We always had a Christmas tree. In those days oranges, nuts and figs were only in the shops at Christmas. Our father had us make endless lists which were altered every night until Christmas Eve when he went to the market to buy them. There always seemed to be a rabbit in a hutch and being country children it didn't seem to bother us that it disappeared at Christmas.'

'The special hour of Christmas Day was about eight o'clock in the evening for me, right up until 1937. In the distance at about that time we would hear hand bells ringing. They were played by four local men, father and sons, every year. After they had reached my grandfather's farmhouse at Holly Farm in Langley and finished their ringing they enjoyed mince pies and all kinds of drinks, but they mainly drank beer and home-made cider. At about nine o'clock they would go on their way to their home.

Then it would be supper time. My grandfather's cat Fluffie would rattle the front door knocker to be let in and sit on the arm of the sofa, to put his paw on grandfather's shoulder to ask for a slice off the large joint of meat. After the meal was over it was time for my parents and me to go home through the plantation to our home at Bugle Horn Farm, Otham.'

'It was Christms 1944. Would it be there this year? I had been asking Father Christmas for it for the last two years. "Times are hard, even for Father Christmas", I was told. We were allowed downstairs, and there it was, the most perfect doll's rocking cradle and a rag doll as well. Thank you Father Christmas, well, thank you to a few older members of my family, as I was later to learn.

My grandfather had managed to get a wooden vegetable box from a farmer and made and painted the cradle. My grandmother had sacrificed one of her white pillowcases to make a mattress and pillow. But best of all was the rag doll, made by great-aunt Phoebe. She used to sit in the corner of my grandmother's kitchen in her long black dress and lace cap. To me she was at least 150 years old. She had stitched the doll so lovingly, with wool for hair, a nightdress to wear to bed and a silk smocked dress for best. Now, where did the silk come from in the middle of the war? My sister had passed the exam to go to the grammar school. She needed white blouses and there was no material to be had. My father, who was serving his country, came home with the answer – half a parachute. My sister's blouses were made of silk and my rag doll had a real silk dress. The best Christmas present I ever had.'

Index

254

List of Contributing Institutes

Contributions were received from the following West Kent Women's Institutes:

Allington, Allington Castle, Aperfield, Ash & Ridley, Badgers Mount, Barming, Bearsted & Thurnham, Bearsted Green, Beckenham, Biddenden, Borstal, Boughton Monchelsea, Brasted, Bredhurst, Brenchley Evening, Bromley Common, Burham & Wouldham, Cage Green, Capel, Chalk Afternoon, Chart Sutton, Chelsfield, Chelsfield Evening, Chevening, Chipstead, Chislehurst, Cobham & Luddesdown, Collier Street, Cowden, Coxheath, Cranbrook, Crayford, Crockham Hill, Detling, Ditton, Downe, East Peckham, Edenbridge Afternoon, Edenbridge Evening, Eynsford, Fairfield (Dartford), Farnborough, Fordcombe, Frindsbury, Frindsbury Extra, Golden Green, Goudhurst, Hadlow, Halling, Harrietsham, Hartley, Hartley Afternoon, Hawkenbury, Hayes, Headcorn, Hever, Hextable & Swanley Village, Higham, Highgate Hawkhurst, High Halden, High Halstow, Hildenborough Evening, Horsted, Horton Kirby & South Darenth, Ide Hill, Iden Green, Istead Rise, Joydens Wood, Keston, Kingswood, Knockholt, Ladycroft, Langton Green, Larkfield, Leeds, Lenham, Leybourne, Longfield Hill, Loose, Luton Valley (Chatham), Maidstone Centre, Marden, Matfield, Meopham, Nashenden, Nevill, Northfleet Perry Street, Otford, Otham, Pembury, Plaxtol, Pratts Bottom, Rainham, Ravenswood, Rolvenden, Roseacre, Rowhill, Ryarsh, St George's Beckenham, St John's Tunbridge Wells, St Mary & St Paul's Cray, St Mary's Platt, Sandhurst & Newenden, Sandown, Sennocke, Shoreham, Shorne & Thong, Sidcup, Southborough, South Park, Southfleet, Speldhurst, Stockbury, Sutton Valence, Swanley Evening, Tatsfield, Teston, The Farleighs, Underriver, Vinters Park, Wateringbury, Westerham Darenth, West Malling, West Peckham, Willington, Wilmington.